RULERS OF EVIL

Useful Knowledge About Governing Bodies

F. TUPPER SAUSSY

Copyright © 1999 by Frederick Tupper Saussy

All rights reserved. No part of this book may be reproduced or transmitted in any form or by any means, electronic or mechanical, including photocopying, recording, or by any information storage or retrieval system, without permission in writing from the publisher.

Published by Ospray Bookmakers, Reno, Nevada

ISBN   0-9673768-0-7
First Edition

Reprint Edition by Last Century Press
ISBN 9781937920296

> "The worst thing you can do in life is underestimate your adversary."
>
> —PRESIDENT WILLIAM J. CLINTON ,
> CBS News, March 31, 1999

CONTENTS

	Introduction:	ix
	Preface	ix
	Foreword	xi
	Orientation	xiii
1:	Subliminal Rome	1
2:	Missionary Adaptation	9
3:	Marginalizing the Bible	15
4:	Medici Learning	19
5:	Appointment at Cyprus	27
6:	The Epitome of Christian Values	35
7:	The Fingerstroke of God	43
8:	Moving In	55
9:	Securing Confidence	63
10:	Definitions	77
11:	The Thirteen Articles Concerning Military Art	85
12:	Lorenzo Ricci's War	97
13:	The Secret Bridge	117
14:	The Dogma of Independence	129

CONTENTS

15:	The Madness of King George III	135
16:	Tweaking the Religious Right	147
17:	A Timely Grand Tour	155
18:	The Stimulating Effects of Tea	167
19:	Death and Resurrection of Lorenzo Ricci	187
20:	American Grafitti	203
21:	Jupiter's Earthly Abode	227
22:	The Immaculate Conception	235
23:	The Dome of the Great Sky	247
24:	The Mark of Cain	265
25:	The Two Ministries	279
	Appendix	293
	A: Fifty Centuries of the Annu Signature	293
	B: Superior Generals of the Society of Jesus	296
	C: Glossary	298
	D: Notes	303
	E: Bibliography	313
	F: Index	318

RULERS OF EVIL

Introduction

PREFACE

THE ONLY PEOPLE in the world, it seems, who believe in the conspiracy theory of history are those of us who have studied it. While Franklin D. Roosevelt might have exaggerated when he said "Nothing happens in politics by accident; if it happens, it was planned that way," Carroll Quigley – Bill Clinton's favorite professor at Georgetown University – boldly admitted in his *Tragedy & Hope* (1966) that (a) the multitudes were already under the control of a small but powerful group bent on world domination and (b) Quigley himself was a part of that group.

Internet conspiracy sites strive to identify the conspiratorial factions. We get pieces here and pieces there. The world is run by Freemasons, some say. Other say Skull & Bones, and a loose confederation of secret societies. CIA gets lots of votes, along with Mossad (though I suspect these factions are merely tools) and, of course, "the British." A major frontrunner is the International Banking Cartel. When Victor Marsden published *The Protocols of the Elders of Zion* in 1906, which purported to be a Jewish plan to take over the world, Jewish writers denied responsibility, charging a Catholic plot to defame Jewry. Whose side was Marsden on? You can get so deep into conspiracies that the suspects start canceling each other out. It can become frustrating.

I'm happy to report that F. Tupper Saussy has come to our emotional rescue. During his ten years as a fugitive from the Department of Justice (convicted of a crime that cannot be found in the lawbooks), Saussy occupied himself with an investigation into the powers that be. It was an investigation the likes of which, as far as I know, has never before been undertaken. The fruit of his amazing legwork is *Rulers of Evil,* a powerful book that in less loving hands might have been angry and judgmental.

Saussy's thesis: There is indeed a small group that runs the world, but we can't call it a conspiracy because it identifies itself with signs, mottoes, and monuments. Signs, mottoes, and monuments? you ask. *Quick:* what occupies the highest point on the U.S. Capitol building? It's probably the most *oft-published* statue on earth, and you can't name it? As long as you don't know whose feet are firmly planted atop your country's legislative center, or how she got there, or whence she came, the group that controls America remains invisible. Once you know these things, the fog begins lifting.

Saussy has analyzed hundreds of signatory clues left by the true rulers of the world, clues that we have perhaps been trained to ignore. He's traced them to their origins, and matched them to facts of history going back six thousand years – all balanced against the most reliable human reference work there is, the Bible. The result: an unavoidable touchstone for all future works on the subject.

Rulers of Evil is an indispensable study book that you'll probably deface from cover to cover with highlighting. By all means keep it on your lower library shelf, within close reach of inquisitive children.

— *Pat Shannon*
Journalist-at-Large, MEDIA BYPASS

Introduction

FOREWORD

WHETHER OR NOT it's appropriate for a literary agent to write his client's Foreword, I don't know. If I'm breaking the rules here, well, this is a rule-breaking book. Example. During last spring's Bookexpo in Los Angeles, I agently introduced my client, Tupper Saussy, to one of New York's most unshockable publishing executives. As Tupper articulately summarized *Rulers of Evil* for him, I personally witnessed the brow of this fearless executive develop a twitch. I saw him actually gulp. With my own ears I heard him say, "This is a little too *extreme* for us."

The twitch developed as Tupper was saying "the Roman Catholic Church really does run the world, including the United States government, and this is openly declared in monuments and emblems and insignia as well as official documents..." By the time Tupper calmly reached his payoff – "And this is good, because it's divinely ordained" – the exec was staring into space.

All right, *Rulers of Evil* is extreme. (Does that frighten you?) It was researched and written during a decade of flight that probably saved the author's life from vindictive federal authorities. I wanted to represent this book from the moment I read the first draft back in 1993, completely unaware that its author could claim the classic *Miracle On Main Street* as his own. (Tupper Saussy's identity was not revealed to me until his capture in 1997. He can keep a secret.)

Like no book I've seen in my thirty years of literary-agenting, *Rulers of Evil* lays out who's *really* who in world power, pegs them as evil (about as evil as the rest of us, more or less), and then explains how spiritual wickedness in high places works for the ultimate good of mankind. It's the book about conspiracies that doesn't advocate throwing the bums out.

Rulers of Evil is almost a self-help product. The useful knowledge it imparts reveals the world structure as it really is. Once we can see, our choices increase, our pathways widen, and our lives improve.

But don't expect a breeze. Parts of the book are so rich in historical detail that your brain might feel over-burdened. When that happens, just flip to more readable parts. Or study the pictures. My client doesn't mind being read casually, back to front, front to back, middle out, a few pages at a time. Enjoy freedom of movement. If a chapter doesn't fit today's mood, find another that does. Use a bookmark, or the dustjacket flaps.

Ultimately, you'll get it all. And when you do, I predict you'll be a different person. You'll have a new worldview, one shaped by evidence that has never been assembled quite this way before. I can say this with confidence because *Rulers of Evil* is still influencing my own life, having begun in me a process of answering many of the heretofore unanswerable questions of our time.

— *Peter Fleming*
THE PETER FLEMING AGENCY

Introduction

ORIENTATION

> "The only new thing in this world is the history you don't know."
> — PRESIDENT HARRY S. TRUMAN

ON FRESHMAN ORIENTATION day at the University of the South in Sewanee, Tennessee, I took a seat across the table from my faculty advisor. He was a professor of botany named Edmund Berkeley. Dr. Berkeley studied the tab on my manila file folder as though it were some rare species of leaf. Suddenly his eyes leapt into my face. Giddy eighteen-year-old that I was, I gulped and tried to smile.

"'Saussy,'" he mused calmly. "Good Huguenot name."

The word stumped me. "Huguenot?"

"'Saussy' is a French name," he lectured. "Sewanee is a Protestant university. Your people must have been Huguenots."

I silently forgave my father for never having told me our name was French and that our ancestors might have been something called "Huguenots."

"What exactly are Huguenots?" I inquired.

"French Protestants," declared my advisor. "Massacred by soldiers ordered by Catherine d'Medici in cahoots with the Jesuits.

The survivors were exiled. Some established in England, others in Prussia. Some came to America, as your people obviously did."

"Jesuits." Now that was a familiar word. In Tampa, my hometown, there was a high school named Jesuit. Jesuit High was greatly esteemed academically and athletically. I was aware of a connection between the Jesuits and the Roman Catholic Church, but little else.

"What are Jesuits?" I asked.

"Oh, the Jesuits are members of the Society of Jesus," he replied. "Excellent men. Intellectuals. They work exclusively for the Pope, take an oath to him and him alone. Some people call them the Pope's private militia. Kind of a swordless army. Controversial. They've gotten into trouble meddling with civil governments in the past, trying to bring them under the Pope's dominion, you know, but in this century they've been tamed down considerably. They're wonderful educators."

That night I called my father, who answered Dr. Berkeley's surmise. Yes, our people were Huguenots. They arrived at Savannah harbor in the latter half of the eighteenth century, after a stopover of several generations in Scotland. They had indeed been run out of their beloved country, the same way the Jews were run out of Germany. Nazis chased the Jews, Jesuits chased us. Ah, but that was a long time ago, my father said, and I agreed. Forgiveness is a great virtue, and it's best to let bygones be bygones. So I forgot about Huguenots and Jesuits and plunged into my college career, my future, my life.

I never had occasion to think about my conversation with Edmund Berkeley until some thirty years later, in August of 1984, during a brief but telling encounter with an assistant United States attorney by the name of John MacCoon. We were standing a few paces apart in the marble hallway outside a federal courtroom in Chattanooga, waiting for the morning session to be called. I was on the docket, scheduled to be arraigned on charges of willful failure to file income tax returns for the years 1977, 1978, and 1979.

INTRODUCTION   ORIENTATION

I had no doubt that the charges would be dropped. The statute I had supposedly run afoul of applied to persons "required" to file returns. Yet I possessed a letter signed by the IRS District Director stating that a diligent search of IRS files had failed to disclose any tax liability in my name for those years. People who have no tax liability are not required to file returns. Why was I there?

The booming voice of a lawyer friend broke my concentration. "Tupper," he said, guiding me over to John MacCoon, "have you met your prosecutor?"

He introduced us in a jovial fashion and then rushed off to a huddle of other litigants.

MacCoon and I shook hands. "John," I asked, feeling the need to make small talk, "are you from Chattanooga?"

"No," he replied, "I came from Washington."

Something inside told me to press. "So you're originally from Washington?"

"No, originally I'm from New Orleans."

"I have lots of cousins in New Orleans," I beamed. He seemed to get a little edgy.

"Well, the name Saussy is not unknown there," he said.

"One of my favorite cousins lives in New Orleans," I said, and named my cousin.

"He's your cousin? Why, he and I were ordained together."

"Ordained?" I asked. "My cousin is a Jesuit priest. Are you a Jesuit?"

"Yes," said my prosecutor, now visibly agitated. "You know, I might have to recuse myself...."

"I've got a better idea, drop the charges."

"Oh no, I couldn't do that."

The dialogue ended suddenly with the hoarse drawl of a bailiff announcing that court was now in session.

So John MacCoon was a Jesuit! The media, spoon fed by his offices, had already branded me a "tax protestor." What was going on? Were the Jesuits chasing Protestants again?

Actually, I had not protested any taxes at all. I had merely discovered some truths about the tax and monetary laws and had dared to stand on them. As with the Huguenots and the truths they'd discovered about Christianity, authorities were offended. Wasn't it interesting that both of us – my ancestors and me – were branded as antisocial, repugnant, as people who disturb good order by daring to "protest"? Was this a religious persecution here? Was my stand on Truth somehow so offensive that the Pope had dispatched one of his swordless warriors to do me in? And then there was the date. The charges against me were filed on July 31st. That happens to be the Feast Day of St. Ignatius Loyola, the founding father of the Society of Jesus. According to the dogma of the Roman Liturgical Calendar, any cause initiated on a saint's feast day is especially worthy of the saint's attention.

A bizarre series of furtive proceedings occurred over the next eleven months. Exculpatory evidence was ignored or suppressed. There were prosecutorial improprieties, which the court excused. When I attempted to avoid the consequences of the improprieties, I was punished. Few precedents for such judicial steam-rolling could be found outside the annals of the Roman Inquisition, which I learned had been administered since 1542 by the Jesuits. What was this – the American Inquisition? All the while, the IRS, John MacCoon, and the media kept labeling me "tax protestor." Sometimes they would slip and call me a "tax evader," even though I had never been accused of the much more serious crime of tax evasion.

Ultimately, a jury acquitted me of willfully failing to file income tax returns for 1978 and 1979. But for 1977 they found willfulness, and the higher courts upheld their verdict. It was only a misdemeanor. The last defendant in my district to be convicted on the same count had been sentenced to six weeks. But the court sentenced me to a full year, the maximum allowed by statute. This was due to what the prosecutor called my "unrepentance." Some say I should have wept crocodile tears and promised to mend my ways. But that would be gameplaying. How can you repent of willfully failing to do something that was never required in the first place?

INTRODUCTION   ORIENTATION

WHEN I soberly reviewed the long list of prosecutorial absurdities, I decided that I was being punished for something not remotely connected to willfulness in filing tax returns. I was being punished for mobilizing what turned out to be the only constitutional issue no court in the United States will fully entertain – the money issue.

Back in the late seventies, I discovered that constitutional government was contravening every American's right to an economy free of fluctuating monetary values. I wrote a book *The Miracle On Main Street: Saving Yourself and America from Financial Ruin* (1980), in which I compared American money as mandated by the Constitution – gold and silver coin – with American money currently in use – notes, computer entries, and base-metal tokens. Not only was the money in use inferior to constitutional money, but also it had been introduced without a constitutional amendment. Since our values were denominated in units of lawless money, we had become a lawless nation. Quality of life follows quality of money. I urged the people to take the initiative in nudging government officials to restore the kind of monetary system established by the Constitution. The ultimate payoff would be a wholesome society. Main Street activism would have worked a miracle.

MOMS caught on very quickly. Activists began asserting economic rights in many creative ways. To assist and document their work, I launched "The Main Street Journal." Published more or less monthly, the MSJ reported in detail the interesting, sometimes frightening consequences of economic rights activism.

By July 1984, my book and my journal had expanded into a growing bibliography of historic and legal materials related to the money issue. I was speaking all over the country, and holding well-attended seminars in Tennessee. We had history on our side. The Framers of the Constitution had unanimously voted down the kind of monetary system that was destroying modern America, and had unanimously voted for the system we were advocating. We had the law on our side. The Supreme Court had never ruled that America's lawless monetary system was constitutional. What we didn't have on our side was the entity having most to gain from lawless money – the governing bodies. We were deeply offending their appearance of legitimacy. As one Tennessee village lawyer said, in returning *Miracle On Main Street* to the friend who'd loaned it to him, "This book won't get Saussy killed, but they'll figure out a humane way of shutting him up."

THERE was an interval of two years between my trial and the Supreme Court's decision on it. About midway during that interval, I received a postcard from the most famous prisoner in Tennessee, James Earl Ray. Mr. Ray, the self-convicted assassin of Dr. Martin Luther King, wanted me to help him write his autobiography. I interviewed him personally, examined his manuscript, and conducted some research of my own. The evidence persuaded me that Mr. Ray did not deserve to be called, in Life Magazine's words, "the world's most hated man." He had been tortured into pleading guilty. Far from punishment for murder, his confinement was the government's way of concealing the true assassins, and at the Tennessee taxpayers' expense. I felt that he, like myself, was being maliciously used by governing bodies for the purpose of deceiving the public.

I worked closely with Mr. Ray, publishing his autobiography under the title *Tennessee Waltz: The Making of A Political Prisoner*. I included an epilogue of my own, "The Politics of Witchcraft," in which I discussed how Dr. King's murder benefitted no one as much as it did the economic powers of government. About a month before *Tennessee Waltz* would be coming off the press, I was notified that the U.S. Supreme Court had denied my appeal. Then the District Judge ordered me to surrender myself to Atlanta Federal Prison Camp on or before April 10, 1987. A friend happened to say, "You know, if your previous writings brought about the tax prosecution, think what *Tennessee Waltz* might provoke them to, with you in custody...."

And so, when the moment came for me to pass through the Prison Camp gates, something got in the way. I can only call it a spirit, an irresistible spirit. It was the same spirit that had directed me to stand on the truth in my writing and speaking. It was the

INTRODUCTION   ORIENTATION

same spirit that had led me to interrogate John MacCoon at our first encounter in that marble hallway back in 1984, the same spirit that had moved him to tell me he was a Jesuit. This spirit turned me away from the prison gate and led me into a fugitive lifestyle.

I felt an overwhelming obligation to love my enemies by studying them in intricate detail. I wanted to know the extent of Jesuit involvement in United States government, presently and historically. What I discovered was a vast Roman Catholic substratum to American history, especially the Revolution that produced the constitutional republic. I found that Jesuits played eminent and under-appreciated roles in moving the complacent New Englanders to rebel against their mother country. I discovered facts and motives strongly suggesting that events that made Great Britain divide in 1776 were the outworkings of an ingenious Jesuit strategy. This strategy appears to have been single-handedly designed and supervised by a true founding father few Americans have ever heard of – Lorenzo Ricci (known to British Jesuits as Laurence Richey). In fact, investigating Jesuit involvement in the formation of the United States turned up a whole host of hitherto little-known names, such as Robert Bellarmine, Joseph Amiot, the Dukes of Norfolk, Daniel Coxe, Sun-Tzu, Lord Bute, Francis Thorpe, Nikolaus von Hontheim, and the Carrolls, Daniel, Charles, and John. In their way, these men were as essential to our constitutional origins as Jefferson, Paine, Adams, Washington, Locke, and George III.

My investigation began in 1987. It coursed ten years, and ranged – with the help of our Lord and many courageous friends, to whom this book is dedicated – from the Florida Keys to Puget Sound, from the District of Columbia to southern California. The mounting evidence inexorably changed the way I perceived constituted authority, and my relationship to it. Finally, on the thirteenth minute of the thirteenth hour of the thirteenth day of November, 1997, the journey that had begun with the filing of charges against me thirteen years earlier reached its destination. I was captured without violence by three U.S. Marshals outside my office on the canals in Venice, California. A valuable personhood

I was prepared to deny forever was given back to me. For sixteen months, the Bureau of Prisons afforded me the opportunity to discuss the fruits of my investigation with intelligent prisoners in California, Georgia, Tennessee, Oklahoma, and Mississippi. Their straightforward questions, comments, insights, and criticisms helped further prepare my manuscript for a general audience.

Now that my liberties are fully restored, I am able finally to relate my findings to you in my own true voice, tried in adversity, seasoned by time.

F. Tupper Saussy

RULERS OF EVIL

Chapter 1

SUBLIMINAL ROME

> *"The Roman Catholic Church is a State."*
> — BISHOP MANDELL CREIGHTON, LETTERS

WHEN A PULITZER PRIZE-winning reporter announced in his 1992 Time Magazine cover story that a "conspiracy" binding President Ronald Reagan and Pope John Paul II into a "secret, holy alliance" had brought about the demise of communism, at least one reader saw through the hype.

Professor Carol A. Brown of the University of Massachusetts fired off a letter to Time's editors saying,

> Last week I taught my students about the separation of church and state. This week I learned that the Pope is running U.S. foreign policy. No wonder our young people are cynical about American ideals.

What Brown had learned from Carl Bernstein I had discovered for myself over several years of private investigation: the papacy really does run United States foreign policy, and always has. Yes,

Bernstein noted that the leading American players behind the Reagan/Vatican conspiracy, to a man, were "devout Roman Catholics" – namely,

William Casey
Director, CIA

Alexander Haig
Secretary of State

Richard Allen
National Security Advisor

Vernon Walters
Ambassador-at-Large

Judge William Clark
National Security Advisor

William Wilson
Ambassador to the Vatican State

But the reporter neglected to mention that the entire Senate Foreign Relations committee was governed by Roman Catholics, as well. Specifically, Senators

Joseph Biden
Subcommittee on European Affairs

John Kerry
Terrorism, Narcotics, and International Communications

Paul Sarbanes
International Economic Policy, Trade, Oceans, and Environment

and...

Daniel P. Moynihan
Near Eastern and South Asian Affairs

Christopher Dodd
Western Hemisphere and Peace Corps Affairs

Bernstein would have been wandering off-point to list the Roman Catholic leaders of American domestic policy, such as Senate majority leader George Mitchell and Speaker of the House Tom Foley.

In fact, when the holy alliance story hit the stands, there was virtually no arena of federal legislative activity, according to *The 1992 World Almanac of US Politics*, that was not directly controlled by a Roman Catholic senator or representative. The committees and subcommittees of the United States Senate and House of Representatives governing commerce, communications and telecommunications, energy, medicine, health, education and welfare, human services, consumer protection, finance and financial institutions, transportation, labor and unemployment, hazardous materials, taxation, bank regulation, currency and monetary policy,

CHAPTER I   SUBLIMINAL ROME

oversight of the Federal Reserve System, commodity prices, rents services, small business administration, urban affairs, European affairs, Near Eastern & South Asian affairs, terrorism/narcotics/ international communications, international economic/trade/ oceans/environmental policy, insurance, housing, community development, federal loan guarantees, economic stabilization measures (including wage and price controls), gold and precious metals transactions, agriculture, animal and forestry industries, rural issues, nutrition, price supports, Food for Peace, agricultural exports, soil conservation, irrigation, stream channelization, flood-control, minority enterprise, environment and pollution, appropriations, defense, foreign operations, vaccines, drug labeling and packaging, drug and alcohol abuse, inspection and certification of fish and processed food, use of vitamins and saccharin, national health insurance proposals, human services, legal services, family relations, the arts and humanities, the handicapped, and aging – in other words, virtually every aspect of secular life in America – came under the chairmanship of one of these Roman Catholic laypersons:

Frank Annunzio	Edward Kennedy	Daniel Moynihan
Joseph Biden	John Kerry	John Murtha
Silvio Conte	John LaFalce	Mary Rose Oakar
Kika De la Garza	Patrick Leahy	David Obey
John Dingell	Charles Luken	Claiborne Pell
Christopher Dodd	Edward Madigan	Charles Rangel
Vic Fazio	Edward Markey	Dan Rostenkowski
James Florio	Joseph McDade	or Edward Roybal.·
Henry Gonzalez	Barbara Mikulski	
Thomas Harkin	George Miller	

Vatican Council IPs *Constitution on the Church* (1964) instructs politicians to use their secular offices to advance the cause of Roman Catholicism. Catholic laypersons, "whoever they are, are called upon to expend all their energy for the growth of the Church and its continuous sanctification," and "to make the Church present and operative in those places and circumstances where only through them can it become the salt of the earth" (IV, 33). Vatican II further instructs all Catholics "by their competence in secular disciplines and by their activity [to] vigorously contribute their effort so that ... the goods of this world may be more equitably distributed among all men, and may in their own way be conducive to universal progress in human and Christian freedom ... and [to] remedy the customs and conditions of the world, if they are an inducement to sin, so that they all may be conformed to the norms of justice and may favor the practice of virtue rather than hinder it" (IV, 36).

Vatican II affirms Catholic doctrine dating back to 1302, when Pope Boniface VIII asserted that "it is absolutely necessary for the salvation of every human creature to be subject to the Roman Pontiff." This was the inspiration for the papacy to create the United States of America that materialized in 1776, by a process just as secret as the Reagan-Vatican production of Eastern Europe in 1989. What? American government Roman Catholic from the beginning?

Consider: the land known today as the District of Columbia bore the name "Rome" in 1663 property records; and the branch of the Potomac River that bordered "Rome" on the south was called "Tiber."[3] This information was reported in the 1902 edition of the *Catholic Encyclopedia's* article on Daniel Carroll. The article, specifically declaring itself "of interest to Catholics" in the 1902 edition, was deleted from the *New Catholic Encyclopedia* (1967). Other facts were reported in 1902 and deleted from 1967. For example, when Congress met in Washington for the first time, in November, 1800, "the only two really comfortable and imposing houses within the bounds of the city" belonged to Roman Catholics. One was Washington's first mayor, Robert Brent. The other was Brent's brother-in-law, Notley Young, a Jesuit priest.

Daniel Carroll was a Roman Catholic congressman from Maryland who signed two of America's fundamental documents, the Articles of Confederation and the United States Constitution. Carroll was a direct descendant of the Calverts, a Catholic family to whom King Charles I of England had granted Maryland as a feudal barony. Carroll had received his education at St. Omer's Jesuit College in Flanders, where young English-speaking Catholics were

CHAPTER I   SUBLIMINAL ROME

trained in a variety of guerrilla techniques for advancing the cause of Roman Catholicism among hostile Protestants.

In 1790, President George Washington, a Protestant, appointed Congressman Carroll to head a commission of three men to select land for the "federal city" called for in the Constitution. Of all places, the commission chose "Rome," which at the time consisted of four farms, one of which belonged to... Daniel Carroll. It was upon Carroll's farm that the new government chose to erect its most important building, the Capitol.

THE American Capitol abounds with clues of its Roman origins. "Freedom," the Roman goddess whose statue crowns the dome, was created in Rome at the studio of American sculptor Thomas Crawford. We find a whole pantheon of Roman deities in the great fresco covering the dome's interior rotunda: Persephone, Ceres, Freedom, Vulcan, Mercury, even a deified George Washington. These figures were the creation of Vatican artist Constantino Brumidi.

The fact that the national Statehouse evolved as a "capitol" bespeaks Roman influence. No building can rightly be called a capitol unless it's a temple of Jupiter, the great father-god of Rome who ruled heaven with his thunderbolts and nourished the earth with his fertilizing rains. If it was a *capitolium,* it belonged to Jupiter and his priests.

Jupiter's mascot was the eagle, which the founding fathers made their mascot as well. A Roman eagle tops the governing idol of the House of Representatives, a forty-six-inch sterling silver-and-ebony wand called a "mace." The mace is "the symbol of authority in the House."[4] When the Sergeant-at-arms displays it before an unruly member of Congress, the mace restores order. Its position at the rostrum tells whether the House is in "committee" or in "session."

America's national motto *"Annuit Coeptis"* came from a prayer to Jupiter. It appears in Book IX of Virgil's epic propaganda, the *Aeneid,* a poem commissioned just before the birth of Christ by Caius Maecenas, the multi-billionaire power behind Augustus

Caesar. The poem's objective was to fashion Rome into an imperial monarchy for which its citizens would gladly sacrifice their lives.

Fascism may be an ugly word to many, but its stately emblem is apparently offensive to no one. The emblem of fascism, a pair of them, commands the wall above and behind the speaker's rostrum in the Chamber of the House of Representatives. They're called *fasces*, and I can think of no reason for them to be there other than to declare the fascistic nature of American republican democracy.

A fasces is a Roman device. Actually, it originated with the ancient Etruscans, from whom the earliest Romans derived their religious jurisprudence nearly three thousand years ago. It's an axe-head whose handle is a bundle of rods tightly strapped together by a red sinew. It symbolizes the ordering of priestly functions into a single infallible sovereign, an autocrat who could require life and limb of his subjects. If the fasces is entwined with laurel, like the pair on the House wall, it signifies Caesarean military power. The Romans called this infallible sovereign *Pontifex Maximus*, "Supreme Bridgebuilder." No Roman was called *Pontifex Maximus* until the title was given to Julius Caesar in 48 BC. Today's *Pontifex Maximus* is Pope John Paul II.

As we shall discover in a forthcoming chapter, John Paul does not hold that title alone. He shares it with a mysterious partner, a military man, a man holding an office that has been known for more than four centuries as *"Papa Nero,"* the Black Pope. I shall present evidence that the House fasces represent the Black Pope, who indeed rules the world.

Later, I will develop what is sure to become a controversial hypothesis: that the Black Pope rules by divine appointment, and for the ultimate good of mankind.

APOSTOLIC NUNCIATURE, UNITED STATES OF AMERICA
3339 Massachusetts Avenue NW
Washington, D.C.

Chapter 2

MISSIONARY ADAPTATION

F EW PEOPLE SEEM to be aware that the Roman Catholic Church in America is officially recognized as a State. How this came about makes interesting reading.

Early in his administration, President Ronald Reagan invited the Vatican City, whose ruling head is the Pope, to open its first embassy in Washington, D.C. His Holiness responded positively, and the embassy, or Apostolic Nunciature of the Holy See, opened officially on January 10, 1984.

Shortly thereafter, a complaint was filed against President Reagan at U.S. District Court in Philadelphia by the American Jewish Congress, the Baptist Joint Committee on Public Affairs, Seventh Day Adventists, the National Council of Churches, the National Association of Evangelicals, and Americans United for Separation of Church and State.The plaintiffs sought to have the Court declare that the administration had unconstitutionally granted to the Roman Catholic faith privileges that were being denied to other establishments of religion.

On May 7, 1985 the suit was thrown out by Chief Judge John Fullam. Judge Fullam ruled that district courts do not have jurisdiction to intervene in "foreign policy decisions" of the executive branch. Bishop James W. Malone, President of the U.S. Catholic Conference, praised Judge Fullam's decision, noting that it settled "not a religious issue but a public policy question."[1] The plaintiffs appealed. The Third Circuit denied the appeal, noticing that "the Roman Catholic Church's unique position of control over a sovereign territory gives it advantages that other religious organizations do not enjoy."[1] The Apostolic Nunciature at 3339 Massachusetts Avenue N.W. enables *Pontifex Maximus* to supervise more closely American civil government – "public policy" – as administered through Roman Catholic laypersons. (One such layperson was Chief Judge Fullam, whose Roman Catholicism apparently escaped the attention of the plaintiffs.)

This same imperium ran pagan Rome in essentially the same way. The public servants were priests of the various gods and goddesses. Monetary affairs, for example, were governed by priests of the goddess Moneta. Priests of Dionysus managed architecture and cemeteries, while priests of Justitia, with her sword, and Libera, blindfolded, holding her scales aloft, ruled the courts.[2] Hundreds of priestly orders, known as the Sacred College, managed hundreds of government bureaus, from the justice system to the construction, cleaning, and repair of bridges (no bridge could be built without the approval of *Pontifex Maximus),* buildings, temples, castles, baths, sewers, ports, highways, walls and ramparts of cities and the boundaries of lands.[3]

Priests directed the paving and repairing of streets and roads, supervised the calendar and the education of youth. Priests regulated weights, measures, and the value of money. Priests solemnized and certified births, baptisms, puberty, purification, confession, adolescence, marriage, divorce, death, burial, excommunication, canonization, deification, adoption into families, adoption into tribes and orders of nobility. Priests ran the libraries, the

CHAPTER 2   MISSIONARY ADAPTATION

museums, the consecrated lands and treasures. Priests registered the trademarks and symbols. Priests were in charge of public worship, directing the festivals, plays, entertainments, games and ceremonies. Priests wrote and held custody over wills, testaments, and legal conveyances.

Constantine

By the fourth century, one half of the lands and one fourth of the population of the Roman Empire were owned by the priests.[4] When the Emperor Constantine and his Senate formally adopted Christianity as the Empire's official religion, the exercise was more of a merger or acquisition than a revolution. The wealth of the priests merely became the immediate possession of the Christian churches, and the priests merely declared themselves Christians. Government continued without interruption. The pagan gods and goddesses were artfully outfitted with names appropriate to Christianity.[1] The sign over the Pantheon indicating "To [the fertility goddess] Cybele and All the Gods" was re-written "To Mary and All the Saints." The Temple of Apollo became the Church of St. Apollinaris. The Temple of Mars was reconsecrated Church of Santa Martina, with the inscription "Mars hence ejected, Martina, martyred maid / Claims now the worship which to him was paid."

Haloed icons of Apollo were identified as Jesus, and the crosses of Bacchus and Tammuz were accepted as the official symbol of the Crucifixion. Pope Leo I decreed that "St. Peter and St. Paul have replaced Romulus and Remus as Rome's protecting patrons."[2] Pagan feasts, too, were Christianized. December 25 – the celebrated birthday of a number of gods, among them Saturn, Jupiter, Tammuz, Bacchus, Osiris, and Mithras – was claimed to have been that of Jesus as well, and the traditional Saturnalia, season of drunken merriment and gift-giving, evolved into Christmas.

Bacchus was popular in ancient France under his Greek name

Sketch of Mithras (left), from a stone carving. Mithras was *"Sol Invictus"* the "unconquerable Sun," an imperial Roman god since the third century BC Under Constantinian Christianity, artisans re-consecrated him Jesus and other biblical names. In the silver dish made on Cyprus in the eighth century AD, Mithras (note the peculiar stance) slaying the Cosmic Bull became David killing a lion.

Dionysus – or, as the French rendered it, Denis. His feast, the *Festurn Dionysi,* was held every seventh day of October, at the end of the vintage season. After two days of wild partying, another feast was held, the *Festum Dionysi Eleutherei Rusticum* ("Country Festival of Merry Dionysus"). The papacy cleverly brought the worshippers of Dionysus into its jurisdiction by transforming the words Dionysos, Bacchus, Eleutherei, and Rusticum into... a group of Christian martyrs. October seventh was entered on the Liturgical Calendar as the feast day of "St. Bacchus the Martyr," while October ninth was instituted as the "Festival of St. Denis, and of his companions St. Eleuthere and St. Rustic." *The Catholic Almanac* (1992 et seq) sustains the fabrication by designating October ninth as the;

> Feast Day of Denis, bishop of Paris, and two companions identified by early writers as Rusticus, a priest, and Eleutherius, a deacon martyred near Paris. Denis is popularly regarded as the apostle and patron saint of France.

CHAPTER 2   MISSIONARY ADAPTATION

PLAYING loose with truth and Scripture in order to bring every human creature into subjection to the Roman Pontiff is a technique called "missionary adaptation." This is explained as "the adjustment of the mission subject to the cultural requirements of the mission object" so that the papacy's needs will be brought "as much as possible in accord with existing socially shared patterns of thought, evaluation, and action, so as to avoid unnecessary and serious disorganization."[1]

Rome has so seamlessly adapted its mission to American secularism that we do not think of the United States as a Catholic system. Yet the rosters of government rather decisively show this to be the case.

By far the greatest challenge to missionary adaptation has been Scripture – that is, the Old and New Testaments, commonly known as the Holy Bible. Almost for as long as Rome has been the seat of *Pontifex Maximus,* there has been a curious enmity between the popes and the Bible whose believers they are presumed to head. In the next chapter, we shall begin our examination of that enmity.

ROME vs. SCRIPTURE
Pope Gregory IX (1227-41), founder of the Inquisition
and champion of Aristotle, excommunicates Holy
Roman Emperor Frederick II, upside down with Bible.
(From the painting by Vasari.)

Chapter 3

MARGINALIZING THE BIBLE

EVERY RULED SOCIETY has some form of holy scripture. The holy scriptures of Caesarean Rome were the prophecies and ritual directions contained in the ten Sibylline gospels and Virgil's *Aeneid*.

The *Aeneid* implied that every Roman's duty was to sacrifice his individuality, as heroic Aeneas had done, to the greater glory of Rome and *Pontifex Maximus*. The Sibyllines, borrowing from Isaiah's much earlier prophecy of Jesus Christ, prophesied that when Caesar Augustus succeeded his uncle Julius as *Pontifex Maximus* he would rule the world as "Prince of Peace, Son of God." Augustus would issue in a "new world order," as indeed he did.

The Sibyllines and the *Aeneid* were so beloved by the government priests that they were considered part of the Roman constitution. The same scriptures were made part of the United States Constitution when the mottoes *"ANNUIT COEPTIS"* and *"NOVUS ORDO SECLORUM,"* taken from the *Aeneid* and the Sibyllines respectively, were incorporated, by the Act of July 28, 1782, into the Great Seal of the United States.[1]

The Sibyllines and the *Aeneid* were open only to priests and certain privileged persons. The people learned their sacred content by the trickle-down of priestly retelling. When the Old and New Testaments were adopted as the Empire's official sacred writings they, too, were given to the exclusive care of the priests. And in accord with Roman tradition, the people learned sacred content from discretionary retelling. This had to be, for the sake of the Holy Empire. For should the people acquire biblical knowledge, they would know that *Pontifex Maximus* was not a legitimate Christian entitlement. Knowing this, they would not bow to his supremacy. The Empire could collapse. And so the monarchial Roman Church forcibly suppressed the Bible's intelligent reading. This is why the millennium between Constantine and Gutenberg is known as "the Dark Ages."

Sprinkled throughout the Empire, however, were isolated Christian assemblies who had preserved Scripture from the days of the early Church. For them the Bible invited an ongoing, personal communion with the Creator of the universe. They lived by the writings of which Rome was so jealous. By the thirteenth century, these assemblies had grown so vibrant that Pope Gregory IX declared unauthorized Bible study a heresy.[2] He further decreed that "it is the duty of every Catholic to persecute heretics." To manage the persecution, Gregory established the Pontifical Inquisition.

The Inquisition treated the slightest departure from the life of the community as proof of direct communion with the Bible or Satan. Either instance was a sin worthy of death.[3] Cases were prosecuted according to a strict routine. First, the inquisitors would enter a town and present their credentials to the civil authorities. In the pope's name, they would require the governor's cooperation. Next, the local priest would be ordered to summon his congregation to hear the inquisitors preach against heresy, which was defined as anything the least bit opposed to the papal system. A brief grace period followed the sermon, wherein the people were

CHAPTER 3   MARGINALIZING THE BIBLE

given an opportunity to step forward and accuse themselves of crimes. Those who did were usually punished mildly. Later, the inquisitors would receive at their lodgings unverified accusations, guaranteeing in the pope's name the anonymity of informants. Many innocent lives were ruined by false testimony.

Trials were conducted arbitrarily and secretly by tribunals consisting of the inquisitors, their staffs, and their witnesses, all concealed under hoods. The accused were never told the charges against them, and they were forbidden to ask. No defense witnesses were permitted. The accused had but one option: to confess guilt and die. Those who refused to confess (and witnesses who balked at testifying) were carried to the dungeon for torture sessions (boys under fourteen and girls under twelve exempted). Inquisitors and executioners were commanded by papal edict to show no mercy. No acquittal was ever recorded. Every fully prosecuted case ended in the death of the defendant and the forfeiture of his or her property, since it was assumed (as in American forfeiture cases since 1984) that the property was gained in sin. Sometimes the property of family members for generations to come was forfeited. These forfeitures were paid out in expenses to the scribes and executioners, half of the remainder going into the papal treasury and half to the inquisitors. Although popes and inquisitors amassed great fortunes from the Inquisition, its greatest beneficiary was, and has been, the Roman system.[4]

The Inquisition was most effective against the isolated truth-seeker in an ignorant community. As communities became more literate, the Inquisition grew subtler. What brought literacy to communities was the epidemic of Bible-reading made possible by the perfection of Johannes Gutenberg's invention of movable type.

NOMINATION
Charles Habsburg (right, King of Spain and
Holy Roman Emperor) confides to Pope
Clement VII (Giulio d'Medici) his choice of the
man to stop defections to Protestantism.
(After the painting by Vasari.)

Chapter 4

MEDICI LEARNING

G UTENBERG CHOSE the Bible to demonstrate movable type not so much that the common man might be brought nearer to God, but that he and his backer, Dr. Johannes Faust, might make a killing in the book trade.

Prior to 1450, Bibles were so rare they were conveyed by deed, like parcels of real estate. A Bible took nearly a year to make, commanding a price equal to ten times the annual income of a prosperous man. Johannes Gutenberg intended his first production, a folio edition of the 6th-century Latin Bible (known as the Vulgate), to fetch manuscript prices. Dr. Faust discreetly sold it as a one-of-a-kind to kings, nobles, and churches. A second edition in 1462 sold for as much as 600 crowns each in Paris, but sales were too sluggish to suit Faust, so he slashed prices to 60 crowns and then to 30.

This put enough copies into circulation for Church authorities to notice that several were identical. Such extraordinary uniformity being regarded as humanly impossible, the authorities charged that Faust had produced the Bibles by magic. On this pretext, the Archbishop of Mainz had Gutenberg's shop raided and a fortune in counterfeit Bibles seized. The red ink with which they were embellished was alleged to be human blood. Faust was arrested for conspiring with Satan, but there is no record of any trial.

Meanwhile, the pressmen, who had been sworn not to disclose Gutenberg's secrets while in his service, fled the jurisdiction of Mainz and set up shops of their own. As paper manufacture improved, along with technical improvements in matrix cutting and type-casting, books began to proliferate. Most were editions of the Vulgate. In the decade following the Mainz raid, five Latin and two German Bibles were published. Translators busied themselves in other countries. An Italian version appeared in 1471, a Bohemian in 1475, a Dutch and a French in 1477, and a Spanish in 1478.

As quickly as our generation has become computer-literate, the Gutenberg generation learned to read books, and careful readers found shocking discrepancies between the papacy's interpretation of God's Word and the Word itself.

In 1485, the Archbishop of Mainz issued an edict punishing unauthorized Bible-reading with excommunication, confiscation of books, and heavy fines. The great Renaissance theologian Desiderius Erasmus challenged the Archbishop by publishing, in 1516, the first printed edition of the Greek New Testament. He addressed the anti-Bible mentality in his preface with these words:

> I vehemently dissent from those who would not have private persons read the Holy Scriptures nor have them translated into the vulgar tongues, as though either Christ taught such difficult doctrines that they can only be understood by a few theologians, or the safety of the Christian religion lay in ignorance of it. I should like all women to read the Gospel and the Epistles of Paul. Would that they were translated into all languages so that not only the Scotch and Irish, but Turks and Saracens might be able to read and know them.

A Catholic monk named Martin Luther, against the advice of his superiors, plunged into the New Testament of Erasmus. He was

CHAPTER 4   MEDICI LEARNING

shocked by the absence of scriptural authority for so many Church traditions. Of the seven Church Sacraments only two, Baptism and the Lord's Supper, were grounded in Scripture. The remaining five – Confirmation, Absolution, Ordination, Marriage, and Extreme Unction – were the inventions of post-biblical councils and decrees. Luther found no scriptural mandate for celibacy of monks and nuns, or for pilgrimages and the veneration of sacred relics. The Church taught that prayer, good works, and regular participation in the Sacraments might save man from eternal damnation. Luther found this to be opposed to the teaching of Scripture. According to Scripture, only one thing can save man from the consequences of his sins: God's grace, and that alone.

Martin Luther

The most explosive result of Luther's Bible-reading was its attitude toward the papacy. Nowhere in Scripture could the passionate monk find that God had ordained an imperious Roman "Vicar of Christ" to rule over a vast economy based on selling rights to do evil. These rights were called indulgences. They had been a Church tradition since Pope Leo III had begun granting them in the year 800, payable in the money coined by Pope Adrian I in 780.

Indulgences were floated on the Church's credibility, rather like government bonds are issued on the credibility of states today. In 1491, for example, Innocent VII granted the 20-year *Butterbriefe* indulgence, by which Germans could pay 1/20th of a guilder for the annual privilege of eating dairy products even while meriting from fasting. The proceeds of the *Butterbriefe* went to build a bridge at Torgau.. Rome's indulgence economy was as extensive as America's income tax system today. And it was every bit as fueled by the people's trembling compliance, voluntarily, to a presumption of liability.

In 1515 Pope Leo X issued a Bull of Indulgence authorizing letters of safe conduct to Paradise and pardons for every evil imaginable,² from a 25-cent purgatory release (the dead left purgatory the instant one's coins hit the bottom of the indulgence-salesman's bucket) to a license so potent that it would excuse someone who had raped the Virgin Mary. For the payment of four ducats, one could be forgiven for murdering one's father. Sorcery was pardoned for 6 ducats. For robbing a church, the law could be relaxed for only 9 ducats. Sodomy was pardoned for 12 ducats. Half the revenues from Leo's indulgence went to a fund for the building of St. Peter's Cathedral, and the other half to paying 40% interest rates on bank loans subsidizing the magnificent works of art and architecture with which His Holiness was establishing Rome as the cultural capital of the Renaissance. Historians have glorified Leo, whose father happened to be the great Florentine banker Lorenzo d'Medici, by marking the sixteenth century as "the Century of Leo X."

In early 1521, Martin Luther formally protested the indulgence racket by nailing his famous *Ninety-five Theses Upon Indulgences* to the door of the castle church of Wittenburg. The church was said to own a lock of the Holy Virgin's hair worth two million years of indulgences. Luther's *Theses* exhorted Christians "to follow Christ, their Head, through penalties, deaths, and hells," rather than purchase "a false assurance of peace" from Church indulgence-salesmen.

Leo had Luther arrested and detained for ten months in Wartburg Castle. While in custody, Luther managed to translate the Greek New Testament of Erasmus into German. Its publication alarmed the broadest reaches of Roman authority. D'Aubigne, in his *History of the Reformation,* tells us that "Ignorant priests shuddered at the thought that every citizen, nay every peasant, would now be able to dispute with them on the precepts of our Lord."

Meanwhile, Leo X died. The new pope, Adrian VI, hardly eulogized Leo when confessing to the Diet of Nuremberg that "for many years, abominable things have taken place in the Chair of Peter, abuses in spiritual matters, transgressions of the Commandments, so that everything here has been wickedly perverted."³

CHAPTER 4   MEDICI LEARNING

Adrian died shortly after speaking these lines, to be succeeded by the Cardinal who had been handling Martin Luther's case all along, another Medici, Leo X's first cousin, Giulio d'Medici. Giulio took the papal name Clement VII.

Just as Leo X's corruption had ignited Luther, Clement VII's shrewdness determined how the Church would deal with the proliferation of Bibles. Clement was personally advised by the cagey Niccolo Machiavelli, inventor of modern political science, and Cardinal Thomas Wolsey, Chancellor of England. Machiavelli and Wolsey opined that both printing and Protestantism could be turned to Rome's advantage by employing movable type to produce a literature that would confuse, diminish, and ultimately marginalize the Bible. Cardinal Wolsey, who would later found Christ Church College at Oxford, characterized the project as *"to put learning against learning."*[4]

Against the Bible's learning, which demonstrated how man could have eternal life simply by believing in the facts of Christ's death and resurrection, would be put the learning of the gnostics. Gnosticism held out the hope that man could achieve everlasting life by doing good works himself. To put it succinctly, Bible-learning was Christ-centered; gnostic learning was man-centered.

An enormous trove of gnostic learning had been brought from the eastern Mediterranean by agents of Clement VII's great-grandfather, Cosimo d'Medici. Suppressed since the Emperor Justinian had piously shut down the pagan colleges of Athens back in 529, these celebrated mystical, scientific and philosophical scrolls and manuscripts flattered humanity. They taught that human intelligence was competent to determine truth from falsehood without guidance or assistance from any god. Since, as Protagoras put it, "man is the measure of all things," man could control all the living powers of the universe. If elected and initiated into the secret knowledge, or *gnosis,* man could master the *cabalah* – the "royal science" of names, numbers, and symbols – to create his very own divinity.

Cosimo had stored huge quantities of this pagan material in his library in Florence. The Medici Library, whose final architect was

Michaelangelo, welcomed scholars favored by the papacy. These scholars, not surprisingly, soon began emulating the papacy in focusing more upon humanity than upon the Old and New Testaments. So extensive was the Medici Library's philosophical influence that even scholars today consider it the cradle of Western civilization.

Martin Luther, seeing that *learning against learning* was the future of Christianity, voiced an "Appeal to the Ruling Classes" (1520), in which he wrote, rather prophetically:

> Though our children live in the midst of a Christian world, they faint and perish in misery because they lack the Gospel in which we should be training and exercising them all the time. I advise no one to place his child where the Scriptures do not reign paramount. Schools will become wide-open gates of hell if they do not diligently engrave the Holy Scriptures on young hearts. Every institution where men are not increasingly occupied with the word of God must become corrupt.

It was one thing to recommend *learning against learning,* and quite another to manage its multiple dimensions. *Learning against learning* amounted to no less than making war on the Bible. To wage such a war, the papacy needed a new priestly order of pious soldiers conditioned to wield psychological weapons on a battlefield of... *human thought.* But first, there had to be a general. The man chosen to lead the assault on the Bible was a swashbuckling adventurer from the proud Basque country of northern Spain.

IGNATIUS OF LOYOLA

Chapter 5

APPOINTMENT AT CYPRUS

His name was Iñigo de Loyola. He was born in 1491 to a rich family, youngest of eight boys, one of thirteen children. His older brother had sailed to the New World with Christopher Columbus.

Iñigo served as a page in the court of King Ferdinand and Queen Isabella of Spain. He became friends with Ferdinand's Belgian grandson, Charles Habsburg, whose other grandfather was Holy Roman Emperor Maximilian. (The Holy Roman Emperor was a kind of secular pope who presided over the Christian kingdoms of the western world.) Charles was propelled to great authority before his twenty-first birthday by the deaths of his two grandfathers within a space of two years. From Ferdinand, Charles inherited Spain. From Maximilian, he inherited the Holy Roman Empire. Charles Habsburg was King Charles I of Spain, Emperor Charles V of Rome. He was the most powerful secular figure in Europe. And he was Iñigo's friend.

In 1518, Iñigo was part of a legation negotiating for Charles with Spain's traditional rival, France, at the court of the Duke of Najera in Valladolid. While the summit was in session, Catherina, the Emperor's sister, was presented to the Najera court. Iñigo fell in love with her. He was twenty-seven and she was eleven. (The Emperor was eighteen.) The match, however, was not to be.

On Monday, May 20, 1521, while commanding a garrison at the Duke's fortress in Pamplona, Iñigo was struck by a French cannonball. His right leg was shattered, and with it – since a well-shaped leg was among a courtier's most prized assets – the prospects for a romantic life with Catherina, or any other woman. An honor guard of French soldiers bore the wounded champion on a stretcher to his family's castle in the Spanish Pyrenees. Surgeons butchered his leg and reset the bones. He lost appetite and was told he might die. He made confession and was given last rites. But a few days after the feast of Sts. Peter and Paul, he was pronounced out of death's immediate grasp. He credited this recovery to his devotion to St. Peter.

Iñigo remained bedridden for nearly a year. Under the concerned if distant eye of the youthful Emperor, he spent his time "searching for substitutes for the shattered ideals, ambitions, and values that had been so central to his sense of himself."[2] He gazed obsessively at a small icon of Saint Catherine, a gift from Queen Isabella to his sister-in-law. The icon sparked dreams of Catherina, which only throttled his heart with desolation. He turned to books, Ludolph of Saxony's *Life of Christ* and Voragine's *Lives of the Saints* – the only two volumes in the family library despite the fact that a Spanish Bible had been available for forty years.

The icon and the books gave him visions. The visions, in turn, led him to develop a process of "preparing and disposing the soul to rid itself of all inordinate attachments, and, after their removal, of seeking and finding the will of God."[3] Iñigo called this process "the Spiritual Exercises."

In the Exercises, a Director leads a Retreatant through Four Weeks of intense prayer, meditation, and dialogue with the Blessed Virgin Mary, Jesus, and God the Father. Frequent repetition of

CHAPTER 5   APPOINTMENT AT CYPRUS

"Anima Christi," Loyola's own habitual prayer for disorientation and sensory deprivation ("Blood of Christ, inebriate me"), is advised. The First Week is spent considering and contemplating sins, creating vivid mental pictures of "hell in all its depth and breadth, putting your five senses at the service of your imagination." The Second Week explores the life of Christ up to Palm Sunday inclusively; the Third Week undertakes the Crucifixion, in which the Retreatant is directed to "imagine Christ our Lord present before you on the Cross, and begin to speak with him ... and ask 'What have I done for Christ? What am I doing for Christ? What ought I to do for Christ?'"[4] The Fourth Week is occupied with the Resurrection and Ascension, after which the Retreatant prays "for a knowledge of the deceits of the rebel chief and help to guard myself against them; and also to ask for a knowledge of the true life exemplified in the sovereign and true Commander, and the grace to imitate him."

By the time the Exercises have run their course, the Retreatant's purified imagination is totally dominated by mental pictures of Jesus resurrected, Jesus the King Militant. One can now answer the King's call to conquer Protestantism and its rebel chief ("the enemy of human nature") with the selfless fidelity of a chivalrous knight. One's consciousness has been altered. One's soul and brain have been washed. One's liberty has been sacrificed to authority. One's individuality has been surrendered to the Christ of Rome. One no longer has a will of one's own. One volunteers for *any* assigned task no matter how adverse.

Martin Luther spent Loyola's year of recovery imprisoned at Wartburg Castle for insulting the papacy with his *Ninety-Five Theses*. Remarkably, while one prisoner experienced mystical visions that urged him to defend the Church's honor in the romantically chivalrous manner of the Knights Templar, the other was translating (with the miraculous permission of his keepers) the New Testament into German so that ordinary people might learn the will of God directly. These parallel, simultaneous quests for holiness would define modern life's underlying conflict: Which Master Do I Serve, Rome or the Word of God?

PURIFIED by the Spiritual Exercises, Iñigo's sensual attachment to Princess Catherina was transformed through Saint Catherine into a higher, spiritual attachment to a higher femininity – to Mary, the Queen of Heaven. An apparition of the Virgin appeared to him one night and validated that he was free of fleshly lusts and was now worthy of a pilgrimage to Jerusalem. In Martin Luther's opinion, "as far as God is concerned, Jerusalem and all the Holy Land are not one whit more, or less, interesting than the cows in Switzerland."[5] But to a spiritual warrior preparing to lead the Church to war against Scripture, a touchdown in Jerusalem was absolutely necessary. Jerusalem was the domain of King Solomon's Temple, the geo-spiritual center of the Knights Templar. If Iñigo was to revive the Templars, as the Emperor desired, it was liturgically imperative that his newly-washed spirit present itself in the Sacred City for initiation into the mysteries of holy warfare.

All pilgrims to the Holy Land were required by law to apply to the pope at Easter for permission to proceed. In early March 1522, more than a year in advance, Iñigo set out for Rome in all his aristocratic finery, riding on the back of a mule. The corrupt Leo X had died suddenly of malaria in December 1521, and on January 9, 1522, Charles Habsburg (King and Emperor) had engineered the nearly unanimous election of his former tutor, Adrian Dedal, to succeed Leo as Adrian VI. Iñigo headed for Rome coincidentally with Adrian's journey across Spain to Barcelona, the point of embarcation for voyages to Italy. The new pope stopped in Navarre, in northern Spain, for an official reception by the Duke of Najera's successor. Iñigo, too, stopped at Navarre to do some undescribed business at the Duke's residence at Navarette. Perhaps Adrian gave him a discreet audience.

Further on, the pilgrim kept an all-night vigil at a chapel of the Virgin of Aranzazu, Protectress of the Basques, vowing his chastity to her small, dark statue. He continued on to Montserrat, where he lodged in a Benedictine abbey. There, he rededicated himself to God's service before another statue of the Virgin, the Black Madonna of Montserrat, Protectress of Catalonia, Patroness of Christian Conquest. The spiritual exercise here must have been

CHAPTER 5   APPOINTMENT AT CYPRUS

intense, for in the late afternoon of the third day, Iñigo traded clothes with a beggar, hung his sword and dagger on the Madonna's shrine, and gave his mule to the abbey.

While Adrian VI proceeded on to Barcelona, Iñigo detoured on foot to the village of Manresa for ten months of penances, spiritual preparation, and note-taking. Stripped of everything but sackcloth, a gourd for drinking, and a pilgrim's staff, he adopted the lifestyle of the early Knights Templar, begging food and alms. He was initiated into the *Illuminati,* the "Enlightened Ones," a secret society of gnostic fundamentalists who preached that all matter is absolutely and eternally evil.

The gnostics taught that humanity itself is of Satanic origin. Adam and Eve were the offspring of devils. Humanity can achieve salvation from death and eternal punishment, however, by freeing soul from body for absorption into the pure light of Godliness. This is done by withdrawing from sensual pleasure and intuitively discovering hidden truths as conveyed by the cabalah. (The gnostics' contempt for anything having to do with the physical side of existence translated into wildly ironic behavior. Some practiced radical celibacy because they believed the result of sexual intercourse, conception, would only imprison more souls in physical bodies. Others practiced unbridled sexual libertinism in order to prove they were completely free from all physical inhibition. Still others combined the two, pursuing hypocritical lives of celibate fornication, of which "safe sex" is the modern institution. Loyola's particular cult apparently chose the asceticism of self-flagellation, for Iñigo wandered many nights about the Manresa countryside whipping himself with a scourge studded with iron barbs. Later in life, he would decide that the whips and barbs "sapped one's strength," that the Godhead could as adequately be sought by the more humane self-mortification of the Spiritual Exercises.)

While Iñigo was outlining the Exercises in Manresa, Luther's translation of the New Testament was introducing readers and listeners in Germany, Switzerland, France, Bohemia, and England to a different form of spiritual exercise, one in which God's will, ancient and immutable, was expressed not within the private imagination but publicly, in the printed Word, for all to see. People devoured the New Testament even before it reached the bindery. In one contemporary's words, "The sheet, yet wet, was brought from the press under someone's cloak, and passed from shop to shop."[6]

THE pilgrim sailed from Barcelona to the Italian port city of Gaeta, and walked the remaining distance to Rome, arriving there on Palm Sunday, March 29, 1523. Two days later, according to Vatican archives, "Iñigo de Loyola, cleric of the diocese of Pamplona" received permission from Pope Adrian VI to visit Jerusalem.

From Rome, Iñigo proceeded to Venice, where one of Charles Habsburg's agents received him graciously and introduced him to the Doge, Andrea Gritti, the highest official in Venetian civil government. A famed diplomat and linguist, Gritti arranged free passage for Iñigo aboard a small ship whose name – the *"Negrona"* – was appropriate for an evangelist dedicated to the Black Virgin of Christian Conquest.

On July 14, 1523, the *Negrona* left Venice, arriving a month later at the island of Cyprus. At Cyprus, one Diego Manes and his servant, along with several Cypriot officials, boarded ship for the rest of the voyage to Haifa. Diego Manes was a Commander of the Knights Hospitallers of St. John of Jerusalem.[7] Since 1312, the Hospitallers had held title to the vast wealth of the Knights Templar. They had been drawing upon these assets to defend the Roman economy against Islamic marauders in the east. But when the Turks attacked the Hospitallers' headquarters on the Island of Rhodes, the assets were frozen by the pope and his former pupil, the Holy Roman Emperor Charles. No assistance in any form was forthcoming from either party. Consequently, in December 1522, the Hospitallers had no choice but to surrender Rhodes and retreat to what would become their final domicile, Malta. The message was clear. Now that Luther's German-language New Testament was in print, Protestantism loomed a greater menace to Rome than Islam ever did.

It is possible that in a Jerusalem-bound ship named *Negrona*,

CHAPTER 5   APPOINTMENT AT CYPRUS

Commander Diego Manes turned over the litanies, lists, secret codes, formulae, cabalah, and other portable assets comprising the Knights Templar resources to Iñigo. If this indeed happened, the western world's secret infrastructure was now Loyola's to populate and manipulate in the cause of *learning against learning.* That is my hypothesis. What is not hypothesis is that as soon as the pilgrim returned from Jerusalem he began vesting himself with Medici learning.

The idea of uniting the Templars with the Hospitallers was first argued publicly in a book published in 1305 by Raimon Llull, a renowned *illuminatus* from Majorca. Llull's book, *Libre de Fine,* ("Free At Last") appeared in the midst of a raging controversy between the French monarchy and the Roman papacy over who held jurisdiction over the Templars. That is the subject of our next chapter.

THE BAPHOMET

Chapter 6

THE EPITOME OF CHRISTIAN VALUES

SINCE THEIR FOUNDING on French soil in 1118, the Knights Templar had grown from a pair of self-impoverished knights hoping to keep Muslim terrorists from molesting pilgrims in the Holy Land to a mammoth organization controlling international finance and politics. The founders, Hugh de Payen and Godfroi de St. Omer, organized a group of excommunicated knight-crusaders and secured their absolution by a bishop. After placing the restored knights under oaths of poverty, chastity, secrecy, and obedience, they pledged the organization to rebuilding Solomon's Temple. Given space adjacent to an Islamic mosque situated upon the Temple's supposed ruins, they took the corporate name "Poor Knights of Christ and of the Temple of Solomon."

Bernard, Abbot of Clairvaux, the leading propagandist of the day, extolled the Templars as "the epitome and apotheosis of Christian values." Bolstered by such unprecedented promotion, the Poor Knights attracted the best and the brightest young men of Europe to become Crusaders, to vow celibacy and leave their families in defense of Christ's tomb against Muslim terrorists.

The mission failed within nine years. Even so, Bernard's propaganda caused the Templars to be received as conquering heroes when they returned to France. They set up their permanent lodge at Troyes under the patronage of the court of Champagne. (For nearly a century, Troyes had been Europe's leading school for the study of the cabalah, which may explain why the city is laid out in the shape of a champagne cork.)

For making the Templars a world power, Bernard shares credit with Cardinal Aimeric of Santa Maria Nuova. Aimeric was the Church's highest judicial officer. It was his unlawful connivance that created Honorius II, the pope who ordained the Templars as the Church's most highly-esteemed religious order. It was Aimeric, too, who devised a radical "inner renewal of the Church," which inspired noblemen throughout England, Scotland, Flanders, Spain, and Portugal to shower the Templars with donations of land and money – over and above the properties required of all initiates upon joining the Order.

When Honorius died in 1130, Aimeric led a minority of cardinals in another connivance resulting in the election of Innocent II, who was consecrated pope in Aimeric's titular church of Santa Maria Nuova. In 1139, Innocent issued a bull placing the Templars under an exclusive vow of papal obedience – a measure by which Aimeric effectively put all Templar resources at the disposal of the papacy. Within another decade, the Knights were given exclusive rights by Pope Eugenius III to wear the *rose croix,* the rosy cross, on their white tunics. As their list of properties lengthened with donations from Italy, Austria, Germany, Hungary, and the Holy Land, the Templars built hundreds of great stone castles. Wealthy travelers lodged in these castles because of their unmatched security. Convinced they were building a new world, the Templars called each other *frère maçon* ("brother mason"). Later, this term would be anglicized into "Freemason."

CHAPTER 6   THE EPITOME OF CHRISTIAN VALUES

The Templars invented modern banking by applying an oriental invention to their commerce. Agents of the Chinese emperor Kao-tsung, inventor of paper currency called *fei-chi'en*, "flying money," sought trade with the middle east during the period of Templar occupation.[2] Kao-tsung's was the first government on earth to enforce circulation of drafts as legal tender for debts. Evi-dently, Kao-tsung's agents introduced the Knights to this new medium of exchange created out of merchant drafts. The Templars enhanced their already booming business of (1) accepting current accounts, deposit accounts, deposits of jewels, valuables and title deeds, (2) making loans and advances (charging "fees" because the Church forbade interest), and (3) acting as agents for the secure transmission of such things by (4) adding circulating letters of credit – flying money – to serve as paper currency. To supply the Templars' currency needs may explain why paper in France was first manufactured in the Poor Knights' hometown of Troyes.

By 1300, presiding over the world economy from their Paris office,[3] the Templars had become an international power unto themselves. Engaged in diplomacy at the highest levels of state from the Holy Land westward, they set the tastes, the goals, the morality, the rules of the civilized world. Kings did their bidding – when Henry III of England threatened to confiscate certain of the Order's properties, he was upbraided by the Master Templar in the city of London:

> "What sayest thou, O King? So long as thou dost exercise justice, thou wilt reign. But if thou infringe it, thou wilt cease to be King."[4]

But suddenly, at their very zenith, the Poor Knights suffered a strange reversal of fortunes. In 1302, King Philip IV of France dared to challenge their sovereignty on his own soil. He asserted that in France everyone, Knights Templars included, was subject to the King. Pope Boniface VIII jumped in and declared that France, the King, the Templars, all of them, and everybody else as well, belonged to *Pontifex Maximus* – "It is absolutely necessary for the salvation of every human creature to be subject to the Roman

Pontiff." Philip then accused the pope of illegitimacy, sexual misconduct, and heresy. Boniface prepared a bull excommunicating Philip, but before it could be published, a band of the Philip's mercenaries stormed the Vatican and demanded the pope's resignation. Although the intruders were driven off, the shock to body and soul was too much for Boniface, and he died a month later.

Two successor popes held firm against Philip, until Bertrand de Got, Archbishop of Bordeaux, was elected in 1305. Crowned in Lyons with the papal name Clement V, de Got moved the papacy to Avignon, and began a long train of concessions to Philip's royal prerogative. Finally, on Friday, October 13, 1307, Philip arrested all but thirteen of the Templars in France, tried them and, upon evidence of their practice of the cabalah, found them guilty of blasphemy and magic. At least fifty knights were burned at the stake.

From captured documents it was learned that the Templars, from the very beginning, had renounced what Roman theologians called "the religion of St. Peter." They had been initiated into a secret gnostic branch of the Eastern Church known as "the Primitive Christian Church." Because the Primitive Christians' apostolic succession claimed to flow from John the Baptist and the apostle John they were called "Johannites."[5]

The Johannites believed that although Jesus was "imbued with a spirit wholly divine and endowed with the most astounding qualities," he was not the true God. Consistent with gnostic logic, the true Johannite God would never lower Himself to become vile human matter. Jesus was in fact a false Messiah sent by the powers of darkness. He was justly crucified – although when his side was pierced he did repent of his pretensions and receive divine forgiveness. Thanks to his repentance, Jesus now enjoys everlasting life in the celestial company of the saints.

Regarding miracles, the Johannites believed that Jesus "did or may have done extraordinary or miraculous things," and that "since God can do things incomprehensible to human intelligence, all the acts of Christ as they are described in the Gospel, whether acts of human science or whether acts of divine power"

CHAPTER 6 THE EPITOME OF CHRISTIAN VALUES

can be accepted as true – except for the Resurrection, which is omitted from the Templars' copy of the Gospel of St. John.[6] Therefore, for all his wonderful attributes, Christ "was nothing, a false prophet and of no value." Only the Higher God of Heaven had power to save mankind.[7]

But the Higher God avoided human matter, and so lordship over the material world belonged to Satanael, the evil brother of Jesus. Satanael alone could enrich mankind. Templar cabalah represented Satanael as the head of a goat emblazoned with, sometimes contained within, a pentagram.[8] This symbol is deeply rooted in Old Testament cabalah, in which the goat is identified with power in the world and separation from God. On the greatest Israelite feastday, *Yom Kippur,* the Day of Atonement, one goat was spared the sacrificial knife, and was sprinkled with the blood of another goat killed for the sins of Israel. The spared goat, the scapegoat, was then banished from the congregation to bear Israel's sins into the wilderness, which typified the world.[9] The scapegoat escaped with his life, his freedom.

King Solomon conferred with evil spirits,[10] but Scripture describes the spirits only generally. However, the Zohar, or "Book of Splendor," one of the main works of ancient cabalistic literature, tells us evil spirits appeared to the Israelites *"under the form of he-goats* and made known to them all that they wished to learn."[11] The Templars called this goat-idol "Baphomet," from *baphe*-and--metis, Greek words combined to mean "absorption" into wisdom. Baphomet encapsulates the career of Solomon, who Scripture says was absorbed into the wisdom of God more than any other human being,[12] yet finished out his life in communion with he-goatish evil spirits.[13] By the Templars' Johannite standard, communing with the evil spirits was the secret to controlling the world. By the biblical standard, however, Solomon represents the impossibility of human perfectibility. Perfectibility is indeed attainable, according to Scripture, but only through the redemptive process shown in the New Testament which Rome kept the Templars from reading.

ON March 22, 1312, Clement V dissolved the Knights Templar with his decree *Vox clamantis* ("War Cry"). But the dissolution proved a mere formality to further appease Philip. More importantly, it permitted the Templars, in other manifestations, to continue enriching the papacy. For Grand Master Jacques de Molay, just prior to his execution in 1313, sent the surviving thirteen French Templars to establish four new Metropolitan lodges: one at Stockholm for the north, one at Naples for the east, one at Paris for the south, and one at Edinburgh for the west. Thus, the Knights *remained* the militant arm of the papacy. Except that their wealth, their secrecy, their gnostic cabalism, and their oath of papal obedience were obscurely dispersed under a variety of corporate names.

A subtle provision in *Vox clamantis* transferred most Templar estates to the Knights of St. John of Jerusalem, who took possession after King Philip's death. In Germany and Austria, the Templars became "Rosicrucians" and "Teutonic Knights." The Teutonic Knights grew strong in Mainz, birthplace of Gutenberg's press. Six centuries later, as the "Teutonic Order," the Knights would provide the nucleus of Adolf Hitler's political support in Munich and Vienna.

The Edinburgh lodge would become the headquarters of Scottish Rite Freemasonry, which Masonic historians call "American Freemasonry" because all but five of the signers of the Declaration of Independence are said to have practiced its craft. In Spain and Portugal the Templars became the *"Illuminati"* in whom Iñigo had taken membership at Manresa, and "Knights of Christ." It was under the red pattée cross of the Knights of Christ that Columbus had taken possession of what he called *"las Indias"* for King Ferdinand V of Spain, grandfather of Iñigo's discreet patron, Charles I and V, the Holy Roman Emperor.

As early as August of 1523, as I hypothesized in the previous chapter, this vast yet fragmented subterranean empire – Roman Catholicism's unseen root-system binding together the world – belonged to Iñigo de Loyola. His spiritual dynasty, which continues to this day, would use this system to cause God-fearing men

CHAPTER 6   THE EPITOME OF CHRISTIAN VALUES

who hated the papacy to perform, without realizing it, exactly how the papacy wanted them to.

But what of Iñigo's education? His rise in academe is the subject of the next chapter.

"Hoc EST DIGITUS DEI!"
Pope Paul III declares Loyola's plan for the Company of Jesus an Act of God. (From a Jesuit altar)

Chapter 7

THE FINGERSTROKE OF GOD

Determined on a priestly life, Iñigo de Loyola returned to Barcelona from Jerusalem in the spring of 1524. He spent the next three years in Spain getting the requisite Latin. Since direct contact with the Bible was prohibited by law, his reading coursed the humanities.

With the esoteric experience of his Spiritual Exercises, he charmed the wives of important men. He received frequent invitations to dine at elegant tables, but preferred to beg food door to door and distribute the choice pickings to the poor and sick. He lived in an attic and slept on the floorboards, trying desperately to persuade God of his worthiness. He prayed for six hours each day, attended mass three times a week, confessed every Sunday, and continued whipping himself. He devised secret penances, such as boring holes in his shoes and going barefoot in winter.

Sometimes the Exercises aroused in his followers instances of bizarre conduct – swooning, long spells of fainting or melancholia, rolling about the ground, being gripped with corpse-like rigidity. The Spanish Inquisition investigated him on suspicion of preaching gnostic illuminism. When Iñigo insisted that he was not preaching at all, but was merely talking about the things of God in a familiar way, the Inquisitor released him. In successive frays, the Inquisition ordered Iñigo (1) to get rid of his eccentric clothing and dress like other students, (2) to refrain from holding meetings until he had completed four years of study, and (3) to refrain from defining what constituted a grave sin. Wearying of the harassment, he decided to seek his four years of education beyond the Inquisition's reach.

He set out for the University of Paris with a pack mule carrying his belongings. He arrived at the University on February 2, 1528, and soon afterward registered in the run-down old College of Montaigu. John Calvin, who would become Protestantism's great theological systems designer, was leaving Montaigu just as Loyola arrived. Erasmus, the College's most famous alumnus, remembered graduating from Montaigu "with nothing except an infected body and a vast array of lice." The student body consisted mostly of wayward Parisian boys kept under harsh discipline; Iñigo was thirty-seven.

Paris was expensive, even for students. Much of the funds Iñigo had raised in Barcelona had been stolen by one of his disciples. In early 1529 he went into Belgium, where it is believed he received money from people close to the Holy Roman Emperor. One of these was Juan de Cuellar, Treasurer of the Kingdom of Spain. Another was Luis Vives, personal secretary to the Emperor's aunt, Queen Catherine of England, and private tutor to her daughter, Princess Mary (afterward the "Bloody" Queen). Iñigo returned to Paris much better off. He upgraded his lodgings.

In October, he left Montaigu and enrolled at the College of Ste. Barbe across the street. He pursued a course in arts and philosophy that would last three and a half years. His name appears on the Ste. Barbe registry as "Ignatius de Loyola." Some Jesuit historians have guessed he adopted the name in veneration of Ignatius of Antioch, an early Christian martyr. It was at Ste. Barbe

CHAPTER 7 THE FINGERSTROKE OF GOD

that Iñigo began earnestly organizing his army, but not before traveling again to Belgium to ask Juan de Cuellar and Luis Vives for yet more money.

Armed with his command of the Templar secrets and with introductions provided by the Emperor and Vives, Ignatius crossed to England. This significant voyage is mentioned only once in his autobiography. He admits that he "returned with more alms than he usually did in other years." Perhaps Queen Catherine, the Emperor's aunt, introduced him to the Howards and the Petres, known to be among the first families to receive and nourish Jesuits sent to England.

Starting with his two Ste. Barbe roommates, Ignatius soon gathered a circle of six close friends ranging in age from teens to early twenties. Somewhat like himself, they were adventurous, impressionable, intelligent, and unpersuaded of the Bible's supreme authority. Their fondest dream was to save the Holy Land from the Muslims by performing heroic Templaresque exploits. One by one Ignatius gave them the Spiritual Exercises, and one by one they became disciples. Within a few years they were calling themselves *La Compañia de Jesus,* the Company of Jesus.

On August 15, 1534, Feast Day of the Assumption of the Virgin into heaven, the companions swore oaths of service to the Blessed Virgin in Ste. Marie's Church at Montmartre, and to St. Denis, patron saint of France, in his chapel. (The experience of the Montmartre Oaths must have been intense, for Francis Xavier, who would become St. Francis, Apostle to the East, made the Spiritual Exercises with "a penitential fervor," says Broderick in *Origin of the Jesuits,* "that nearly cost him the use of his limbs.") They vowed poverty, chastity, and to rescue Jerusalem from the Muslims. However, should the rescue prove infeasible within a year, they vowed to undertake without question whatever other task the pope might require of them.

Well before a year had passed, Clement VII died and the Jerusalem dream was overwhelmed by more present dangers. Luther's Bible in German was creating defection in record numbers throughout Germany, Norway, Sweden, and Denmark. In

France, the response to LeFevre's Bible was so decisive that King Francis I exclaimed that he would behead his own children if he found them harboring the blasphemous heresies acquirable through direct contact with scripture. England was lost in its entirety, due not to Bible reading, which Henry VIII prosecuted as avidly as any pope, but to the royal love life. Henry had demanded that Clement VII grant him a divorce from the Emperor's aunt Catherine, and then recognize the Protestant-oriented Anne Boleyn as his new Queen. When Clement stood mute, Henry took all of England away from Rome and made himself "complete owner of the lands and tenements [of England], as well at law as in equity."[1]

Giulia Farnese, with metal blouse

Clement VII was succeeded by the oldest cardinal, an erudite humanist with formidable diplomatic skills, 66-year-old Alessandro Farnese. Cardinal Farnese had been privately educated in the household of Lorenzo d'Medici and had been appointed Treasurer of the Vatican in 1492. He was crowned Pope Paul III. Vatican wags called Farnese "Cardinal Petticoat" because his strikingly beautiful sister Giulia had been mistress to the licentious Pope Alexander VI, for which the same wags nicknamed her "Bride of Christ." Giulia posed undraped for the statue of the Goddess Justice that still reclines voluptuously on Paul III's tomb in St. Peter's Basilica. Two centuries later, at the command, in the interests of decency, of Pius IX, the first pope to be officially declared infallible, Giulia's exposed breasts were fitted with a metal blouse.[2]

Paul III is a major figure in the history of the Society of Jesus, and consequently of the United States of America, since it was he who approved, in the summer of 1539, Ignatius de Loyola's business plan. Ignatius proposed a "minimal society" that would "do battle in the Lord God's service under the banner of the Cross." The militia would be very small, no more than sixty members, and

CHAPTER 7　　THE FINGERSTROKE OF GOD

each would have to take four vows – of poverty, chastity, obedience to the Church, and a vow of special obedience to the pope. They would not be confined to any specific parish but would be dispersed throughout the world according to the papacy's needs. They would wear no particular habit, but would dress according to the environment in which they found themselves. They would infiltrate the world in an unpredictable variety of pursuits – as doctors, lawyers, authors, reforming theologians, financiers, statesmen, courtiers, diplomats, explorers, tradesmen, merchants, poets, scholars, scientists, architects, engineers, artists, printers, philosophers, and whatever else the world might demand and the Church require.

Their head would be a Superior General. In the Constitutions which Ignatius was writing, the Superior General would be "obeyed and reverenced at all times as the one who holds the place of Christ our Lord."[3] The phrase "holds the place of Christ" means that the Superior General would share with the Pope, at a level unperceived by the general public, the divine title of "Vicar of Christ" first claimed by Gelasius I on May 13, 495. Loyola's completed *Constitutions* would repeat five hundred times that one is to see Christ in the person of the Superior General.[4] The General's equal status with the Pope, advantaged by an obscurity that renders him virtually invisible, is why the commander-in-chief of the Society of Jesus has always been called *Papa Nero*, the Black Pope.

The Superior General's small army would be trained by the Spiritual Exercises to practice a brand of obedience Loyola termed *contemplativus in actione*, active contemplation, instantaneous obedience with all critical thought suppressed. As stated in Section 353.1 of the Exercises, "We must put aside all judgment of our own, and keep the mind ever ready and prompt to obey in all things the hierarchical Church." But Jesuit obedience would be more than mere obedience of the will. An obedient will suppresses what it would do in order to obey what a superior wants done. Ignatius demanded obedience of the *understanding*. An obedient understanding alters its perception of reality according to the superior's dictates. Section 365.13 declares, "We must hold fast to the following principle: *What seems to me white, 1 will believe black if the hierarchical Church so defines.*" Francis Xavier would later describe this quality of submission in a vow that unintentionally summarized the Jesuit mission: "I would not even believe in the *Gospels* were the Holy Church to forbid it."

The Society does not open its extreme oath of obedience to public inspection. However, a script alleged to be a true facsimile was translated by Edwin A. Sherman and deposited in the Library of Congress with the number BX3705.S56. According to this document,

> when a Jesuit of the minor rank is to be elevated to command, he is conducted into the Chapel of the Convent of the Order, where there are only three others present, the principal or Superior standing in front of the altar. On either side stands a monk, one of whom holds a banner of yellow and white, which are the Papal colors, and the other a black banner with a dagger and red cross above a skull and crossbones, with the initials 'I.N.R.I.,' and below them the words *'ICSTUM NACAR REGES IMIOS,'* the meaning of which is 'It is just to annihilate impious rulers.' [Biblically, these initials represent the Roman inscription above Christ's head on the cross: 'Jesus of Nazareth King of the Jews.']
>
> On the floor is a red cross upon which the postulant or candidate kneels. The Superior hands him a small black crucifix, which he takes in his left hand and presses to his heart and the Superior at the same time presents to him a dagger, which he grasps by the blade and holds the point against his heart, the Superior still holding it by the hilt....
>
> The Superior gives a preamble, and then administers the oath:
>
> I,_____, now, in the presence of Almighty God, the Blessed Virgin Mary, the blessed Michael the Archangel, the blessed St. Paul and all the Saints and sacred Hosts of Heaven, and to you, my Ghostly Father, the Superior General of the Society of Jesus, founded by Ignatius Loyola, in the Pontificate of Paul the Third, and continued to the present, do by the Womb of the Virgin, the Matrix of God, and the Rod of Jesus Christ, declare and swear, that His Holiness the Pope is Christ's

CHAPTER 7 THE FINGERSTROKE OF GOD

Vice-Regent and is the true and only Head of the Catholic and Universal Church throughout the earth; and that by virtue of the keys of binding and loosing, given to His Holiness by my Saviour, Jesus Christ, he hath power to depose heretical kings, princes, states, commonwealths and governments, all being illegal without his sacred confirmation, and that they may safely be destroyed.

Therefore, to the utmost of my power, I shall and will defend this doctrine and His Holiness' right and custom against all usurpers of the heretical or Protestant authority whatever, especially the Lutheran Church of Germany, Holland, Denmark, Sweden and Norway, and the now pretended authority and churches of England and Scotland, and branches of the same now established in Ireland and on the Continent of America and elsewhere; and all adherents in regard that they be usurped and heretical, opposing the sacred Mother Church of Rome.

I do now renounce and disown any allegiance as due to any heretical king, prince, or state named Protestants or Liberals, or obedience to any of their laws, magistrates or officers.

I do further declare that the doctrines of the churches of England and Scotland, of the Calvinists, Huguenots and others of the name Protestants or Liberals to be damnable, and they themselves damned and to be damned who will not forsake the same.

I do further declare that I will help, assist and advise all or any of His Holiness' agents in any place wherever I shall be, in Switzerland, German, Holland, Denmark, Sweden, Norway, England, Ireland, or America, or in any other kingdom or territory I shall come to, and do my uttermost to extirpate the heretical Protestants or Liberals' doctrines and to destroy all their pretended powers, regal or otherwise.

I do further promise and declare that, notwithstanding I am dispensed with, to assume any religion heretical, for the propagating of the Mother Church's interest, to keep secret and private all her agents' counsels from time to time, as they may entrust me, and not to divulge, directly or indirectly, by word, writing, or circumstance whatever; but to execute all that shall be proposed, given in charge or discovered unto me, by you, my Ghostly Father, or any of this sacred convent.

I do further promise and declare that I will have no opinion or will of my own, or any mental reservation whatever, even as a corpse or cadaver, but will unhesitatingly obey each and every command that I may receive from my superiors in the Militia of the Pope and of Jesus Christ.

That I will go to any part of the world whithersoever I may be sent, to the frozen regions of the North, the burning sands of the desert of Africa, or the jungles of India, to the centres of civilization of Europe, or to the wild haunts of the barbarous savages of America, without murmuring or repining, and will be submissive in all things whatsoever communicated to me.

I furthermore promise and declare that I will, when opportunity presents, make and wage relentless war, secretly or openly, against all heretics, Protestants and Liberals, as I am directed to do, to extirpate and exterminate them from the face of the whole earth; and that I will spare neither age, sex, or condition; and that I will hang, burn, waste, boil, flay, strangle and bury alive these infamous heretics, rip up the stomachs and wombs of their women and crush their infants' heads against the walls, in order to annihilate forever their execrable race. That when the same cannot be done openly, I will secretly use the poisoned cup, the strangulating cord, the steel of the poinard or the leaden bullet, regardless of the honor, rank, dignity, or authority of the person or persons, whatever may be their condition in life, either public or private, as I at any time may be directed so to do by any agent of the Pope or Superior of the Brotherhood of the Holy Faith, of the Society of Jesus.

In confirmation of which, I hereby dedicate my life, my soul, and all my corporeal powers, and with this dagger which I now receive, I will subscribe my name written in my own blood, in testimony thereof; and should I prove false or weaken in my determination, may my brethren and fellow soldiers of the Militia of the Pope cut off my hands and my feet, and my throat from ear to ear, my belly opened and sulphur burned therein, with all the punishment that can be inflicted upon me on earth and my soul be tortured by demons in an eternal hell forever!

All of which I,_____, do swear by the blessed Trinity and blessed Sacrament, which I am now to receive, to perform and on my part to keep inviolably; and do

CHAPTER 7   THE FINGERSTROKE OF GOD

call all the heavenly and glorious host of heaven to witness these my real intentions to keep this my oath.

In testimony hereof I take this most holy and blessed Sacrament of the Eucharist, and witness the same further, with my name written with the point of this dagger dipped in my own blood and sealed in the face of this holy Convent.

He receives the wafer from the Superior and writes his name with the point of his dagger dipped in his own blood taken from over the heart....

WHEN Ignatius concluded his presentation, the Pope reportedly cried out *"Hoc est digitus Dei!"* – "This is the fingerstroke of God!" On September 27, 1540, Paul III sealed his approval with the highest and most solemn form of papal pronouncement, a document known as a "bull" (from the Latin *bulla,* meaning "bubble," denoting the attached ovoid or circular seal bearing the pope's name). Paul's bull ordaining the Jesuits is entitled *Regimini militantis ecclesiae,* "On the Supremacy of the Church Militant." The title forms a cabalistic device common to pagan Roman divining. Known as *notariqon,* this device is an acronym that enhances the meaning of its initialized words, in the way "MADD" tells us that Mothers Against Drunk Drivers are more than "against" drunken drivers, they're very angry. *"Regimini militantis ecclesiae"* produces the notariqon "R[O]ME," the empire whose salvation the Society of Jesus was ordained by this bull to secure through the arts of war.

The following April, the original six and a few other members elected Ignatius de Loyola their first Superior General. What had been approved as a minimal society soon multiplied to a thousand strong. Ignatius did this by administering to only sixty the extreme oath of obedience to the pope, while admitting hundreds more under lesser oaths. Ever since, the exact size of the Society has been known only to the Superior General. As the world gained increasing numbers of doctors, lawyers, authors, reforming theologians, financiers, statesmen, courtiers, diplomats, explorers, tradesmen, merchants, poets, scholars, scientists, architects, engineers, artists, printers, and philosophers, it was extremely difficult for an ordinary citizen to tell which were Jesuits and which were not. Not even Jesuits could say for sure, because of a provision in the Constitutions (Sections 81-86 of Part I) which authorizes the Superior General to "receive agents, both priestly agents to help in spiritual matters and lay agents to give aid in temporal and domestic functions." Called "coadjutors," these lay agents could be of any religious denomination, race, nationality, or sex. They took an oath which bound them "for whatever time the Superior General of the Society should see fit to employ them in spiritual or temporal services." This provision was availed by so many black popes that the French had a name for people suspected of being Jesuit agents: *les robes-petites* ("short-robes"). The English called them "short-coats" or "Ignatians."

Within two years of *Regimini militantis ecclesiae,* Paul III appointed the Society to administer the Roman Inquisition (not to be confused with the Spanish Inquisition, which reported only to the Spanish crown). When the Jesuits were comfortable with the Inquisition, Paul made his move to "reconcile" with the Protestants.

THE SPIRIT OF TRENT
Sketch from the Sebastiano painting of the
Psychopomp directing Paul III (left center)
and his cardinals to the Council of Trent.

Chapter 8

MOVING IN

THE TERM "PROTESTANT" was coined in 1529 to describe the large number of princes and delegates of fourteen cities, largely German, who protested Emperor Charles Habsburg's attempt to enforce the Edict of Worms. This edict bound the Empire's three hundred princely states and free cities to Roman Catholicism. The Protestants proposed a compromise formula – basically a statement of the Lutheran faith – known as the Augsburg Confession.

For fifteen years the Edict of Worms and the Augsburg Confession kept Catholic and Protestant rulers in a Mexican standoff. Then, on December 13, 1545, Paul III called both factions to the small German-speaking northern Italian cathedral city of Trent. The promise was to resolve differences peacefully in an ecumenical council.

The Council of Trent had not been seated four months before it decreed that the books and biblical translations of Luther,

LeFevre, Zwingli, Calvin, and other "unapproved persons" were "altogether forbidden [and] allowed to no one, since little advantage, but much danger, generally arises from reading them."[1]

Then the Jesuits moved in. Diego Lainez, Alfonso Salmeron, two of the original companions, and Claude LeJay, all three in their early thirties, distinguished themselves at Trent early on by spurning the grand style of the other delegates. They set up housekeeping in a "narrow, smoke-blackened baker's oven" and wore clothing so heavily patched and greasy that other priests were embarrassed to associate with them.[2] They carried with them intricate advisories from Ignatius himself, written from the delegates' point of view, as for example:

> When the matter that is being debated seems so manifestly just and right that I can no longer keep silent, then I should speak my mind with the greatest composure and conclude what I have said with the words 'subject of course to the judgment of a wiser head than mine.' If the leaders of the opposing party should try to befriend me, I must cultivate these men, who have influence over the heretics and lukewarm Catholics, and try to win them away from their errors with holy wisdom and love....

Most of the eighteen-year lifetime of the Council of Trent consisted of two intermissions spanning four and ten years each. At the beginning of the second intermission, Ignatius founded a special college in Rome for German-speaking Jesuits called the Germanicum. Three years later, the Peace of Augsburg established the principle *cuius regio, eius religio,* "whose the region, his the religion." The Peace of Augsburg was Jesuit paydirt. They could now bring whole populations to Rome simply by winning over a few princes. And so they did. By 1560, the Society had returned virtually all of South Germany and Austria to the Church.

The fruits of the Germanicum were so successful that when the Council of Trent finally adjourned on December 4, 1563, its decrees and canons conceded nothing to the Protestant reformers. Indeed, under the spiritual direction of Superior General Diego Lainez – Ignatius had died in 1556 – the Council denied every

CHAPTER 8   MOVING IN

Protestant doctrine point by point. Anathematized (eternally damned) was anyone who believed that salvation is God's free gift to His faithful and does not depend upon partaking of Church sacraments. Anathematized was anyone who looked to the Bible for the ultimate authority on "doctrine, reproof, correction, and instruction in righteousness"[3] rather than to the teaching Church. Anathematized was anyone who regarded as unworthy of belief such unscriptural doctrines as (1) the efficacy of papal indulgences, (2) of confession alone to a priest as necessary to salvation, (3) of the mass as a true and real sacrifice of the body of Christ necessary to salvation, (4) the legitimacy of teachings on purgatory, (5) the celibate priesthood, (6) invoking saints by prayer to intercede with God, (7) the veneration of relics, and (8) the use of images and symbols.

The Council of Trent hurled one hundred twenty-five anathemas – eternal damnations – against Protestantism. Then, as an addendum to its closing statements, the Council recommended that the Jesuits "should be given pride of place over members of other orders as preachers and professors." It was at Trent that the Roman Catholic Church began marching to the beat of the Black Papacy.

A generation later, the guidelines of the Roman Inquisition under Jesuit direction were published at the command of the Cardinals Inquisitors General. This *Directorium Inquisitorum* (1584) was dedicated to Gregory XIII, the pope who bestowed upon Jesuits the right to deal in commerce and banking, and who also decreed that every papal legate should have a Jesuit advisor on his personal staff.[4] Here follows a summary of the *Directorium Inquisitorum* (translated by J. P. Callender, 1838):

> He is a heretic who does not believe what the Roman Hierarchy teaches— A heretic merits the pains of fire____By the Gospel, the canons, civil law, and custom, heretics must be burned.... For the suspicion alone of heresy, purgation is demanded.... Magistrates who refuse to take the oath for defense of the faith shall be suspected of heresy____Wars may be commenced by the authority of the Church.... Indulgences for the

57

remission of all sin belong to those who signed with the cross for the persecution of heretics____Every individual may kill a heretic. Persons who betray heretics shall be rewarded.... Heretics may be forced to profess the Roman faith.... A heretic, as he sins in all places, may everywhere be judged.... Heretics must be sought after, and be corrected or exterminated.... Heretics enjoy no privileges in law or equity.... The goods of heretics are to be considered as confiscated from the perpetration of the crime... The pope can enact new articles of faith.... Definitions of popes and councils are to be received as infallible.... Inquisitors may torture witnesses to obtain the truth.... It is laudable to torture those of every class who are guilty of heresy___The Pope has power over infidels.... The Church may make war with infidels— Those who are strongly suspected are to be reputed as heretics___He who does not inform against heretics shall be deemed as suspected— Inquisitors may allow heretics to witness against heretics, but not for them.... Inquisitors must not publish the names of informers, witnesses, and accusers.... Penitent heretics may be condemned to perpetual imprisonment___Inquisitors may provide for their own expenditures, and the salaries of their officers, from the property of heretics.... Inquisitors enjoy the benefits of a plenary indulgence [a full papal forgiveness of sin] at all times in life, and in death.

The Inquisition's effect, of course, was to send the more resourceful of the "heretics, Protestants and Liberals" who escaped torture or execution scurrying underground, or into the burgeoning world of commerce, or into regions where Protestant civil authorities kept Inquisitors at bay. Yearning for a less intrusive religious experience, they joined attractive philosophical fraternities where they could speak freely against Roman Catholicism. For this ostensible reason, these fraternities or cults or lodges operated in secrecy. In fact, they were the remnants of the Templar network – Rosicrucians, Teutonic Knights, the numerous and various rites of Freemasonry. Like the Templars and the Jesuits, they were religious hierarchies of strict obedience. They differed from the Jesuits, however, in that their pyramid culminated in an ultimate authority no brother could identify with certainty. The highest master of

CHAPTER 8   MOVING IN

a Lodge received commandments from an "Unknown Superior," a Superior whose will the master's whole struggle up the degrees had trained him to obey without question. What the masters never realized was that this mysterious personage, as we shall examine in more detail later, was in fact none other than the Black Pope.

A century after Trent, a descendant of Paul III, Ranuccio Farnese, commissioned the great Venetian painter Sebastiano Ricci to commemorate the genesis of this definitive Council. Sebastiano produced his famous "Paul III and the cardinals en route to Trent." The work is breathtakingly candid. In the air, above the pope's head, hovers a deity, directing the entourage onward. The deity is not Jesus or Mary or Yahweh, God of the Bible. It is Mercury of the Sibylline and Virgilian gospels – the holy scripture of Caesarean Rome.

Mercury is the celebrated god of commerce. The metal most essential to commercial fluidity is named for him. Metallic mercury is known to scientists as the element Hg (derived from the Latin *hydrargyrum,* "liquid silver"). It is Hg's unique chemical nature that produces refined gold, the fundamental substance in which commercial value is denominated. Liquid at room temperature, Hg draws impurities out of gold ore and binds them into an amalgam. When the amalgam is heated, the heat drives away both Hg and the impurities. What is left is pure gold suitable for further amalgamation into coin.

Mercury's theological life began in ancient Babylon, where he was known as Marduk. The Bible calls him Merodach, the Hebrews called him Enoch, the Egyptians called him Thoth, the Scandinavians worshiped him as Odin, the Teutons as Wotan, and the Orientals as Buddha. Livy says he was introduced to the Romans in 495 BC as a Latinate version of the Greek god Hermes.[5]

By whatever name, in whatever culture, Mercury is considered the god of the Universal Mind, of Writing, Number, and Thought. Just as Mercury the metal draws out impurities and binds them into a mass that is burned and discarded, Mercury the deity uses his intellectual brilliance to play Pied Piper to impure humanity.

He attracts followers and leads their souls to Hades, for which the Greeks gave him the title *Psychopompas* (from *psycho-* "soul" and *pompous*, "director"). Because Hades is not the most desirable of destinations, the Psychopomp had to construct elegant missionary adaptations. He had to charm souls, *deceive* them into following him any way he could – whether by words, sights, or sounds. Like Hg, his metallic form, Mercury could change his shape instantaneously. Did you see the villain in the movie *Terminator II?* With his ever-changing voices, physiognomies, and identities, he is state-of-the-art Psychopomp. In many cultures, Mercury's ingenious deceptions earned him the title of "The Trickster." He was patron deity of deceivers. And of thieves – even as a baby, Mercury couldn't resist stealing Apollo's cattle....

Was Sebastiano Ricci telling us that Mercury was the dominating spirit of the Council of Trent? Certainly the Council required, and still requires, Roman Catholics to honor many traditions which the Bible either condemns or does not authorize. Yet the Council also required, and still requires, that the Bible be honored as divinely inspired. Honoring the Bible by advocating unbiblical norms? This calls for a skill worthy of the Psychopomp, a skill that makes one believe that black is white. As we've seen, this is the Jesuit skill – securing obedience of the subject's understanding. If indeed the Society of Jesus performs the function of Mercury, it is participating in a natural process known to pagan and biblical scriptures alike, a process by which impure humanity is attracted to oblivion, leaving behind only the pure. The theological implications of this process we shall discuss toward the end of this book.

With the Inquisition and the Council of Trent to pave their way, the Society of Jesus quickly became what Loyola had dreamed it would become: the resurrected Knights Templar. In the next chapter, we shall examine the continuation of their meteoric rise as developers of the modern world.

IGNATIUS IN HEAVEN
Padre Pozzo's spectacular ceiling at the Church of St. Ignatius in Rome. Note how the light emanates from Ignatius rather than Jesus Christ, who still bears His cross.

Chapter 9

SECURING CONFIDENCE

STRENGTHENED BY Trent's unqualified endorsement, the Jesuits quickly became the Church's most popular confessors. Ignatius directed that "a Jesuit should not allow anyone to leave the confessional entirely without comfort." If a confessant's opinion on any matter could be found in the least bit defensible, Ignatius said, "he should be permitted to adhere to it, even when the contrary opinion can be said to be more correct."

People relished confessing to Jesuits. "Always go to the Jesuits for confession," it was said in Germany, "for they put cushions under your knees and under your elbows, too."

Merchants, aristocrats, courtiers, and crowned heads insisted that Jesuit confessional direction was the best in all Christendom. They considered the Jesuits to be the greatest converters of hardened sinners, the surest moral guides through life's bewildering complexities. Indeed, for two centuries, all the French kings, from Henry III to Louis XV, would confess to Jesuits. All German emperors after the early seventeenth century would confess to Jesuits, too. Jesuits would take the confessions of all Dukes of Bavaria after 1579, most rulers of Poland and Portugal, the Spanish kings in the eighteenth century, and James II of England.

The sacrament of confession kept Jesuit information channels loaded with vital state secrets. It also furnished the Society an ideal vehicle for influencing political action. One of the most dramatic instances is found in the famous memoir of François de la Chaize, Jesuit confessor to the painfully diseased King of France from 1675 until 1709. "Many a time since," wrote La Chaize,

> when I have had him [Louis XIV] at confession, I have shook hell about his ears, and made him sigh, fear, and tremble, before I would give him absolution.[1] By this I saw that he had still an inclination to me, and was willing to be under my government; so I set the baseness of the action before him by telling the whole story, and how wicked it was, and that it could not be forgiven till he had done some good action to balance that, and expiate the crime. Whereupon he at last asked me what he must do. I told him that he must root out all heretics from his kingdom.

Louis obeyed his confessor by revoking the Edict of Nantes (October 1685), which immediately resulted in:

> the demolition of all the remaining Protestant temples throughout France, and the entire prohibition of even private worship under penalty of confiscation of body and property; the banishment of all Protestant pastors from France within fifteen days; the closing of all Protestant schools; the prohibition of parents to instruct their children in the Protestant faith; the injunction upon them, under a penalty of five hundred livres in each case, to have their children baptized by the parish priest, and brought up in the Roman Catholic religion; the confiscation of the property and goods of all Protestant refugees who failed to return to France within four months; the penalty of the galleys for life to all men, and of imprisonment for life to all women, detected in the act of attempting to escape from France.[1]

CHAPTER Q   SECURING CONFIDENCE

It was inevitable that the Council of Trent would establish the Jesuits as the schoolmasters of Europe. With money from royalty and commerce (and not so much as a pfennig from the Church), the Society built an extensive system of schools and colleges. No tuition was charged, but each prospective student was thoroughly examined to see if he had aptitudes the Society could use. With the founding of the first Jesuit school at Coimbra, Portugal, by the Emperor's youngest sister Catherina (Iñigo's romantic interest who had since married the King of Portugal), the principal Jesuit occupation became teaching. By 1556, three-fourths of the Society's membership were dedicated in 46 Jesuit colleges to "learning against learning," to indoctrinating minds with the learning of illuminated humanism as opposed to the learning of Scripture. This network would expand by 1749 to 669 colleges, 176 seminaries, 61 houses of study, and 24 universities partly or wholly under Jesuit direction.

Many Protestant families sent their sons to Jesuit schools, despite Martin Luther's early warning in An *Appeal to the Ruling Class* (1520) that "unless they diligently train and impress Scripture upon young students, schools will prove to be widening gates of hell." The Jesuit curriculum, or *ratio studiorum* ("method of study"), gave Scripture significant inattention. Part IV, Section 351 of Loyola's Constitutions prescribes courses in "the humane letters of different languages, logic, natural and moral philosophy, metaphysics, scholastic and positive theology," with "Sacred Scripture" bringing up the rear. How rigorously any one of these subjects was to be studied depended upon "circumstances of times, places, persons, and other such factors, according to what seems expedient in our Lord to him who holds the principal charge." Section 366 puts Scripture at the mercy of these factors: "The scholastics should acquire a good foundation in Latin before they attend lectures on the arts, and in the arts before they pass on to scholastic theology; and in it before they study positive theology. Scripture may be studied either concomitantly or later on." If Scripture should be studied at all, the commentary and critical interpretation of Protestant scholastics were to be ignored: "In the case of Christian authors, even though a work may be good it should not be lectured on when the author is bad, lest attachment to him be acquired."

"The curriculum of the Jesuit colleges came to be adopted to a great extent as the basis of the curricula in the European colleges generally," wrote Dr. James J. Walsh, Dean of Fordham University Medical School., Moreover, according to Dr. Walsh;

> The Founding Fathers of our American Republic, that is to say the groups of men who drew up and signed the Declaration of Independence, who were the leaders in the American Revolution, and who formulated the Constitution of the United States ... were, the majority of them, educated in the colonial colleges or in corresponding colleges abroad ... which followed ... almost exactly the Jesuit *Ratio Studiorum*. The fact has been missed to a great extent in our histories of American education....

Embedded in the *ratio studiorum* were the elements of entertainment, of dramatic production – composition, rhetoric, and eloquence. These courses interlinked with the Spiritual Exercises to intensify the experientiality of Catholic doctrine over Scripture and Protestantism. They resulted in a genre of spectacular plays that won distinction as "Jesuit theatre."

The first Jesuit theatre was performed in Vienna in 1555, nearly forty years before the emergence of Shakespeare. It was instantly popular and quickly spread to other parts of Europe. Between 1597 and 1773 more than five hundred Jesuit theatricals were staged in the lower Rhine regions alone. Jacob Bidermann's play *Cenodoxus* ("Newfangled Beliefs"), a point-by-point rebuttal of Luther's teachings, proved the power of entertainment to achieve political reform. "Such a wholesome impression was made," wrote Father Bidermann recalling the 1609 opening of *Cenodoxus* in Munich, "that a full fourteen persons of the highest rank of the Bavarian court retired into solitude during the days that followed, to perform the Spiritual Exercises and to reform their manner of living. Truly a hundred sermons would not have done so much good."[4]

CHAPTER 9   SECURING CONFIDENCE

An exemplary Jesuit drama, performed in 1625 at the College of St. Omer in honor of Belgian royalty, allegorized the glorious end to civil war in Belgium brought by the advent of Princess Isabella and her husband, Albert. The play, as reviewed by a contemporary official,

> represented a country, long heavily oppressed under the Iron Age, supplicating the help of Jupiter, who, after having summoned a council of the gods, sent down Saturn, lately married to Astraea. These visitors were received with much pomp by twelve zodiacs or princes sent by Mercury. They then dispatched four most potent heroes, Hercules, Jason, Theseus and Perseus from the Elysian Fields, with commands to conquer Iron Age, War, Error, and Discord. The heroes expelled those terrible monsters from the country and substituted in their stead Golden Age, Peace, Truth, and Concord. The Princess with the whole assembly were highly delighted.₅

The faculty of Munich College praised the way Jesuit theatre captivated Protestants, especially the parents of school-aged youngsters: "There is no better means of making friends out of the heretics and the enemies of the Church, and filling up the enrollment of the school than good high-spirited playacting." Moliere's Jesuit theatricals in Paris were so popular that even the dress rehearsals were sold out. Mozart, at the age of eleven, was commissioned to write music for a play at the Jesuit college in Salzburg, where his father was musical director to the Archbishop. Even from the West Indies a Jesuit missionary reported that "nothing has made a more forceful impression on the Indians than our play."

In England, Jesuit theatre was not known as such because of Queen Elizabeth's statute making it a capital crime to be, or even to assist, a Jesuit within her orbit. But if the purpose of Jesuit theatre was to capture that share of man's spiritual attention which might otherwise have been directed toward the Bible, then England certainly produced the greatest Jesuit playwright of them all. Shakespeare occupies us with the human process in a way that subtly marginalizes the Bible – exactly pursuant to the Jesuit mission.

Shakespearian characters do preach, and they preach a religion, but it is not the Gospel of Jesus Christ. It is the gnostic illumination of Medici learning that Shakespeare preaches, the stuff of Jesuit schools. Not surprisingly, the secret tradition of Templarism claims Shakespeare, at least the writer of his plays, to have been a Rosicrucian steeped in Medici learning:

> The philosophic ideals promulgated throughout Shakespearian plays distinctly demonstrate their author to have been thoroughly familiar with certain doctrines and tenets peculiar to Rosicrucianism; in fact, the profundity of the Shakespearian productions stamps their creator as one of the *illuminati* of the ages....
>
> Who but a Platonist, a Qabbalist, or a Pythagorean could have written *The Tempest, Macbeth, Hamlet,* or *The Tragedy of Cymbeline*? Who but one deeply versed in Paracelsian lore could have conceived A *Midsummer Night's Dream*?

Yet, as Garry Wills in his book *Witches & Jesuits* points out, *Macbeth* is an elaborate condemnation of the Jesuits as satanists, murderers, witches. *Macbeth* is one of many of its period's "powder plays," a genre in which certain buzz words, well understood by contemporaries, memorialize the guilt and execution of eight Jesuits for having schemed the Gunpowder Plot of November 5, 1605. The Plot aimed to blow up the entire government of Great Britain, including the royal family, in a single catastrophic explosion under the Houses of Parliament.

How could a play defaming Jesuits be of service to the Jesuit agenda? As we shall see, warfare in defense of the papacy requires extravagant measures. In fact, both the Gunpowder Plot, which failed, and the celebration of its detection, which lives on in *Macbeth,* served Rome abundantly. King James I, who declared himself the Plot's divinely-illuminated discoverer, blamed the Plot on "Jesuits and papists." But at the same time, James exonerated "less fanatical Catholics."⁶ According to Wills, "the Plot gave [James] his best opportunity to separate loyal and moderate Catholics from the mad extremists of the Plot." In short, the Plot secured England

CHAPTER 9   SECURING CONFIDENCE

for "loyal and moderate" Roman Catholicism. In the reasoning of a Superior General, particularly the General of the Gunpowder Plot and Shakespearian theatre, Claudio Acquaviva, the sacrifice of eight Jesuits was a small tactical price to pay for moving the King of England to express confidence in the pope's British subjects, estimated at half the population of the realm.

CERTAINLY the most elaborate single Jesuit theatrical event was produced by Gregory XV, the first Jesuit pupil to be elected Pope. This was the canonization of Ignatius de Loyola, the climax of Gregory's brief pontificate (he reigned only three years). Canonization is authorized nowhere in the Bible. Rather, it is a process adapted from the pagan tradition of "apotheosis," whereby the priestly college declared a particularly effective mortal to be a god. In Roman Catholicism, the Sacred Congregation of Rites conducts a lengthy inquisition into the works of a deceased candidate. The inquisition can take dozens, even hundreds of years. The candidate's works are defended before a tribunal of three judges against a "devil's advocate." A final judgment is declared by the Pope, who orders the Church to believe that the candidate's soul is in Heaven, and to venerate the person with the title of "Saint." (The Bible teaches that anyone who hears and does the commandments of Jesus is a saint. Without any hierarchical red tape, he or she avoids judgment and goes to heaven immediately upon physical death.)

Loyola's canonization was celebrated on March 12, 1622 in a ceremony that was "an unprecedented display of ecclesiastical pomp, pageantry, and extravagance."[7] One eyewitness described the event as "an expression of the reborn spirit of the Catholic Church, of the triumph of the Blessed Virgin over Luther and Calvin."[8]

RIDING the crest of humanist exuberance following Loyola's canonization, Jesuit priest Athenasius Kircher (1602-1680) contributed powerfully to Jesuit theatre as sensory experience. With his megaphone, which enabled the voice of one to reach thousands, Kircher invented broadcasting. He also fathered modern camera theory with his perfection of the *lanterna magica*. The magic lantern projected sharp images through a lens upon a screen, giving audiences the illusion of burning cities and conflagrations. Kircher's work influenced the creation of the phenakistoscope (1832), the zoetrope (1860), the kinematoscope (1861), the kineograph (1868), the praxinoscope (1877), and finally, Thomas Alva Edison's kinetograph for filming action to be projected onto a screen through his kinetoscope (1894). Edison had a pet name for the tar-papered studio in West Orange, New Jersey, where all his prototypical films were made. He called it "Black Maria," a term that aptly described the image to whom Iñigo de Loyola dedicated his life in 1522 – the Black Madonna of Montserrat.

The American cinema's earliest subject matter to capture the popular imagination – the "cowboy" – was a Jesuit contribution as well. Eusebio Kino, whose statue is one of two representing Arizona in the U.S. Capitol building, was a Jesuit professor from Ingolstadt College in Bavaria. Between 1687 and 1711 Kino introduced cattle and their management to southern Arizona. For this he is gratefully remembered as "Father of the Cattle Business." Pondering the works of Kircher and Kino, we come to a rather astonishing awareness: Kino's cowboys, as projected through Kircher's magic lantern, indoctrinated America's earliest movie audiences with the underlying message of Jesuit theatre and Roman Catholic theology – that knowing and obeying Scripture is not necessary in comprehending the ways of good and evil, or in doing justice under natural law.

Using cinema and radio to unite Catholic laypersons with the Roman hierarchy was a main purpose of "Catholic Action." Catholic Action was inaugurated in 1922 by Pius XI, whose two confessors, Fathers Alissiardi and Celebrano, were Jesuits. The first pope to install a radio station at the Vatican (1931) and to establish national film review offices (1922), Pius XI ordered Catholics into politics. In the letter *Peculari quadam* ("Containing the flock") he warned that "the men of Catholic Action would fail in their duty if, as opportunities allow it, they did not try to direct the pol-

CHAPTER 9   SECURING CONFIDENCE

itics of their province and of their country."

The men of Catholic Action did try. Their first major effort was to employ Black Pope Vladimir Ledochowski's strategy of bringing the Catholic nations of central and eastern Europe together into a pan-German federation. To head the federation, Ledochowski required a charismatic leader charged with subduing the communistic Soviet Union on the east, Protestant Prussia, Protestant Great Britain, and republican France on the west.[9] Ledochowski chose the Catholic militarist Adolf Hitler, who told Bishop Bernind of Osnabruch in 1936 that

> there was no fundamental difference between National Socialism and the Catholic Church. Had not the church, he argued, looked on Jews as parasites and shut them in ghettos? 'I am only doing,' he boasted, 'what the church has done for fifteen hundred years, only more effectively.' Being a Catholic himself, he told Berning, he 'admired and wanted to promote Christianity.'[10]

To promote Christianity as taught him by Roman Catholicism, Hitler appointed Leni Riefenstahl to create the greatest fascist films ever produced. Her deification of Hitler and romanticization of autocracy in spectacles like *Triumph of the Will* are, in themselves, the history of German cinema in the thirties and early forties. In print, Ledochowski's pan-German manifesto took the form of Hitler's autobiographical *Mein Kampf* ("My Struggle"), ghostwritten by the Jesuit Father Staempfle[11] and placed beside the Bible on the altars of German churches.[12]

After World War II, during September 1957, Pope John XXIII gave Jesuit theatre even broader horizons with his encyclical *Miranda prorsus* ("Looking ahead"), saying,

> Men must be brought into closer communion with one another. They must become socially minded. These technical arts (cinema, sound broadcasting, and television) can achieve this aim *far more easily than the printed word.* [Italics mine] The Catholic Church is keenly desirous that these means be converted to the spreading and advancement of everything that can be

truly called good. Embracing, as she does, the whole of human society within the orbit of her divinely appointed mission, she is directly concerned with the fostering of civilization among all peoples.

To Catholic film producers and directors, *Miranda prorsus* delivered;

> a paternal injunction not to allow films to be made which are at variance with the faith and Christian moral standards. Should this happen – which God forbid – then it is for the Bishops to rebuke them and, if necessary, to impose upon them appropriate sanctions.

John XXIII urged that Pius XI's national film reviewing offices;

> be entrusted to men who are experienced in cinema, sound broadcasting, and television, under the guidance of a priest specially chosen by the Bishops.... At the same time, we urge that the faithful, and particularly those who are militant in the cause of Catholic Action [Jesuits and their protégés], be suitably instructed, so that they may appreciate the need for giving to these offices their willing, united, and effective support.

In 1964, Pope Paul VI amplified *Miranda prorsus* with the decree *Inter mirifica* ("Among the Wonders"), saying "it is the Church's birthright to use and own ... the press, the cinema, radio, television and others of a like nature." Paul cited;

> a special responsibility for the proper use of the means of social communication [which] rests on journalists, writers, actors, designers, producers, exhibitors, distributors, operators, sellers, critics – all those, in a word, who are involved in the making and transmission of communications in any way whatever.... They have power to direct mankind along a good path or an evil path by the information they impart and the pressure they exert. It will be for them to regulate the economic, political, and artistic values in a way that will not conflict with the common good....

CHAPTER 9   SECURING CONFIDENCE

The quality of entertainment's content was decreed in a section of *Inter mirifica* encouraging "the chronicling, the description or the representation of moral evil [which] can, with the help of the means of social communication and with suitable dramatization, lead to a deeper knowledge and analysis of man and to a manifestation of the true and the good in all their splendor." Emboldened by this papal decree, social communicators since 1965 have pushed the constitutional guarantees of "free speech" to the limit by chronicling, describing, and representing moral evil with such progressively vivid, repulsive, prurient, yet often appealing detail that entertainment has become, in the opinion of many, a veritable *technological "how to"* of moral evil. It clearly does not lead audiences to a deeper appreciation of Holy Scripture. This fact identifies entertainment today as a successful Jesuit theatrical mission.

During its four centuries of existence, the Jesuit educational/theatrical enterprise has produced a proud, poised, and imaginative graduate. He or she is enlightened by the Medici Library's humanities, facile in worldly matters, moved by theatricality, and indifferent toward Holy Scripture. Producing Jesuitic graduates has become the aim of modern public education, despite the heavy price of ignoring Scripture (which, as Luther warned and the Columbine murders attest, has indeed turned the public schools into "widening gates of hell"). Jesuit theatre and the Spiritual Exercises, whose original purpose was to bring human understanding into papal subservience through esoteric emotional experiences, have evolved into the full panoply of contemporary social communication.

The great objective of obscuring Scripture has operated to discourage the formal study of the basics of which the Bible is the cornerstone – literature, science, and history. Research by the National Association of Scholars (NAS) of U.S. News & World Report's annual listing of "America's Best Colleges" (including both private and public) disclosed startling figures.[15] In 1914, nearly all of these institutions had required courses in English composition; by 1964 the figure was 86%; in 1996, 36%. In 1914, 82% of the best colleges and universities had traditional mathematics requirements; by 1964 only 36% did; by 1996, 12%. In 1914, 1939 and 1964, more than 70% of the institutions required at least one course in the natural sciences; that figure fell to 34% in 1996. Literature courses were required at 75% of the institutions in 1914, and at 50% in 1939 and 1964. Today, not one of the "best" institutions has a literature requirement. Most colleges today are turning out graduates who have studied little or no history. In 1914, 90% of America's elite colleges required history; in 1939 and 1964 more than 50% did; by 1996 only one of the 50 best schools offered a required history course. The day is approaching, perhaps, when the only historians will be amateurs who study history as self-help, who examine the past in order to make sense of the present and not be caught unprepared by the future.

America's understanding has been systematically bent to the will of the Church Militant, while the intellectual means for sensing the capture have been disconnected. Most of the content of modern media, whether television, radio, print, film, stage, or web, is state-of-the-art Jesuit *ratio studiorum*. The Jesuit college is no longer just a chartered institution; it has become our entire social environment - the movies, the mall, the school, the home, the mind. Human experience has become a Spiritual Exercise managed by charismatic spiritual directors who know how to manipulate a democracy's emotions. Logic, perspective, national memory, and self-discipline are purged to the point that "unbridled emotional responses," as economist Thomas Sowell put it, "are all we have left."

Despite its ascendancy over American life, few Americans understand the term "Jesuit." In our next chapter, we shall examine how this term is defined in our basic reference works. These definitions will help us to better understand the kind of character produced by Ignatian psychological technique.

B.C. 1452.

en. 56. 17.
Chr. 7. 30.

en. 46. 20.

osh. 17. 1.
Chr. 7. 14,

alled,
biezer,
sh. 17. 2
dg. 6. 11,
34.

en. 46. 24.
hr. 7. 13.

43 All the families of the Shu'-hăm-ites, according to those that were numbered of them, *were* threescore and four thousand and four hundred.

44 ¶ *Of* the children of Ăsh'-ẽr after their families: of Jĭm'-nă, the family of the Jĭm'-nītes: of Jĕs'-ū-ī, the family of the Jĕs'-ū-ītes: of Bĕ-rī'-ăh, the family of the Bĕ-rī'-ītes.

45 Of the sons of Bĕ-rī'ăh: of Hē'-bẽr, the family of the Hē'-bẽr-ītes: of Măl'-chī-ĕl, the family of the Măl-chī-ē'-lītes.

46 And the name of the daughter of Ăsh'-ẽr *was* Sâr'-ăh.

47 These *are* the families of the sons of Ăsh'-ẽr according to those that were numbered of them; *who were* fifty and three thousand and four hundred.

48 ¶ *Of* the sons of Năph'-tă-lī after their families: of Jăh'-zēel, the family of the Jăh'-zēel-ītes: of Gu'-nī, the

Chapter 10

DEFINITIONS

THE TERM "Jesuit" was first used to describe a member of the Society of Jesus in 1559. It did not originate from within the Society, but from outsiders. Whether intended derisively or respectfully, "Jesuit" does appear to have been inspired.

We find in the Bible (Numbers 26:44) the mention of "Jesuites." These Jesuites were the progeny of Jesui, whose name in Hebrew, *Yishviy,* means "level." The Jesuits certainly levelled the Protestant menace.

Jesui was a great-grandson of Abraham. His father was the Israelite tribal chieftan Asher (Asher, "happy"). At Genesis 49:20, Asher's posterity is divinely prophesied to "yield royal dainties *(ma-adanim,* 'delights')." Their uniquely privileged access to the minds and wills of kings has certainly enabled the Jesuits to yield copious harvests of royal delights.

But in fulfilling their scriptural prophecy, the Jesuits seem to have alienated themselves from people who use the English language. This does not disappoint St. Ignatius. "Let us hope," he once wrote, "that the Society may never be left untroubled by the hostility of the world for very long."

America's first indigenous dictionary was compiled by Noah Webster and published in 1828. His *American Dictionary of the English Language* reflects the place held by Jesuits in the opinion of a public whose senior citizens had brought forth the Declaration of Independence and the Constitution (Webster himself was forty-one when the Constitution was ratified):

> **Jesuit.** One of the society of Jesus, so called, founded by Ignatius Loyola; a society remarkable for their cunning in propagating their principles.
> **Jesuited.** Conforming to the principles of the Jesuits.
> **Jesuitess.** A female Jesuit in principle.
> **Jesuitic, jesuitical.** Pertaining to the Jesuits or their principles and arts. **2.** Designing; cunning; deceitful; prevaricating.
> **Jesuitically.** Craftily.
> **Jesuitism.** The arts, principles and practices of the Jesuits. **2.** Cunning; deceit; hypocrisy; prevarication; deceptive practices to effect a purpose.

One hundred seventy-eight years later, Webster's *Third New International Dictionary* (1986) informs us that the language has not repented:

> **Jesuit: 1:** a member of a religious society for men founded by St. Ignatius Loyola in 1534. **2:** one given to intrigue or equivocation: a crafty person: CASUIST
> **Jesuited:** jesuitic
> **Jesuitic or jesuitical: 1:** of or relating to the Jesuits, Jesuitism, or Jesuitry. **2:** having qualities thought to resemble those of a Jesuit - usu. used disparagingly
> **Jesuitize:** to act or teach in the actual or ascribed manner of a Jesuit: to indoctrinate with actual or ascribed Jesuit principles
> **Jesuitry:** principles or practices ascribed to the Jesuits, as the practice of mental reservation, casuistry, and equivocation

CHAPTER 10   DEFINITIONS

Webster's online dictionary, *WWWebster* (1999), is particularly revealing. Here we read that "Jesuit" means "a member of the Roman Catholic Society of Jesus founded by Saint Ignatius Loyola in 1534 and devoted to missionary and educational work," and that a Jesuit is "one given to intrigue or equivocation." *WWWebster* defines "to intrigue" as meaning "to cheat, trick, plot, and scheme," and "to equivocate" as "to use equivocal language especially with intent to deceive; to avoid committing oneself in what one says." "Equivocal" language, according to the same source, is language "subject to two or more interpretations and usually used to mislead or confuse; of uncertain nature or disposition toward a person or thing; of doubtful advantage, genuineness, or moral rectitude."

The Jesuit discipline has elevated mental reservation, casuistry, and equivocation to high arts - you will not find a more hilarious defense of these arts than Blaise Pascal's classic "Pastoral Letters"(1657), freely available on the internet. Purportedly written to a friend, the "Letters" report conversations Pascal is having with a Jesuit casuist. The Jesuit defends his arts thusly:

> Men have arrived at such a pitch of corruption nowadays that, unable to make them come to us, we must e'en go to them, otherwise they would cast us off altogether; and, what is worse, they would become perfect castaways. It is to retain such characters as these that our casuists have taken under consideration the vices to which people of various conditions are most addicted, with the view of laying down maxims which, while they cannot be said to violate the truth, are so gentle that he must be a very impracticable subject indeed who is not pleased with them. The grand project of our Society, for the good of religion, is never to repulse any one, let him be what he may, and so avoid driving people to despair.

Jesuit moral theology hardly needs a satirist. Its humor is self-contained. Consider Hermann Busenbaum, one of the Society's most venerated moral theologians. Busenbaum literally wrote the book on self-serving logic. His celebrated *Medulla theologiae moralis*

("The Marrow of Moral Theology," 1645) enjoyed more than two hundred printings and was required ethics reading in all the Jesuit colleges. A man of stout appetites, Busenbaum constructed an equivocation to relieve himself of the obligation to eat fish on Fridays: "On Fridays every good Catholic must eat only creatures that live in the water, which justifies ordering a nice roast duck!"

Busenbaum demonstrated how mental reservation could enable a criminal to escape a charge of breaking and entering:

> "Did you force the window to gain felonious entry into these premises?" asks the judge. "Certainly not!" replies the accused, qualifying his denial with the mental reservation "I *entered through the skylight.*"

Father Gury, who taught moral theology at the Roman College from his book *Casus Conscientire* (1875), approved of the way an adulterous wife, having just received absolution for her sin from a priest, used mental reservation to mislead her husband:

> To the entreaties of her husband, she absolutely denied the fault: "I have not committed it," she said; meaning "adultery such as I am obliged to reveal;" in other words, "I have not committed an adultery." She could deny her sin as a culprit may say to a judge who does not question him legitimately: "I have not committed any crime," adding mentally, "in such a manner that I should reveal it." This is the opinion of St. Liguori, and of many others.

The "St. Liguori" to whom Gury refers is Alphonse Liguori, declared Patron Saint of Confessors and Moralists by Pope Pius XII. St. Liguori was not a Jesuit himself, but he was devoted to them. He facilitated adultery by means of an equivocation: "An adulteress questioned by her husband, may deny her guilt by declaring that she has not committed 'adultery,' meaning 'idolatry,' for which the term 'adultery' is often employed in the Old Testament."

Casuistry is the process of applying moral principles falsely in deciding the rights or wrongs of a case - the word "casuistry"

CHAPTER 10   DEFINITIONS

comes from "cases." *WWWebster* equates casuistry with rationalization, "to cause something to seem reasonable; to provide plausible but untrue reasons for conduct." (In early 1999, President Clinton's biographer, David Maraniss, could be seen remarking on talkshows that the President owed his formidable skills as a criminal defendant to "his training in casuistry at Georgetown University.") The great Jesuit casuist Antonio Escobar pardoned evildoing as long as it was committed in pursuit of a lofty goal. "Purity of intention," he declared in 1627, "may justify actions which are contrary to the moral code and to human laws." Hermann Busenbaum ratified Escobar with his own famous maxim *"Cum finis est licitus, etiam media sunt licita,"* "If the end is legal, the means are legal." Escobar and Busenbaum boil down to the essential doctrine of terrorism: "The end justifies the means."

Casuistry solved the problem of usury. Although the voice of Jesus commanded "lend, hoping for nothing again; and your reward will be great" (Luke 6:35), Jesuit lenders often charged exorbitant interest. Father Gury explained the principle:

> If lending one hundred francs you are losing ten francs by it, you lend really one hundred and ten francs. Then you shall receive one hundred and ten francs.

Indeed, casuistry has set the moral tone of world economics. In his *Universae theologiae moralis* ("Catholic Moral Theology", 1652-66), Antonio Escobar rendered the opinion that "The giving of short weight is not to be reckoned as a sin when the official price for certain goods is so low that the merchant would be ruined thereby." By this reasoning, the international network of central banks (beginning with the Knights Templars and sustained by the Society of Jesus) has been absolved of manipulating monetary values if doing so helps individual sovereign nation-states manage their subjects. Subjects are cyclically required to part with true value - that is, hard-earned gold and silver coinage - in exchange for intangible credit denominated in paper notes whose official promises to repay in precious coinage... are cyclically broken. As the most powerful office in Roman Catholicism, the black papacy might have promoted stable national economies by means of the divinely fair monetary system commanded in the Bible at Leviticus 19 -

> Ye shall do no unrighteousness in measure. Just balances, just weights, shall ye have: I am the Lord your God, which brought you out of the land of Egypt.

Instead, it has promoted Escobar's casuistry, which directs merchants to survive official value manipulations by cheating one another. There are significant sociological consequences. When giving short weight becomes policy, a moral paradigm is set. That paradigm governs more than just commercial transactions. It affects human relationships, as well. Partners in friendships, marriages, and families begin giving short weight - giving less than represented. This results in one-sided, frustrating, dysfunctional emotional transactions, and ultimately an aberrant society. The ultimate beneficiary of aberrant societies, of course, is *Pontifex Maximus,* whose profession is their regulation.

If we depend solely on dictionary definitions, we learn that Jesuits are churchmen and teachers of a doubtful moral rectitude who are likely to cheat, trick, plot, scheme, deceive, and confuse us while avoiding to commit themselves verbally. When we study their published moralists, we sense a rather vibrant presence of The Trickster. But in the Society's defense, it must be said these are *legitimate* character traits for a militia empowered by a declaration of war, and we must remember that Paul III's bull ordaining the Society of Jesus, *Regimini militantis ecclesiae,* is just such a declaration. Human life in a declared war becomes subject to the first great rule of war, *belli legum dormit,* "in war the law sleeps." When the law sleeps, the unarmed priest's only weapons are the intrigue, deceit, equivocation, casuistry, and mental reservation with which the Jesuits have made themselves so notorious and so often despised.

In forthcoming chapters, we shall be examining how the Society of Jesus made war against Great Britain and the British colonies during the second half of the eighteenth century, and

CHAPTER 10 DEFINITIONS

then against the sovereign American States a century later. In each instance, the warfare was of the highest sophistication. It was so subtly conceived and so masterfully executed, that neither of the major combatants could discern the presence of Jesuits in the equation. The amazing technology of Jesuit warfare - that is the subject of our next chapter.

ART MILITAIRE DES CHINOIS,

OU

RECUEIL

D'ANCIENS TRAITÉS SUR LA GUERRE,

composés avant l'ere chrétienne,

PAR DIFFÉRENTS GÉNÉRAUX CHINOIS.

Ouvrages sur lesquels les Aspirants aux Grades Militaires sont obligés de subir des examens.

ON Y A JOINT

Dix Préceptes adressés aux Troupes par l'Empereur YONG-TCHENG, pere de l'Empereur régnant.

Et des PLANCHES GRAVÉES pour l'intelligence des Exercices, des Evolutions, des Habillements, des Armes & des Instruments Militaires des Chinois.

Traduit en François, par le P. AMIOT, Missionnaire à Pe-king, revu & publié par M. DEGUIGNES.

A PARIS,

Chez DIDOT L'AINÉ, Libraire & Imprimeur, rue Pavée, près du quai des Augustins.

M. DCC. LXXII.

AVEC APPROBATION, ET PRIVILEGE DU ROI.

Chapter 11

THE THIRTEEN ARTICLES CONCERNING MILITARY ART

BEFORE THE American Revolution, Roman Catholics were barred from voting or holding public office throughout the British colonies. They were a persecuted minority everywhere but in the proprietary domain of William Penn (Pennsylvania and Delaware). Some of their most energetic persecutors, in fact, were the very Huguenots whom the Catholics had chased out of France in the wake of Louis XIV's revocation of the Edict of Nantes.

The basis of Roman Catholic persecution was political. Catholics owed allegiance to *Pontifex Maximus*, the Bishop of Rome. The Bishop of Rome was a foreign ruler who, as a matter of public policy, regarded the British king and his Protestant Church as heretics to be destroyed. From the American colonists' standpoint, to allow Catholics to vote or hold office was tantamount to surrendering their colonies to a foreign conqueror. A crucial part of maintaining personal liberty in Protestant colonial America was keeping Roman Catholics out of government. But then came the Revolution. The colonial citizenry fought for and won their independence from Great Britain. They established a Constitution that amounted to... *surrendering their country to a foreign conqueror.* Consider the legalities. Before the Constitution was ratified, American Catholics had few civil rights; after ratification, they had them all. Article VI, section 3 provides that "no religious test shall ever be required as a qualification to any office or public trust under the authority of the United States," while the First Amendment denies Congress the power "to make any law respecting an establishment of religion, or prohibiting the free exercise thereof." With Article IV Section 3 and the First Amendment, the Constitution welcomed agents of *Pontifex Maximus,* the world's chief enemy of Protestantism, into the ranks of government.

Of the 2,500,000 enumerated inhabitants in 1787 America, the Roman Catholic population consisted of no more than 16,000 in Maryland, 7,000 in Pennsylvania, 1,500 in New York, and 200 in Virginia.[1] Once the Constitution was in place, a steady influx of European immigrants transformed Roman Catholicism from America's smallest to largest religious denomination. By 1850, the higher powers at Rome could view the United States as a viable tributary, if not another papal state.

This awesome result did not just happen. I submit that it was brilliantly designed and commanded by a man I am pleased to honor as the American republic's least known founding father, Lorenzo Ricci (pronounced "Richey.") Ricci was a Tuscan aristocrat by birth, a stoical philosopher by reputation, and a Jesuit father by profession. He was Superior General of the Society of Jesus during the formative years of the American Revolution, from 1758 until 1775. He also may be credited with having written the most celebrated treatise on war ever published, a work entitled *The Thirteen Articles Concerning Military Art.*

The reputed author of this work is a quasi-historical Chinese general believed to have lived in the sixth century BC named Sun-tzu. Sun-tzu was unknown to western languages until Joseph-Marie Amiot, astronomer to the Emperor of China, brought forth a

CHAPTER 11 THE THIRTEEN ARTICLES CONCERNING MILITARY ART

French edition of the *Thirteen Articles* in 1772. Amiot was a Jesuit priest under obedience to General Ricci. I base my inference that Ricci is the author of Amiot's Sun-tzu on a remark from today's premier Jesuit spokesman, Malachi Martin, retired professor at the Pontifical Institute in Rome, to the effect that a book written by a Jesuit, due to the obedience factor, can be presumed "in essence" to be the work of his Superior General.² Amiot's Sun-tzu, then, can be presumed to have been "written" by Lorenzo Ricci.

The black pope's decision to publish Sun-tzu prior to the outbreak of the Revolution he had engineered demonstrates, I believe, his confidence that divine authority had already delivered victory to him. Ricci knew that circumstances had reached the point at which there was nothing which his enemy, the forces of Protestantism on both sides of the Atlantic, could do to alter the outcome. He was like a chess master who sees the inevitability of checkmate four moves ahead and reveals his winning method out of courtesy to the imminent loser. His method was so sublimely Sun-tzuan that his opponents never even perceived his army to be an opponent - just as Protestants today are unaware that extirpating their credo is still the unrelenting Jesuit mission.

The Thirteen Articles were ignored by Americans until the nineteen-seventies, when our corporate executives discovered that their oriental counterparts were doing business according to Sun-tzuan strategies. As U.S. corporations increased their presence in the Pacific Rim, Sun-tzu became a major survival tool. Since the middle eighties, more than fifty editions of the *Articles* have been published in this country, mostly under the *"Art of War"* title. These editions represent Sun-tzu well enough, but none of them are derived from the 1772 Amiot translation into French (which itself was based on a Tartar-Manchurian version of the older Chinese manuscripts). Amiot's Sun-tzu appears never to have been published in English, although a 1996 commission by La Belle Église produced a very fine manuscript English translation by Hermine F. Garcia. That manuscript is the source of my citations here.

Only the Amiot edition reflects in virtually the Jesuit General's own words how he formed the United States of America by dividing the British Empire against itself, while at the same time dividing the rest of Europe against Britain, against even the General's own army! The Amiot is all the more remarkable for appearing in the very midst of the unfolding of this extraordinary process.

AMIOT begins *The Thirteen Articles* by noting how odd it is that the benign Chinese morality should spawn a warrior of Sun-tzu's magnitude:

> If we are to judge the Chinese by their morals ... and in general by everything one can currently observe of them, we would instantly conclude that this must be the most pacifist Nation in the world, far from having the brilliant qualities necessary for Warriors. Yet, surprisingly, this very Nation, which has subsisted for nearly four thousand years in approximately the same state we see it in today, has always, or almost always, triumphed over its enemies; and when it had the misfortune of being conquered, it gave its laws to the conquerors themselves.

We know this, Amiot says, from the Annals, which contain "admirable accounts of prodigious bravery," and lists of actions and military conduct of various founders of dynasties. He exclaims;

> What Heroes! What Politicians! What Warriors! No Alexander or Caesar could surpass them. Why shouldn't these great men, these powerful geniuses, who made such fine political and civil Laws, have made military laws which were just as fine?

The reference to Caesar is significant. Declaring China's dynastic heroes to be Caesar's equals, Amiot equates Lorenzo Ricci, the reigning bearer of Caesarean authority, with the greatest oriental Warriors. Were the oriental military laws "just as fine" as Caesar's? "It is not up to me to judge this," Amiot answers. "Our Warriors must pronounce themselves in this regard."

If the term "Our Warriors" means "our Jesuit brethren," as I believe it does, then we have before us Ricci's clandestine order that the book be received by the scattered members of the Society

CHAPTER 11 THE THIRTEEN ARTICLES CONCERNING MILITARY ART

as the latest statement of the General's military Law. (Clandestine generals order clandestinely.) Amiot admits that translating a war manual was "contrary to my taste, & so far from the object of my profession." He says that he only undertook the work in hopes that the reader might have "some pleasure conversing with these foreign Heroes and receiving some of their instructions and [finding] something useful." What cannot be denied is that Rome was served by critical events in America and England during the years of Ricci's reign in ways that flow quite discernably from the strategies, laws, and maxims set forth in the *Thirteen Articles*. I believe that anyone reading Amiot's Sun-tzu in 1772, knowing that its translator was a Jesuit, knowing the Jesuit mission, and knowing the nature of Jesuitic obedience, could observe world events with this knowledge, and predict that the dispute between the American colonists and the British Empire would end - as it actually did - in Roman dominance over a new, independent republic.

Before presenting the works of Sun-tzu, Amiot recounts an important legend demonstrating the severity of Sun-tzuan authority. It is a severity that empowers the General to overrule even his Sovereign in order to secure the army's perfect obedience. Hearing that the King of Oo was preparing for war and not wishing to remain idle, Sun-tzu offered his services to the King. The King had read Sun-tzu's book and liked it, but doubted its practicability.

> "Prince," replied Sun-tzu, "I said nothing in my Writings that I had not already practiced in the army. What I have not yet said, but of which I presume to assure Your Majesty today, is that I am capable of transmitting these practices to anyone whomsoever & training them in military exercises when I am authorized to do so."
>
> "I understand," replied the King. "You wish to say that you will easily teach your maxims to intelligent men who are already both prudent and valorous; that you will have no difficulty giving training in military exercises to men accustomed to hard work who are docile & full of good will. But the majority is not of that nature."
>
> "It matters not," replied Sun-tzu. "I said *anyone whomsoever*

and I exclude no one from my offer, including the most mutinous, the most cowardly and the weakest of men."

"To hear you speak," said the King, "you would even inspire women to have the feelings of Warriors; you would train them to bear arms."

"Yes, Prince," replied Sun-tzu in a firm voice, "and I beg Your Majesty to be assured of it."

The King, who in the circumstances in which he found himself was no longer entertained by the customary amusements of Court, took advantage of this opportunity to find a new sort of amusement. He said, "Bring me one hundred eighty of my wives." He was obeyed, & the Princesses appeared. Among them were two in particular whom the King loved tenderly; they were placed ahead of the others. "We will see," said the King, smiling. "We will see, Sun-tzu, if you will be true to your word. I make you General of these new troops. All throughout my palace you need only choose the place which seems the most comfortable to give them military training. When they are sufficiently instructed you will let me know, & I will come myself to render justice to them & to your talent."

The General sensed the ridicule of the role he was asked to play. But he did not back down, and instead appeared quite satisfied by the honor bestowed on him by the King, not only by allowing him to see his wives but also by putting them under his direction. "I will do well with them, Sire," he said in an assured tone, "and I hope that soon Your Majesty will have cause to be satisfied with my services. At the very least, Your Majesty will be convinced that Sun-tzu is not a man who takes risks."

Once the King had retired to his apartments, the Warrior thought only of executing his commission. He asked for weapons & all the military equipment needed for his newly created soldiers. While waiting for everything to be ready, he led his troop into one of the courtyards of the palace which seemed the best suited for his work. Soon the items he had requested were brought to him. Sun-tzu then spoke to the Princesses. "Here you are," he said, "under my direction and my orders. You must listen to me attentively and obey me in whatever I command you to do. That is the first & most essential military law: make sure you don't break it. By tomorrow I want you to perform exercises

CHAPTER 11 THE THIRTEEN ARTICLES CONCERNING MILITARY ART

before the King, & I intend for them to be done perfectly."

After those words he strapped on their swords, put spears in their hands, divided them into two groups, and put one of the favorite Princesses at the head of each. Once that arrangement was made, he began his instructions in these terms: "Can you tell the difference between your chest and your back, & your right hand from your left hand? Answer me." At first the only response he received was some bursts of laughter. But he remained silent and very serious. "Yes, of course," the Ladies then replied in one voice. "If that is so," resumed Sun-tzu, "then listen carefully to what I am going to say. When the drum strikes only one beat, you will remain as you are now, only paying attention to what is before your chest. When the drum strikes two beats, you must turn so that your chest is in the place where your right hand was before. If instead of two beats you hear three, you must turn so that your chest is precisely where your left hand was before. But when the drum strikes four beats, you must turn so that your chest is where your back was, & your back will be where your chest was.

"What I just said may not be clear enough; let me explain. A single drum beat means that you must not change your position & you must be on guard. Two beats means you must turn right. Three beats means you must turn left. And four beats means you make a half turn. I will explain even more.

"This is the order I shall follow. First I will strike one beat: at that signal you will be ready to receive my orders. A few moments later I will strike two beats: then, all together, you will turn to the right with gravity, after which I will not strike three beats but four, & you will make a half-turn. I will then have you return to your first position and, as before, I will strike one beat. At the first signal, be ready. Then I will strike, not two beats but three, & you will turn left; at four beats you will complete the half-turn. Have you well understood what I am saying? If you have any difficulties, you have but to speak to me of them and I shall attempt to explain the matter." "We have understood," replied the Ladies. "If that is so," responded Sun-tzu, "I will begin. Do not forget that the sound of the drum takes the place of the General's voice, but he is the one who is giving you these orders."

After repeating his instructions three times, Sun-tzu again aligned his small army, after which he had the drum strike one beat. At that sound, all the Ladies began to laugh. At two drum beats, they laughed even louder. Ever serious, the General spoke to them thus: "It is possible that I did not explain clearly enough the instructions I gave you. If that is so, it is my fault. I will attempt to remedy it by speaking to you in a way that is more accessible to you (& at once he repeated the lesson three times in other terms), and then we will see," he added, "if you obey me any better." He had the drum strike one beat, and then two. Seeing him look so serious, and given the strange situation they found themselves in, the Ladies forgot to obey him. After attempting in vain to stop the laughter that was choking them, they finally let it burst forth loudly.

Sun-tzu was in no way disconcerted, but in the same tone he had used when speaking to them before, he said: "If I had not explained myself clearly, or if you had not assured me, in unison, that you understood what I said, you would in no way be guilty. But I spoke to you clearly, as you admitted yourselves. Why did you not obey? You deserve punishment, and military punishment. Among the Makers of War, whoever does not obey the orders of his General deserves death. Therefore you will die." After that short preamble, Sun-tzu ordered the women who formed the two lines to kill the two who were leading them. Just then, one of the men whose job it was to guard the women, seeing that the Warrior was not joking, ran to warn the King of what was happening. The King sent someone to Sun-tzu to forbid him from going any farther, & in particular from mistreating the two women he loved the best & without whom he could not live.

The General listened with respect to the words that were spoken on behalf of the King, but he refused to bow to his wishes. "Go tell the King," he replied, "that Sun-tzu believes him to be too reasonable & too just to think he might have changed his mind so soon, & that he truly wishes to be obeyed in what you have just told me on his behalf. The Prince is the lawmaker; he would not give orders which would sully the dignity he vested in me. He asked me to train one hundred and eighty of his Wives as soldiers, he made me their General. The rest is up to me. They

CHAPTER 11 THE THIRTEEN ARTICLES CONCERNING MILITARY ART

disobeyed me, they will die." So saying, he pulled out his sword and with the same calmness he had displayed until then, he cut off the heads of the two who were leading the others. He immediately put two others in their place, and had the drum strike the various beats he had explained to his troops. And it was as if those women had been professional soldiers all their lives; they made their turns silently and impeccably.

Sun-tzu spoke thus to the Envoy: "Go tell the King," he said, "that his wives know how to drill. Now I can lead them to war, make them affront all sorts of perils, & even make them pass through water & fire."

When the King learned what had happened, he was penetrated by the deepest sorrow. With a great sigh he said, "Thus have I lost what was dearest to me in this world.... Have that Foreigner return to his country. I do not want him, nor his services— What have you done, barbarian?... How can I go on living?" ... and so on.

As unconsolable as the King was, time and the circumstances soon made him forget his loss. His enemies were ready to descend upon him. He asked Sun-tzu to return, made him General of his armies, & with his help he destroyed the Chou Kingdom. Those of his neighbors who had formerly been the most worrisome were now penetrated by fear at the mere mention of the glorious acts of Sun-tzu, and thought only of living peacefully under the protection of a Prince who had such a man at his service.

This introduction confirms that Paul III's war declaration *Regimini militantis ecclesiae* is about protecting the life of the nation, which is the Roman Church. Protecting the Church may require the Superior General to sacrifice his soldiers, his citizens, and if need be, his sovereign, the pope. In a very real sense, the great General is so inscrutably alone, so omnipotent, that he is at war with... *everyone*. Sacrificing his own (just as Saturn, the grandfather-god of Rome devoured his own children) in order to defeat an enemy short of coming to blows, this is a great General's legitimate obligation. Sun-tzu writes:

Without giving battle, without spilling a drop of [the enemy's] blood, without even drawing a sword, the clever General succeeds in capturing cities. Without setting foot in a foreign Kingdom, he finds the means to conquer them. He acts in such a way that those who are inferior to him can never guess his intentions. He has them change location, even taking them to rather difficult places where they must work and suffer. When a clever General goes into action, the enemy is already defeated. When he fights, he alone must do more than his entire army, not through the strength of his arm but through his prudence, his manner of commanding, & above all his ruses.

Lorenzo Ricci's most compelling ruse was disestablishing the Society of Jesus, a campaign that mimicked the collapse of the Knights Templar four centuries earlier. With astonishing precision, the Disestablishment ran concurrently with the escalation of hostilities between the American colonies and the British Crown.

It was an amazing juggle that spanned seventeen years. It saw Ricci's secret liaisons in and around the British Parliament buy legislation that inflamed his secret liasons in and around the American colonial governments to formulate a culture of rebellion. It saw his own visible army, mute and defenseless, systematically assaulted by the European powers and eventually suppressed "for all eternity" by a 1773 papal brief. Once the stage was set and the action scripted, it saw the General slip into deeper cover to let the Protestant powers exhaust themselves in wars that within a single generation resulted in a glorious Roman presence where once England had reigned.

Clandestine military operations inspired by the ingenuity of Sun-tzu are virtually impossible to document. If strategic notes were taken, if written commands were given, they were carefully destroyed. Such that survive may have been spared in order to misinform. The mouths of covert operatives are kept shut out of a simple desire to stay alive. Sensational disclosures, too, we can presume to be misinformational. To determine that Lorenzo Ricci did in fact mount any clandestine operation at all requires a careful evaluation of circumstantial evidence. Was there an outcome that

CHAPTER 11   THE THIRTEEN ARTICLES CONCERNING MILITARY ART

benefitted him and his Sovereign? Did he have the authority, the motive, the resources, the ability, and the opportunity to do what created the outcome? As to outcome: English-speaking Protestantism did in fact violently divide, and the victorious party moreover invited Roman Catholic religionists to participate in its political government. As to authority for waging war against Protestantism, *Regimini militantis ecclesiae* authorized the General to prosecute enemies of the Roman faith. As to motive: the Jesuit oath spiritually obligated the extirpation of Protestantism in both America and Great Britain. As to resources, the black papacy, even as its martial strategy brought its own organization to apparent oblivion, had instant call on the vast reserve of Roman Catholic wealth - as the old Spanish proverb goes, *"Don Dinero es muy Catolico."* Ricci's ability to direct an international covert operation was stated and defined by the momentous publication of *The Thirteen Articles* in what was then the language of international diplomacy. Finally, a man commanding unlimited financial resources and unlimited obedience of an unlimited supply of well-trained personnel enjoys unlimited opportunity to do anything possible, and some things deemed impossible. To deny that Lorenzo Ricci orchestrated American Independence may be to ignore his talent and demean his office.

Let us move now to the next chapter, and begin our examination of how the General did it.

LORENZO RICCI A/K/A LAURENCE RICHEY.
(From a painting believed contemporaneous.)

Chapter 12

LORENZO RICCI'S WAR

LORENZO RICCI'S strategy of dividing the British imperial system can be discerned in events occurring as early as 1752. In that year, Catholic interests in America were rather poorly managed by the Congregation for the Propaganda at Rome, depending upon a tangle of ambassadors (or nuncios) and intermediaries in Madrid, Paris, London, and Brussels. The Jesuit mission was to consolidate these often adversarial parts into a dynamic and independent whole governed directly from the mind of the black papacy.

In 1752, the Society of Jesus was brilliantly powerful, and had been so for nearly a century. "Most statesmen," a fine Jesuit historian has written, "reckoned that the Society was a major force in politics, an international Great Power, acting primarily for its own interests.". Lorenzo Ricci had been Spiritual Father of this great power for nearly a year. Although that title assured him of unanimous election as Superior General upon the demise of General

Luigi Centurioni, it presently endowed him with diplomatic oversight embracing the whole world. Ricci's particular geographic interests included France and its possessions in New France - the whole Mississippi valley, from Canada and the Great Lakes down to the Gulf of Mexico; and England and its colonies in New England - all the lands to the south of French Canada and north of Spanish Florida stretching from the Atlantic to the Pacific coasts.

Both empires were to a certain extent Jesuit-driven. Great Britain was run by the Catholic-loathing system of Freemasonry, whose highest adepts obeyed the revered "unknown superior." France was run by Louis XV, who obeyed the same superior through his Jesuit confessor, Père de Sacy. De Sacy's good-natured ministry reduced the King's dinner, on a strict fast day, from eight courses to five, and limited his wine consumption to three glasses per sitting.

Sun-tzu wrote;

> I demand the art of making enemies move as one wishes. Those who possess that admirable art know how to arrange their men & the army they command in such a way that they make the enemy come toward them whenever they judge it appropriate. They know how to make generous gifts when appropriate, even to those they wish to conquer. They give to the enemy & the enemy receives; they abandon things to him & he comes to take them. They are ready for anything, they take advantage of any circumstance. They do not fully trust those whom they employ but choose others to be their overseers. They do not count on their own strength alone but use other means which they believe can be useful to them. They consider the men against whom they must fight to be stones or pieces of wood which they have been asked to roll down a slope. You, therefore, who are commanding an army must act in such a way that the enemy is in your hands like a round stone that you have caused to roll down a mountain a thousand paces high. Thus it will be recognized that you have power & authority, and that you are truly worthy of the position you occupy.

Lorenzo Ricci transformed British and French colonial person-

CHAPTER 12 LORENZO RICCI'S WAR

nel into round stones by creating a crisis between their conflicting imperial claims to dominion in North America. In 1752 his spiritual fatherhood directed French soldiers and their Indian allies to destroy the important British colonial trading center on the upper Great Miami river. Then followed the plundering, capture or killing – not murdering, but papally-absolved extirpating – of every English-speaking trader in the upper Ohio valley that the French and Indians could locate. Although these lands were legally British, dating from a grant to Virginia by King James I in 1609, the important Virginia families failed to empathize with the misfortunes of explorer-inhabitants in such remote and undeveloped wilderness. But when, toward the end of 1752, the Virginia government granted an additional 1,500,000 acres of Ohio valley land, empathies burst into bloom. Suddenly the Virginians had something to lose, and it was being lost to a band of Roman Catholics and their Indian converts.

In 1753, French engineers constructed a chain of forts connecting Lake Erie with the Ohio River. The governor of Virginia dispatched a small militia to confront these Catholic trespassers. Leading the militia was a recent initiate into the Fredericksburg Masonic Lodge, twenty-one-year-old Major George Washington. Washington warned the garrison at Fort LeBoeuf that it was illegally occupying Virginia real estate "so notoriously known to be the property of the Crown of Great Britain." He read aloud the governor's demand that they depart. The French ignored him and he returned home.

Despite the clear indication that the French intended not to concede to the governor's demands, Virginia encouraged the Ohio Company to build a palisaded fort at the fork where the Allegheny and Monongahela Rivers join to create the Ohio River – where Pittsburgh now stands. The government pledged Virginian troops to support the venture.

Construction began in the spring of 1754. Almost immediately, French and Indians descended upon the tiny crew of woodcutters and carpenters and overwhelmed them. By the time Washington, now a Lieutenant Colonel, could reach the scene, he was forced by Catholic fire-power to fall back to Fort Necessity. Here Washington surrendered on July 4. It was this clash between British and French armies that precipitated what was called by contemporary writers "The Maritime War," or "Great War," or "Great War for the Empire," or "Seven Years' War," or "French and Indian Wars." It could more appropriately be called "Lorenzo Ricci's War."

As these rounded stones began rolling, more succumbed to Ricci's gentle touch. The colony most affected by the fighting was meek Pennsylvania, the colony originally settled by adherents of the renowned Quaker leader, William Penn. Penn had been dead a whole generation, and ownership of his colony had devolved upon a British corporation which included some of Penn's descendants and was known austerely as "the Proprietors." The Proprietors wanted wars in Pennsylvania to be fought by Pennsylvanians. The Quakers, who controlled the Assembly, abhorred the notion of Pensylvanians bearing arms. When the Assembly voted to raise a war chest, the Quakers stepped down and out of power. First, however, they appointed their most celebrated member, Dr. Benjamin Franklin, official printer of Pennsylvania's paper currency, to sail to London and represent them against the Proprietors.

Dr. Franklin, who happened to be Grand Master of Pennsylvania Freemasonry, arrived in London to find that King George II, having made peace with France as recently as 1748, favored the Proprietors. The king's attitude was "Let Americans fight Americans." Franklin explained that Virginia's undisciplined militiamen and the pacifists of Pennsylvania were no match for seasoned French regulars and savage Indian braves. France was jeopardizing British imperial interests. The king acquiesced to Franklin's reasoning and ordered General Edward Braddock to take a small army to clear the forks of the Ohio of the French trespassers. He also sent Admiral Edward Boscawen's fleet to the Gulf of St. Lawrence to prevent the arrival of more French reinforcements in Canada. All this was in perfect obedience to Lorenzo Ricci's strategy of establishing a British military presence in America. The Crown ultimately would require the Americans to pay for this presence,

CHAPTER 12 LORENZO RICCI'S WAR

which would expose the colonists to taxation from afar, which they could readily be fomented to resist. The resistance would be met with harassment, which would incite rebellion and, ultimately, division.

The philosophical similarities between Quakers and Loyolan gnosticism should not escape our notice. "Quaker," the term, was first used by an English judge in 1650 to ridicule how the leader of that denomination, George Fox, admonished him to "tremble at the Word of the Lord!" Fox summoned all who sought spiritual truth and peace to come out of the churches and seek an intimate, "personal relationship with Christ." Jesus of the Quakers spoke through inner illumination, a light available to all, having nothing to do with outward forms of ceremony, ritual, or creed. To the Quaker, every person was a walking church; every heart was God's altar and shrine. There was no need, therefore, to attend "steeple houses," or pay taxes to support a state church clergy, or doff a hat to king or commoner, or fight wars, or distinguish between sex or social class. Such doctrine, of course, was highly offensive to the Church of England, and so the Quakers were mercilessly persecuted as treasonous criminals.

They found a haven across the Atlantic in the colony conveniently granted by King Charles II to William Penn, one of the more outspoken English Quakers. Charles granted the land to settle a debt the Crown owed Penn's deceased father, Admiral Sir William Penn. Knowledgeable contemporaries publicly charged the younger Penn with being "a Jesuit in disguise." Actually, all Catholic clergy in England were to a certain extent "in disguise," thanks to a law prohibiting Roman Catholics from wearing clerical garb. Promulgated with the intent of handicapping "Popery," the law might as well have been written by Jesuits, as its effect reduced the Jesuit profile to nothing – the level preferred by covert militias. Eighteenth-century London was teeming with disguised Jesuit missioners trained at places like St. Omer's in moral theology (casuistry, equivocation, mental reservation), as well as espionage, cloak-and-dagger diplomacy, guerrilla tactics, and the manipulation of public opinion.

William Penn's higher education began at Cardinal Wolsey's endowment for the furtherance of papal supremacy, Christ Church College at Oxford. Before completing Oxford, Penn was sent by his father to the small University of Saumer, France. Penn left Saumer an accomplished propagandist less interested in achieving specific biblical objectives ("Much reading is an oppression of the mind," he would later advise his children) than in establishing illuminated social justice through reason and natural understanding. His most influential work, the pamphlet "No Cross, No Crown," published in 1669, agitated for Quaker separatism. Charles II readily accommodated Penn's agitations by launching the Great Persecution of 1682, which created enormous migrations of diehard Protestants and Catholics alike to the American colonies. If Penn was not the Jesuit he was believed to be, he was at least a rather superior Jesuit product, another in a long train of Princes (designated "Proprietor" in Penn's case, deferring to the Quakers' dislike for titles of nobility) well-trained to populate, administer and defend their land-grants in obedience to the will of the Grantor. Penn's example, and Franklin's after him, inspired Franklin's esteemed masonic brother Jean-François Arouet, better known as Voltaire, a founder of the Enlightenment, to memorialize Quakers as the noblest kind of born-again European.

Yet well-informed Englishmen saw neither Quaker nor regeneration in Penn's curiously compromising friendship with James II, who succeeded Charles II in 1685. What possible league could a Quaker have with a King? Worse, a King converted to Roman Catholicism by Jesuits? Certainly no true Quaker could have written Penn's Charter for the City of Philadelphia, which amounted to his gift of that estate to the Church of England. In the Charter's Preamble, Penn stated: "I have, by virtue of the king's letters patent, under the great seal of England, erected the said town into a borough, and do, by these presents, erect the said town and borough into a City."[2] The name "city," in every case, signifies the location of a bishop's *see,* the seat of his authority (from the Latin *sedes),* and the territory under his supervision.[3] No place in England was called a City unless governed by a bishop – as in the See

CHAPTER 12 LORENZO RICCI'S WAR

or City of Canterbury, See or City of York, See or City of London, of Bath and Wells, of Bristol, of Salisbury, etc. With the Philadelphia charter, Penn erected for the persecuting Church of England a nearly invisible mechanism for recycling the very victims of its persecutions. Indeed, Penn's last will and testament, which became effective with his death in England in 1718 at the age of 74, turned all Pennsylvania into the same mechanism with these words: "The government of my province of Pennsylvania, and territories thereunto belonging, and All Powers relating thereto, I give and devise to the most honourable the Earl of Oxford, and Earl Mortimer, and their heirs, upon trust, to dispose thereof to the Queen [Anne], or to any other person, to the best advantage and profit they can." With a stroke of Penn's quill, the children of the Quakers who had followed him out of the Church of England were literally given back. To become free of this bondage, the Quakers were obliged to align themselves with the Church of Rome, at least the black papacy. This alliance was facilitated by Benjamin Franklin, whose political career was built on defending the Quaker interests against the Proprietary heirs, which were the Church of England. Against this common enemy, Franklin and the Quakers united, knowingly or unknowingly, with the designs of the Roman Church Militant.

WHILE these stones rolled unstoppably toward their objective, Jesuit General Luigi Centurioni died. Early in May of 1758 the General Congregation arrived at Rome to choose his successor. On the last day of the month the Congregation unanimously elected Lorenzo Ricci, the Society's Spiritual Father and Secretary, as its eighteenth Black Pope.

Ricci, a professor of philosophy, theology, and the classics at the Roman College, was known for his patient, placid nature, his even temper. He inherited an organization in remarkably good shape. The Latin American missions were flourishing. A mission had just been established in Poland. Everywhere the schools and colleges were prospering. In the natural sciences, Jesuits were counted among the world's leading authorities. Their presence in economic and secular government had never been more imposing. As the papal nuncio to Vienna stated in a letter to his superior at the Vatican, "the Jesuits have the upper hand over everything, even the most prominent ministers of State, and domineer over them if they do not carry out their will."[4]

But the Society's legendary power could hinder Catholic activity in the Protestant missions. To defeat Great Britain without a battle Lorenzo Ricci required the abilities and resources of an important Maryland family, the Carrolls. The three Carroll sons, Daniel, John and their first cousin Charles, all now in their twenties, had been trained in Jesuit warfare at St. Omer's. John was teaching there. Charles was studying law at the Jesuit College Louis-le-Grand in Paris, about to undertake further studies at London's Inner Temple. Daniel – of Daniel's activities between 1753 and 1781, very little is known. What is well-known is that the Carroll lads were among the wealthiest Americans alive. The mother of Daniel and John, Eleanor Darnall, claimed direct descent from the Calverts, the owning family of original Maryland. She had come into possession of much of the land that Daniel would transfer to the District of Columbia. Charles Carroll stood to inherit America's largest private estate; later, John Adams would label him America's richest citizen.

Lorenzo Ricci could not win his War without the overt participation of the Carrolls. But New England was virulently Protestant. What Protestant leader would stoop to cooperate with devout Roman Catholics schooled in trickery by the all-powerful Jesuits? Would uniting with Jesuits not be laying America's future at the feet of the Bishop of Rome? In this consensus Ricci was able to discern a valuable negative weapon. If the stones of envy and hatred were given a gentle nudge, their own weight and momentum could spectacularly blast the Society of Jesus to smithereens. With the Society out of the way, Roman Catholicism would hang in the wind, defenseless. To a Protestant's perception, the Church would no longer be a forceful contender for political power. Sun-tzu advised a ruse known in the lingo of modern covert professionals as "blown cover as cover:"

CHAPTER 12 LORENZO RICCI'S WAR

> There will be times when you will lower yourself, and others when you pretend to be afraid. Sometimes you will feign weakness so that your enemies, opening the door to presumption & pride, come to attack you unwisely.... Give out false information about the state [you] are in ... [The enemy], believing [it] to be true, will act in consequence toward his Generals & all the Officers presently at his service....

Yes, sudden misfortune would bless the Society. Weakness and persecution would be transformed into magnificent new capital for building sympathetic relationships with other weak and persecuted people, such as the British colonists were destined soon to become. Without detailing his strategy (for Sun-tzu says "You will act in such a way that those who are inferior to you can never guess your intentions...."), Lorenzo Ricci affirmed to the General Congregation that stormclouds were gathering on the horizon. The Congregation summarily gave its understanding in obedience to the "hidden design" of their new Superior General – who occupied, after all, the place of Jesus. It issued a call for *esprit* to the brotherhood at large:

> If, God permitting it because of his hidden designs which we could do nothing else but adore, we are to become the butt of adversity, the Lord will not abandon those who remain attached and united to him; and as long as the Society is able to go to him with an open soul and a sincere heart, no other source of strength will be necessary for it.[5]

The Prime Minister of Portugal, Sebastian the Marquis de Pombal, had been conducting what the New Catholic Encyclopedia calls "a long campaign of calumnies, false rumors, distorted manipulation of incidents, all intent on undermining the Jesuits' reputation by ascribing to them nefarious doctrines, purposes, and practices." Among Pombal's allegations were that the Jesuits had incited revolts in Paraguay (a Portuguese colony), had traded illegally, had even conspired to murder the King. Pombal supported his claim with numerous anti-Jesuit tracts and inflammatory pastoral letters, which he submitted to Parliament. In the Society's defense, a group of bishops showered Pope Clement XIII with letters commending the Jesuits for their invaluable work. Clement, known by Jesuit historians as "a Jesuited pope,"[6] hastened to send copies of these endorsements to Lorenzo Ricci for publication under the title "Catholic Ecclesiastical Judgment for the Present Status of the Society of Jesus." Publication of these endorsements would show the world that the Society enjoyed the solid support of the Roman hierarchy. Significantly, *Ricci declined to publish them.*

On January 19, 1759, the Marquis de Pombal procured a royal decree expelling the Jesuits from Portugal and its overseas colonies. More than a thousand Jesuit fathers were crammed into ships and dumped on the shores of the Papal States (then an area in central Italy only slightly more spacious than Switzerland). Two hundred-fifty fathers were cast into dungeons, many perishing from maltreatment. The Portuguese Crown seized all the Society's houses, churches, and colleges, as well.

STONES were then nudged in France. The Superior of a Jesuit mission in the Caribbean, Père LaValette, had obtained commercial credit to finance his mission in Martinique. When it happened that he could no longer pay his debt, a trading firm in Marseilles alleged damages against him of more than two million francs. LaValette asked Lorenzo Ricci for help. *Ricci turned him down.* The firm sued the Society in a French court and won. Ricci then appealed the case to the Parlement in Paris, which was more of a supreme court than a legislative body. His lawyers argued that the Society could not be held liable for personal debts of its members due to a prohibition laid down by St. Ignatius himself in the *Constitutions* against any member's doing business as a principal or partner. Although this claim was easily dismissible as a flimsy legal fiction, the court demanded evidence to support it. This required Lorenzo Ricci to produce the *Constitutions,* which had never before been publicly revealed. When the volumes were brought to court and examined, the government attorneys had a field day. A lawyer

CHAPTER 12 LORENZO RICCI'S WAR

from Brittany named LaChatolais charged that the *Constitutions* was a handbook of "every known form of heresy, idolatry, and superstition, [which] provides tutelage in suicide, legicide, blasphemy, and every kind of impurity, usury, sorcery, murder, cruelty, hatred, vendetta, insurrection, and treason."[7]

As the LaValette case unfolded, during 1759 and 1760 Benjamin Franklin's beloved Voltaire slammed the Jesuits in two satirical plays mounted on the Parisian stage. Educated in the humanities and theatrical arts by Jesuits at the Collège Louis-le-Grand, Voltaire served the Society and the Catholic Church with distinction by becoming their chief critic and debunker, much in the way Will Rogers served Franklin Roosevelt's administration by lampooning New Deal politicians, or in the way Keystone Cops tickled an America being transformed into a police state. Audiences at *Candide* howled at Jesuit buffoons strutting about self-importantly drilling their Paraguayan Indian troops. In *The Account of the Sickness, Confession, Death and Apparition of the Jesuit Berthier,* the editor of a Jesuit literary review who dies of sheer boredom challenges the notion that the Society is even worthy of existence. With his predecessor Blaise Pascal (whose *Provincial Letters* had alerted earlier generations to the egomania of high Jesuitry), Voltaire provided a spirit of ridicule which gave Jesuit-bashing the feel of good sport.

Lorenzo Ricci's handling of the LaValette case resulted in a resolution, passed by Parlement on August 6, 1762, condemning the Jesuits as "endangering the Christian faith, disturbing the peace of the Church, and in general building up far less than they destroy." The resolution continued:

> The Society of Jesus by its very nature is inadmissible in any properly ordered State as contrary to natural law, attacking all temporal and spiritual authority, and tending to introduce into Church and State, under the specious veil of a religious Institute, not an Order truly aspiring towards evangelical perfection, but rather a political organization whose essence consists in a continual activity, by all sorts of ways, direct and indirect, secret and public, to gain absolute independence and then the usurpa-

tion of all authority.... They outrage the laws of nature and as enemies of the laws of France should be irrevocably expelled.

Louis XV being an absolute monarch, parliamentary resolutions were worthless without his signature. Louis being obedient to his Jesuits, it was highly unlikely that he would ever sign a resolution condemning the Jesuits. *Yet sign it he did.* And why he did has remained a point of debate. Some say his mistress, Madame de Pompadour, craved vengeance against court Jesuits for implacably denying her a mass. Others say the king needed Parlement's favor to bail him out of debt. I submit that Louis signed because Lorenzo Ricci wanted him to.

When the resolution became law, Ricci released the French Jesuits from their vows. The Society as an institution ceased to exist on French soil. Louis consented to allow the Jesuits to remain in France, but as "regular clergy." Others went into exile. (Père LaValette, whose financial problems had brought on the debacle, was exiled by Ricci to live the rest of his life as a private citizen in England. When the war that had begun in the Ohio valley reached Martinique, the English occupied that tiny island and took over the Jesuit plantations, selling them, slaves and all, for more than enough money to have paid off LaValette's debts.)

In the midst of their decomposing glory, the Jesuits received from Clement XIII an awesome gift designed to make welcome the most humiliating of circumstances. This was the mass and office of the Sacred Heart, with its icon of a realistically bloody heart plucked from Christ's ribcage and ignited by an eternal flame. Based on visions resulting from the Spiritual Exercises made by Ste. Margaret-Marie Alacoque (1647-90) as promoted by her Jesuit spiritual director, Claude de la Colombière, Sacred Heart is a gnostic Jesuit production centering on the Saviour's perfect humanity. "By devotion to my Heart," Jesus supposedly revealed to Alacoque, "tepid souls shall grow fervent, and fervent souls shall quickly mount to high perfection." Sacred Heart summons true believers to pay a debt of "reparation" for the world's sins. The debt is payable only by prayers, penances, masses, and (significantly for

CHAPTER 12   LORENZO RICCI'S WAR

this epoch in the Society's history) social action. John Carroll, so indispensable for the outworking of the American Revolution, was profoundly devoted to Sacred Heart.

Louis xv was the effective head of the "Family Compact," an agreement between reigning Bourbon monarchs to present a united front before the rest of the world "on important measures." Once he had dissolved the Jesuits in France, he advised other Bourbons to do likewise, although he could not name anything to be gained politically, economically, or financially by the Society's dissolution. The issue "still remains puzzling and problematic" (Professor Martin says[8]) unless considered (I submit) in light of Sun-tzuan ruse.

At any rate, the Bourbon Charles III of Spain followed Louis' advisory. Charles convened a special commission to prepare a master plan for ousting the Jesuits. No one could produce any hard evidence against the Society. But there were plenty of rumors. A mob that had risen up to protest a law Charles had passed forbidding the wearing of wide sombreros was said to have been fomented by Jesuits. A rumor swept across Spain that the Jesuits were nursing a plot to assassinate Charles. The Jesuits supposedly had proof that the king was technically a bastard and should be deposed. None of these rumors were ever substantiated. Moreover, *General Ricci ordered the Jesuits to do nothing to dispel them.* The result was that forty-six of the sixty Spanish bishops decided that Spain should follow the Marquis de Pombal and oust the Society.

And so the commission drafted an expulsion order, which Charles signed on February 27, 1767. The order was executed by ambush, reminiscent of Philip IV's move against the Knights Templar in 1312. Charles sent out sealed envelopes marked "Not to be opened before sunrise of April 2 on pain of death" to all provincial viceroys and military commanders. When sunrise came and the recipients opened their envelopes, they discovered two letters inside. The first ordered them to place troops around the Jesuit residences and colleges during the night of April 2, to arrest all Jesuits, and to arrange for them to be placed aboard waiting ships at certain docks. "If a single Jesuit," concluded the king, "even though sick or dying, is still to be found in the area under your command after the embarcation, prepare yourself to face summary execution."

The second letter was a copy of King Charles' original order of expulsion, which began "Being swayed by just and legitimate reasons which shall remain sealed within my royal breast forever," and went on to say that "all members of the Society of Jesus are to leave my kingdoms [Castille, Aragon, Navarre, and the other formerly independent kingdoms that made up Spain] and all their goods are declared forfeit ... by virtue of the highest power, which the Lord God Almighty has confided into my hands." The king made sure to discourage any investigation into causes: "It is not for subjects to question the wisdom or to seek to interpret the decisions of their sovereign."

Only days before April 2, the Spanish ambassador to the Holy See presented a document from Charles to Pope Clement XIII that explained,

> Your Holiness knows as well as anyone else that a sovereign's first duty is to ensure the peace of his dominions and the tranquillity of his subjects. In the fulfillment of this sovereign task, I have found it necessary to expel all the Jesuits residing in my kingdoms and to commit them directly to Your Holiness' wise stewardship in the States of the Church.... I beg Your Holiness to consider that my decision is unalterable and has been made as the result of mature reflection and all due consideration for the consequences....

Clement, the likelihood of whose submission to the will of Lorenzo Ricci should not be underestimated, responded in a melodramatic vein, as though playing for an audience: "Of all the shocks I have had to endure in the nine unhappy years of my pontificate, this one, of which Your Majesty has informed me, is the worst." The pope had little more to say, except that the king may have placed himself in danger of eternal damnation.

The order was executed during the night of April second and

CHAPTER 12   LORENZO RICCI'S WAR

third. Some six thousand Jesuits were rounded up throughout Spain. They were crammed into the lower decks of twenty-two warships. In May 1767 the gruesome fleet appeared off Civitavecchia, the port of the Papal States, and – amazingly, *was fired upon by shore artillery!* The ships were denied permission to land their human cargo *by order of the pope himself, pursuant to a conference with Lorenzo Ricci!* Historians are at a loss to explain why Clement, so devoted to the Jesuits, would impose such cruelty upon his beloveds in their hour of need. The most plausible answer, I would suggest, is that his understanding was obedient to the inscrutable command of his General, whose exceedingly private objective, after all, was to disqualify the Society of Jesus and the Roman Catholic Church as viable enemies of Protestantism, at least in the North American colonies. No longer enemies, they could develop personal alliances. The suffering priests, the guns of Civitavecchia, were all explained in Amiot's Sun-tzu:

> Your army, accustomed to not knowing your plans, will be equally unaware of the peril which threatens it. A good General takes advantage of everything. But he can only do that because he has operated in the greatest secrecy, because he knows how to remain cool-headed & because he governs with uprightness. At the same time, however, his men are constantly misled by what they see & hear. He manages for his troops never to know what they must do nor what orders they must receive.... If his own people are unaware of his plans, how can the enemy discover them?

Over the next few months, thousands more Jesuits were expelled from the remaining Bourbon states of Naples, Parma, Malta, and Spanish America. Jesuits in French America (Quebec) and New England were left undisturbed, as were those in Austria. In October 1768 the Austrian Empress Maria-Theresa, a Habsburg, wrote her Jesuit confessor, Father Koffler: "My dear father, there is no cause for concern; as long as I am alive you have noth-ing to fear." But Maria-Theresa hoped to marry her two daughters to Bourbon princes, Caroline to the son of the Spanish king,

Marie-Antoinette to the son of Louis XV. Bourbon ambassadors advised her that unless she expelled the Jesuits, she would have to look elsewhere for sons-in-law. The Empress reneged on her promise to Father Koffler, expelled the Jesuits, and the girls got their men. (Marie-Antoinette's marriage would end with the execution of her husband, Louis XVI, in January 1793. Nine months later, she would die the same way, decapitated by the guillotine. This device bears the name of the French Revolutionist who in 1792 first suggested its use in administering the death penalty, Dr. Josef Guillotin. Dr. Guillotin was a disestablished Jesuit.)

In January 1769 the ambassadors from France, Spain, and Portugal visited Clement XIII to demand "the complete and utter suppression of the Society of Jesus." Clement called for a special consistory of the College of Cardinals to deliberate the question. But when the cardinals convened February 3, it was not to discuss Bourbon ultimatums, but to choose Clement's successor. For the 76-year-old pope had died the night before "of an apoplectic attack," said the official record, a heart attack attributed to the pressures applied by the Bourbon diplomats.

For nearly three months, one question charged the turbulent conclave: Should the next pope be for or against the Jesuits? The cardinals' choice of Lorenzo Ganganelli was a triumph for Lorenzo Ricci. Although Ganganelli was a Franciscan, he had colleagued with Jesuits as a special consultant to the Inquisition. His celebrated book *Diatriba theologica* (1743) had been dedicated to Ignatius Loyola. Moreover, Ganganelli literally owed his papacy to Lorenzo Ricci, as it was Ricci who had sponsored his nomination for cardinal in 1759.[9] Almost immediately after receiving the red hat Ganganelli had shown evidence of cooperating with General Ricci's strategy of gradually disestablishing the Society of Jesus. *Oxford Book of Popes* indicates a sudden and unexplainable habit change: "Hitherto regarded as a friend of the Jesuits, Cardinal Ganganelli now distanced himself from them." And now, a decade later, calling himself Clement XIV, Ganganelli presented what the Catholic Encyclopedia calls "in *appearance* a hostile attitude" toward the Jesuits, an *apparent* hostility, a theatrical hostility that masked an

CHAPTER 12 LORENZO RICCI'S WAR

involved loyalty toward the Society. Clement XIV would do whatever was necessary to help the Society win victory without doing battle, even if it meant obliterating the Society.

The Bourbons needed appeasing. Hastily, Clement promised Charles III of Spain forthcoming documents necessary to "proclaim to all the world the wisdom of Your Majesty's decision to expel the Jesuits as unruly and rebellious subjects." He assured Louis XV of France also of a "plan for the complete suppression of this society." On Maundy Thursday 1770, Clement omitted the annual reading of *In coena Domini* ("On the Lord's supper"). The omission was an astonishing statement. This celebrated bull, first proclaimed in 1568 by Pope Pius V, arrogantly reminded kings that they were but vassals of the papacy. Suddenly discontinuing this assertion flattered the royal self-importance, inviting crowned heads to stay on the anti-Jesuit, anti-Church track so necessary for the fulfillment of Lorenzo Ricci's secret designs in England and America. It surely evidences Clement's involvement in the strategy of feigned weakness in order to conceal what Sun-tzu called "an order that nothing can interrupt." The non-reading of In *coena Domini* rang the deathknell of the strong-armed white papacy as manifest by Ricci's political theorist, "Justinius Febronius," in his 1763 masterpiece On *the State of the Church & the Legitimate Power of the Roman Pontiff* – about which more presently.

For more than eighty years, the papacy had supported Rome-based members of the Stuart monarchs exiled from England for being Roman Catholics. Not only did Clement XIV diminish this tradition to almost nothing, in 1772 he began extending a highly visible and most cordial hospitality to the Protestant King George III and his family. This tableau was enormously disturbing to American Protestants, who at that time were having extreme difficulties with George. The prospect of England reuniting with Rome gave them all the more reason to strive for what Lorenzo Ricci wanted, their independence.

Finally, on July 21, 1773, Clement XIV delivered on his promise by signing the brief *Dominus ac Redemptor noster* ("God and our Redeemer"). The brief "dissolved, suppressed, disbanded, and abolished" the Society of Jesus "for all eternity" so as "to establish a real and enduring peace within the Church." All the Jesuits' "offices, authorities, and functions" were declared "null and void, and all their houses, colleges, hospices, and any other places occupied by them to be hereby disestablished, no matter in what province, state, or kingdom they might be found."

Clement appointed five cardinals, an archbishop, a bishop, two theologians, and other ecclesiastical dignitaries to supervise the Disestablishment. None of the confiscated Jesuit records, correspondence, and accounts showed any incriminating evidence.

Although Lorenzo Ricci lived a short walk from the pope's palace at St. Peter's, notice of the Disestablishment was not served upon him until mid-August. Guards took the General into custody at his offices in Number 45 Piazza del Gesu. They removed him to the English College a few blocks away. He remained there five weeks. Things were then happening in England and America that make Ricci's presence in the English College extraordinarily significant. We shall consider those happenings in a forthcoming chapter.

Toward the end of September, Lorenzo Ricci was taken from the English College to Castel Sant'Angelo, a medieval fortress whose dungeons suggest a prison. His detention was probably less demeaning than we might imagine, as Sant'Angelo contained quite elegant rooms. Popes often used them as a convenient resort from administrative stresses. In fact, a secret underground tunnel connected Sant'Angelo to the papal palace at the Vatican. It would be consistent with Lorenzo Ricci's position and strategy for him to stay in personal, secret contact with Clement XIV by means of this tunnel.

View of St. Peter's Basilica from Castel Sant'Angelo

On September 22, 1774, the first anniversary of Ricci's deten-

CHAPTER 12   LORENZO RICCI'S WAR

tion at Sant'Angelo, Clement died. He was sixty-nine. He had suffered the last year of his life in severe depression, it was said, with morbid paranoia over assassination. His corpse decomposed rapidly, feeding rumors of death by poison, rumors which his famous last words tended to confirm: "Mercy! Mercy! *Compulsus feci!*" ("I was compelled to do it!") For many years afterward, historians would wonder just whom Ganganelli was addressing: God? A vengeful Jesuit assassin? Ricci? What was the "it" he was compelled to do? Disestablish the Jesuits? Commit suicide? The definitive answer may never be known, because the pope's personal papers and effects decomposed as rapidly as his flesh. What is quite known, though, is that the death of Clement XIV, in the words of *Oxford Book of Popes,* "brought the prestige of the papacy to its lowest level in centuries." Which is precisely what Lorenzo Ricci needed for his American Revolution to happen.

WE now proceed to examine the structured darkness of the men who led the attack against the Society of Jesus. It was the same darkness from whence came not only the Englishmen who turned their kingdom into a hated tyranny, but also the Americans who advocated rebellion against that tyranny. The darkness is called Freemasonry, and it is the subject of our next chapter.

WASHINGTON IN MASONIC REGALIA
(From a Currier & Ives engraving, 1868.)

Chapter 13

THE SECRET BRIDGE

> "The papal prohibition might even have encouraged Masonry by identifying opposition to the group with Catholic tyranny and superstition."
> — STEVEN C. BULLOCK,
> REVOLUTIONARY BROTHERHOOD, 1996

THE *New Catholic Encyclopedia* identifies the men who attacked the Society of Jesus as "the radical devotees of the rationalistic Enlightenment – richly talented and influential writers, such as Voltaire, Rousseau, and other *'philosophes'* among the Encyclopedists, the followers of Freemasonry, and high placed government officials." Attacking the Jesuits was for them "a step toward their ultimate objective of abolishing all religious orders, the papacy, and finally the Church itself."

The masterpiece of the encyclopedists (most of whom happened to be *philosophes),* was the monumental *Encyclopedia of Sciences, Arts, and Trades* (1743-1751). The *Encyclopedia* was the flame of the Enlightenment, the fulfillment of Cardinal Wolsey's dream of flooding the world with print containing "learning against learning." It brought so much learning (secular learning, as against Scriptural learning) that it became its own paradigm demanding radical change in existing norms. The Enlightenment called for a "new age" that placed Reason above any Church, above even the Bible. The new age issued in the elegant neo-gnostic religion of Deism, the thinking man's alternative to Roman Catholicism and its imperious hold on the human conscience.

Nowhere was Deism more methodically practiced than "around the altars of Freemasonry," as the great Masonic scholar Albert Pike put it. Here, wrote Pike in his influential *Morals and Dogma* (1871), "the Christian, the Hebrew, the Moslem, the Brahmin, the followers of Confucius and Zoroaster, can assemble as brethren and unite in prayer to the one God who is above all gods." The brethren prayerfully climb the gnostic pyramid of successive illumination until, hopefully, a oneness with the supreme God is attained. As Pike explained, the Deists (like the papacy) looked upon the Bible as something of a stumbling block:

> The Freemason does not pretend to dogmatic certainty, nor vainly imagine such certainty attainable. He considers that if there were no written revelation, he could safely rest the hopes that animate him and the principles that guide him, on the deductions of reason and the convictions of instinct and consciousness.
>
> He studies the wonders of the Heavens, the framework and revolutions of the Earth, the mysterious beauties and adaptations of animal existence, the moral and material constitution of the human creature, so fearfully and wonderfully made; and is satisfied that God IS....

Most of the *philosophes,* including Frederick the Great, the Protestant King of Prussia who subsidized the entire *Encyclopedia* project, were Deistic brethren. As were the "high placed government officials" who pushed for the disestablishment of the Jesuits. All the Bourbon monarchs employed as their official advisors "ardent members of the Lodge," to use Professor Martin's phrase.' The Marquis de Pombal of Portugal was a Mason. Charles Ill's advisor the Count de Aranda, Louis XV's Minister de Tillot and the Duc de Choiseul, as well as Maria-Theresa's Prince von Kaunitz and Gerard von Swieten – all belonged to the secret brotherhood.

CHAPTER 13   THE SECRET BRIDGE

Since it was no secret that the Enlightenment aimed to make Roman Catholicism passée, Pope Clement XII promulgated in 1728 the constitution in *eminenti,* which appeared to condemn Freemasonry thusly:

> CONDEMNATIO SOCIETATIS DE CONVENTICULORUM DE FREEMASONS, UNDER THE PENALTY *IPSO FACTO* INCURRED, OR EXCOMMUNICATION; ABSOLUTION FROM IT BEING RESERVED TO PONTIFEX MAXIMUS
>
> Free Masons of whatever sect or religion, confederate together in a close and inscrutable bond, according to secret laws and orders agreed upon between them, and bind themselves as well by strict oath taken on the Bible as by the imprecations of heavy punishments to preserve their mysteries with inviolable secrecy___
>
> The great mischiefs which generally accrue from secret bodies are antagonist to civil and canonical laws.
>
> Wherefore, by the advice of the cardinals and of our mere motion, and from the plenitude of the apostolic power, we do condemn and prohibit the meetings of the above-named society of Free Masons.
>
> We strictly command that no one, under any pretext or color, dare to presume to promote, favor, admit, or conceal in their houses members of assemblies of this abominable order, nor in any way aid or assist in their meeting in any place, or to administer medicine to them in their sickness, or in any manner, directly or indirectly, by themselves or others, afford them counsel or help in their hour of trial and affliction, or persuade others to join said Order....

While *Eminenti's* stern rhetoric, which was renewed by Benedict XIV in 1751, seems to dig a wide ocean between Catholicism and Freemasonry, its fruits tell another story. Why, for example, were the Bourbon monarchs, all of them Roman Catholic, never penalized or excommunicated for admitting, promoting, and favoring Masonic advisors? And why, a decade after the Marquis de Pombal had shipped the Jesuits out of Portugal, did Clement XIV send an appeasing nuncio to the Portuguese court, elevate Pombal's brother to Bishop, and confirm all Pombal's nominees in bishoprics? The answer, of course, is contained in the bull's title, which provides that absolution from penalties or excommunication is "reserved to *Pontifex Maximus.*" That is to say, associating with the abomination of Freemasonry, if done for a cause valuable to the papacy (such as weakening the Jesuits to the point everybody assumes they're no longer a threat to Protestantism), will be absolved by the papacy. Given the historical context, does any other answer make sense?

The leading Jesuit-bashers were not only Freemasons, they were also the product of Jesuit learning against learning. It was the *ratio studiorum* — the Medici Library's gnostic wisdom absorbed in an ambiance of casuistry, equivocation, mental reservation, and obedience of the understanding, combined with smatterings of Holy Scripture usually filtered through the commentaries of Church doctors — that had turned two centuries of Jesuited students into secular *philosophes.* The *ratio studiorum* dictated the form and scope of the *Encyclopedia,* which in turn codified the Enlightenment paradigm, whose Deistic litany was preached "around the altars of Freemasonry."

Hold Freemasonry up to the light and you cannot help but see the black papacy's watermark. Isn't it reasonable, given the circumstances, that the "G" in the center of the familiar Masonic emblem represents the initial of *"Gesu,"* the residence of the black popes at the Jesuits' world headquarters at Number 5, Borgo Sancto Spiritu, in Rome? Freemasons wouldn't suspect this, nor would Jesuits. It would be information reserved uniquely to the unknown superior, who shares what he knows with no one. "Your enemies will serve you without their wishes," said Sun-tzu, "or even their knowledge."

Freemasonry was the natural, the reasonable, the only intelligent way for the Roman Catholic Church to control (a) the ongoing affront of Protestantism, (b) the increase in "divine right" kings heading their own national churches independent of Vatican control, and (c) the incredible explosion of international mercantilism. Like the aquatic creature whose mouth resembles a

CHAPTER 13   THE SECRET BRIDGE

comfortable resting place to its prey, the Lodges were a sagacious recycling of the old Templar infrastructure into a dynamic spiritual and economic brotherhood that gave Protestants, Jews, Buddhists, Muslims, agnostics, and anyone else an opportunity to build a better life outside Roman Catholicism, yet still under the Church's superintending eye. For Sun-tzu said, "The General sees all, hears all, does all, and in appearance is not involved with anything." The Jesuit General is the disembodied eye substituting for the pyramid's missing capstone, the stone the builders rejected.

The Lodge's secrecy and its condemnation by the Church were essential to sustaining the integrity of both institutions. And so the deepest Masonic secret, the secret that not even their Grandest Masters could penetrate, was that all their secrets were known to one man alone, the Superior General of the Society of Jesus. This should not surprise anyone aware of how thoroughly Freemasonry is suffused with Jesuitic technique. Both Freemasonry and the Society of Jesus are (a) humanist religious orders, (b) secretive, (c) fraternal, (d) socially conscientious and politically active – questing, like Aeneas, the prototypical Roman, for the greatest good for the greatest number. Both orders (e) hold Tradition, Reason, and Experience in equal if not greater esteem than the Bible, (f) employ carefully structured programs of gnostic visualization to achieve an ever-increasing knowledge of the divine, (g) condone "the end justifies the means," and (h) require absolute obedience, secured by a blood oath, to a hierarchy of superiors culminating in the Jesuit General, whose orders are so wisely suited to the recipient that they are obeyed as though willed by the recipient himself.

THE first recorded member of American Freemasonry was Daniel Coxe, who was constituted Provincial Grand Master of the provinces of New York, New Jersey, and Pennsylvania on June 5, 1730, on a deputation granted by the Duke of Norfolk, Grand Master of Masons in England.[5] Evidently, Coxe was an industrious recruiter. Minutes of a meeting of the Grand Lodge of London on January 29, 1731 reflect that "Coxe's health was proposed and drank [sic] as 'Provincial Grand Master of North America.'"

Daniel Coxe was actually a junior, according to Sidney Hayden's *Washington and His Compeers* (1868). He was "the son of Dr. Daniel Coxe of England, who was physician to the Queen of Charles II." Dr. Coxe must be presumed a Roman Catholic sympathizer, as both Charles and his Queen were Catholics. The Queen, Catherine of Braganza (Portugal), flaunted a huge Vatican entourage, for which she was continually harassed by death plots. Charles converted to Catholicism in exchange for money from Louis XIV of France under the terms of the Treaty of Dover.

The junior Daniel Coxe deserves wider recognition as an American visionary, or at least the sole apologist of some undisclosed visionary. Thirteen years before Benjamin Franklin's proposal of a "colonial Union" to the Albany congress in 1754, for which Franklin is credited with being the first to suggest a "united States," Coxe published in England a dissertation promoting a scheme to settle "an extensive tract of country lying on the Gulf of Mexico" owned by his father, the Queen's physician. The dissertation, entitled *A Description of the English Province of Carolina, by the Spaniards called Florida, and by the French La Louisiane,* promoted the elder Coxe's tract as an English province allied with New England against the Spanish, French, and Indians. It called for "all the colonies appertaining to the crown of Great Britain, on the northern continent of America, [to] be united under a legal, regular, and firm establishment; over which a lieutenant or supreme governor may be constituted and appointed to preside on the spot, to whom the governors of each colony shall be subordinate." With this union of governments under one president, Coxe foresaw "a great council or general convention of the estates of the colonies" to "meet together, consult and advise for the good of the whole." These "united states" would provide "for their mutual defense and safety, as well as, if necessary, for offense and invasion of their enemies" – independently of the protections of the British Crown. Of course, these imaginings became reality forty years later with the fulfillment of Lorenzo Ricci's strategy for dividing the British Empire. Considering the elements involved – lands owned by the Catholic Queen's physician, lands managed and promoted

CHAPTER 13   THE SECRET BRIDGE

by the physician's son, who is a Freemason deputed to generate an American brotherhood by the eighth Duke of Norfolk, who himself was a member of England's premier Roman Catholic family – Coxe's dissertation appears to be the earliest formatting of the colonial conscience to divisive thinking by agents of the black papacy.

The Duke of Norfolk, "Grand Master of Masons in England," was also known as Thomas Howard, Earl of Arundell. His nephew, Henry, Lord Arundell, occupied Wardour Castle near Tisbury in Wiltshire at the time Clement XIV disestablished the Jesuits. We shall see how, in the autumn of 1773, it was to Lord Arundell's castle that John Carroll repaired when civil authorities closed down the Jesuit school in Liège, Belgium, where Carroll had been teaching. For a year Carroll stayed at Wardour, serving as the Arundell family's tutor and chaplain before sailing for America to participate in the Revolution.

THIRTY-THIRD degree Masonic scholar Manly P. Hall, in his gnostic extravaganza *Secret Teachings of All Ages: An Encyclopedic Outline of Masonic, Hermetic, Qabbalistic and Rosicrucian Symbolical Philosophy* (1988), remarked that "not only were many founders of the United States Government Masons, but they received aid from a secret and August body existing in Europe, which helped them to establish this country for a peculiar and particular purpose known only to the initiated few."

Most histories of the American Government skim over the Masonic presence. Americans like their history told in high-definition icons of good and evil, liberty and tyranny, heroism and treason, might and right. They won't buy a heritage polluted by dark spots of mystery. Yet the greater part of American governmental heritage is almost wholly mysterious.

The man best qualified to become our country's greatest historian, certainly the man with the most complete access to primary sources in the Revolutionary cause, was Charles Thomson. An authentic classical scholar, a discreet Protestant steeped in Medici learning, Thomson was known as "Perpetual Secretary of the Con-

Charles Thomson, the man who talked the truth.

tinental Congress." He inscribed minutes of every Congressional session from 1774 until ratification of the Constitution in 1789. With William Barton, a Freemason, he designed the Great Seal of the United States of America: the choice of its Virgilian mottoes is credited exclusively to Thomson.

Among his contemporaries, Charles Thomson's name was synonymous with Truth. So accurate were his minutes of Pennsylvania's negotiations with the Delaware Indians that the Delawares called him *Wegh-wu-law-mo-end,* "the man who talks the truth." When he would take his daily reports of congressional proceedings to the streets, eager mobs would cry "Here comes Charles Thomson! Here comes the Truth!"

Once the Constitution was ratified, Charles Thomson retired to Harriton, his country home in Bryn Mawr. He destroyed his personal papers relative to the creation of the new republic. An article by Kenneth Boling in the *Pennsylvania Magazine of History and Biography* (1976) says that Thomson actually wrote a lengthy history of the Revolution, which he also destroyed. Thomson biographer J. Edwin Hendricks of Wake Forest suggests a fate other than destruction, alluding to "persistent rumors that the Thomson papers are in the Pennsylvania Masonic records." (Professor Hendricks assured me personally that numerous inquiries have failed to reflect Thomson's membership in Pennsylvania Masonry.) Whether Thomson destroyed his history or surrendered it to the crypt of secrecy, it is clear that he knew there were certain elements in the formation of American government that must, *must* be ignored. "If the truth were known," he told friends darkly, "many careers would be tarnished and the leadership of the nation would be weakened."[4]

And so Charles Thomson occupied the remaining forty years of his life translating the Septuagint, the Greek-language Bible,

CHAPTER 13   THE SECRET BRIDGE

into English. Still, he was frequently requested to write the definitive insider's history of the Revolution. Dr. Benjamin Rush overheard Thomson's reply to one such request and recorded it in his diary:

> "No," said he, "I ought not, for I should contradict all the histories of the great events of the Revolution, and show by my account of men, motives and measures, that we are wholly indebted to the agency of Providence for its successful issue. Let the world admire the supposed wisdom and valor of our great men. Perhaps they may adopt the qualities that have been ascribed to them, and thus good may be done. I shall not undeceive future generations.".[5]

What I believe Thomson was meaning to say is simply that no historical account of the American Revolution can be truthful unless it discloses the role played by *"the agency of Providence."* Notice that Thomson does not use the word *"Providence"* alone, which was understood in his day to mean "God" or "Christ." He does not say *"we are wholly indebted to* God*,"* or *"we are wholly indebted to Christ,"* but rather to the *"agency"* thereof.

If Thomson knew the word "agency" was a synonym for "vicar," and I can't imagine that a professional linguist wouldn't, and if he knew that the popes had been called "vicars of Christ" since the fifth century, and I can't imagine that a biblical scholar of his quality wouldn't, then Thomson was most likely saying *"We are wholly indebted to the Vicar of Christ, that is, the Roman papacy."*

But what a ridiculous statement to the post-Revolutionary American mindset! Who would have believed such an outrageous notion, coming from even the man who talks the truth? The embattled, degenerate, dying papacy could not possibly have effected the Revolution! Anyone foolish enough to run with this idea would have crashed headlong into a wall of ridicule. For Thomson, there was no future in telling what he knew. Since he chose not to undeceive future generations, the American people have lived according to histories that can be contradicted by truth. They have been served by careers and leaders that truth could tarnish and weaken. They seem comfortable in their deception, which is generally the case among consenting subjects to Roman rule.

Let's move now to the next chapter, wherein we shall see how the Jesuits, which we now recognize as the unsung architects of the Enlightenment, supplied the American colonists a philosophical basis for rebelling against Great Britain.

CARDINAL ROBERT BELLARMINE (1542-1641)
(After Passerotti's engraved portrait from life.)

Chapter 14

THE DOGMA OF INDEPENDENCE

THE JESUIT *ratio studiorum* imbued western culture with a purely Catholic political theory. This theory, as articulated by Deist *philosophes* and politicians, ultimately became the rhetorical mainspring of the American Revolution. It so impacted the world that its formulator and original apologist, a Jesuit priest named Robert Bellarmine, was created a Saint in 1930.

Prior to Henry VIII's break with the Roman papacy in the mid-1530s and subsequent creation of the Church of England, kings regarded themselves, within their respective realms, as the anointed vicars of God for secular purposes only. After Henry's schism, Protestant kings assumed God's anointment covered religious purposes as well. They became infallible popes of their own national churches. Following the biblical teaching that the ruler is "God's minister to thee for good," Protestant kings claimed to rule by Divine Right, holding absolute sway over their subjects. In the maxim of Divine Right's greatest champion and James I's private theologian, Sir Robert Filmer, "The King can do no wrong."

Divine Right's staunchest opponent was Robert Bellarmine, private theologian to the pope, Clement VIII (1592-1605), who made him Cardinal Bellarmine in 1599. Cardinal Bellarmine appealed to the self-interest of the common man, something the Divine Right system failed to do. He invented liberation theology. Drawing on Aristotle and St. Thomas Aquinas, Bellarmine maintained that God anointed no kings but instead gave sovereignty directly and naturally to the people. The people were free to confer their sovereignty upon whomever or whatever they chose. Should the people's chosen sovereign prove himself (or itself) unworthy, the people had the right to depose him (or it) and start anew with any form of government they deemed necessary, whether monarchy, aristocracy, or republic.

Understandably, the Protestant monarchs loathed Cardinal Bellarmine. A *Collegio Anti-Bellarminianum* was established at Heidelberg to train Lutherans in how to cope with Bellarmine's democratic egalitarianism. When Queen Elizabeth ordered that Bellarmine be lectured against at Cambridge, the lecturer, while reading the Cardinal to refute him, converted to Roman Catholicism. Theodore Beza, who succeeded John Calvin as head of the Protestant church at Geneva, is said to have declared of Bellarmine's magnum opus, *Christian Controversy,* "This book has ruined us!"

Of the process of "making the enemy move as one wishes," Sun-tzu wrote: "The great science is to make him desire everything you wish him to do & to provide him with all the means to help you in this, without his realizing it." Thus, liberation theology reached the American revolutionaries through the voice and energies of its principal *adversary,* Sir Robert Filmer. Sir Robert spent the first four pages of *Patriarcha* (1680), his illustrious defense of Divine Right monarchy, refuting Cardinal Bellarmine. But his refutation contains so much material from Bellarmine's works that *Patriarcha* amounts to nothing less than a concise *introduction* of Bellarminian theory.

The two most conspicuous reviewers of *Patriarcha* were Alger-

CHAPTER 14   THE DOGMA OF INDEPENDENCE

non Sidney, Puritanism's greatest political philosopher, and John Locke, the voice of Enlightenment in England and America. Algernon Sidney's name means little to modern Americans, but in his day, and for generations after, it was synonymous with individual liberty. Babies and country estates were called "Sidney" in his honor, even though he was beheaded in 1683 for plotting the death of King Charles II. Sidney's philosophical admirers loved his open hostility to Roman Catholicism. They ignored his intrigues with the Jesuits of Louis XIV, and his long visits to Rome. *Discourses concerning Government,* his most celebrated work, was known respectfully as "the noble book." After its republication in 1763, along with an account of his preposterous trial (no indictment, no assistance of counsel, perjured testimony, tainted evidence, packed jury), it could be found in the library of every affluent home in America.

Sidney began *Discourses* with the following sentence: "Having lately seen a book entitled *Patriarcha* written by Sir Robert Filmer concerning the universal and undistinguished right of all kings, I thought a time of leisure might well be employed in examining his doctrine and the questions arising from it: which seem to concern all mankind." Whereupon, quoting Filmer's quotations from Bellarmine, Sidney goes on to attack Filmer and *in the process defends Bellarmine.* How wondrously Sun-tzuan that a trusted Protestant thinker would indoctrinate a nation of fellow-Catholic-bashers with the teachings of a Jesuit Cardinal!

John Locke held such influence over revolutionary intellectuals that historians have labeled him "America's Philosopher." He, too, endorsed Bellarmine by attacking Filmer. On the title page of his *Two Treatises on Government* (1690), Locke advertises that he will refute *Patriarcha* with reasoning wherein "the false principles and foundation of Sir Robert Filmer and his followers are detected and overthrown." He then expounds Cardinal Bellarmine in his own words, words that will become the rationale of the American Revolution: "Men being by nature all free, equal, and independent, no one can be put out of this estate, and subjected to the political power of another, without his consent...."

The personal library of the main author of the Declaration of Independence, Thomas Jefferson, contained a copy of *Patriarcha*, and also a handsome folio of four hundred ninety-seven pages of the discourses of Algernon Sidney. "If Jefferson read but the opening pages of Sidney's and Filmer's books," Bellarminian scholar John Clement Rager wrote in 1926,

> he had the principles of democracy as propounded by Bellarmine, in a nutshell. It is more than likely, however, that the curiosity of Jefferson ... prompted [him] to look more deeply into the original writings of this Catholic Schoolman.
>
> [He] had not far to go. In the library of Princeton University there was a copy of Cardinal Bellarmine's works. James Madison, a member of the committee which framed the Virginia Declaration of Rights, was a graduate of Princeton. Probably he read Bellarmine, for at this period of his life he read everything he could lay his hands on and was deeply versed in religious controversy.
>
> It might be remarked that several members of the committee which drew up the [Virginia] Declaration of Rights had been educated in England, where the writings of Bellarmine were not unpopular even among those who were most inimical to his faith.

The operative philosophy of the Declaration of Independence is easily traceable to Bellarminian liberation theology:

Cardinal Bellarmine	**Declaration of Independence**
"Political power emanates from God. Government was introduced by divine law, but the divine law has given this power to no particular man."	"The people are endowed by their Creator with certain inalienable rights."
"Society must have power to protect and preserve itself."	"To secure these rights, governments are instituted among men."

CHAPTER 14   THE DOGMA OF INDEPENDENCE

Cardinal Bellarmine	**Declaration of Independence**
"The people themselves, immediately and directly, hold the political power."	"Governments are instituted among men, deriving their just powers from the consent of the governed."
"All men are born naturally free and equal."	"All men are created equal."
"For legitimate reason the people can change the government to an aristocracy or a democracy or vice versa."	"Whenever any form of government becomes destructive of these ends, it is the Right of the People to alter or abolish it, and to institute a new goverment."

Interestingly, *Patriarcha* (1680) was not published until twenty-eight years after its author Sir Robert Filmer's death. It arrived in an era of dwindling hopes for Divine Right, the concept having been thoroughly discredited when King Charles I was beheaded in 1625.

Could it be that *Patriarcha* was edited or ghost-written by Jesuits at the command of Superior General John Paul Oliva (1661—1681)? The purpose would have been to induce the enemies of Roman Catholicism to follow Bellarmine by having Bellarminian liberation *attacked* by a *loser,* Filmer, the disgraced champion of a lost Protestant cause. The idea is not far-fetched when one considers actual outcome. For *Patriarcha* did in fact produce the theory of revolution that impelled the colonists to create a nation subservient to the black papacy.

But for liberation theology to translate into the violence necessary to divide the English-speaking world, England had to commit acts of tyranny. How this was accomplished, despite a dazed and confused and rather innocuous young king, is the subject of our next chapter.

JOHN STUART, 3RD EARL OF BUTE
(From the portrait by Alan Ramsay.)

Chapter 15

THE MADNESS OF KING GEORGE III

UPON THE DEATH in 1732 of Thomas Howard, Eighth Duke of Norfolk and real Founder of American Freemasonry, the Norfolk title passed to Thomas' brother Edward. In a curious way, the Ninth Duke of Norfolk played a part in the founding of the United States as well, albeit a cameo role.

Sun-tzu wrote

> Multiply your spies, put them everywhere, in the very Palace of the enemy Prince; have a list of the principal Officers who are at his service. Know their first & last names, the number of their children, their relatives, their friends, their servants. Let nothing happen to them that is not known to you.

Edward, Ninth Duke of Norfolk, was a regular in the crowd of Frederick William, Prince of Wales, and his Princess, Augusta of Saxony. The Waleses were party creatures, and an on-going disappointment to the Prince's father, King George II. The king resented that his son appeared not to have inherited his craving for war — George II was the last British monarch to lead his army into battle, which he did against the Spanish in 1739. George despised his son's Ignatian entourage. When Frederick William ran up an exorbitant tab entertaining foreign ambassadors at St. James's Palace, the king cut his allowance, shooed the ambassadors away, and ordered the couple to move out of St. James's and take up a simpler residency at Leicester House.

In 1738, Augusta gave birth to a son, George William. At the age of six the child was placed under the tutelage of a Dr. Ayscough. Like the Society of Jesus, Ayscough did not wish the head of the Church of England well. "He is chiefly remarkable," says Brittanica, "as an adherent of the opposition." Ayscough's role in history was to keep the future king of England, who suffered emotionally under the ungainly squabbles dividing father and grandfather, virtually illiterate for more than five years.

The Prince of Wales was fond of horse-racing. One afternoon in 1747, so the official story goes, a sudden downpour of rain confined him and a handful of friends to his tent at the Egham races. Determined to play cards, the Prince sent Edward, Ninth Duke of Norfolk, out in the rain to find someone to make up a whist party. The Duke returned with a strikingly handsome Scot, John Stuart, third Earl of Bute. "Bute immediately gained the favour of the prince and princess," says Brittanica, "and became the leading personage at their court." What Britannica omits saying, along with every other source I could find on this leading character in the formation of Anglo-American relations, is that Bute, like Norfolk, was *a secret brother of the Lodge*. This fact is ascertainable only from the keystone of the arch over Bute's mausoleum in St. Mary's Cemetery at Rothesay, Isle of Bute, in the Firth of Clyde west of Glasgow. Carved into that keystone is the familiar Masonic disembodied all-seeing eye.

Born in 1713, educated at Eton, Bute was elected in 1737 to the representative peerage for Scotland. He never opened his mouth in debate. When his bid for re-election failed, he returned

CHAPTER 15 THE MADNESS OF KING GEORGE III

to the family estate on the Isle of Bute, whose remarkably temperate climate produces a lush foliage, even palm trees. There he indulged a passion for botany that can be experienced to this day in the verdant grounds at Mount Rothesay. In 1745, Bute suddenly left Rothesay and took up residence in London. The year 1745 is distinguished by the so-called Jacobite Rebellion, another wondrous Sun-tzuan ruse in which apparent defeat for the Society of Jesus masked a hidden victory.

The Jacobite Rebellion aimed to restore Roman Catholic rule over England by deposing George II and placing James II's grandson Charles Stuart, better known as Bonnie Prince Charlie, on the throne. However, when Charlie marched on London with a band of Scottish devotees, no Catholic politician of any prominence would desert George II. The Rebellion was forced to abort. Charlie escaped to France and the and the Scots were massacred. Clearly, this was a Catholic disaster. Or was it? Such extensive Catholic support for a Protestant king assured England that the monarchy would be forever Protestant. A Catholic England was now an impossible dream. The Jesuits could give up. Englishmen could now relax with them in their midst, just as Jesuits could now go about their business without causing official alarm. The Jacobite Rebellion made England at last... *safe* for the black papacy. The Jesuits secured a new cover by blowing their cover – "blown cover as cover" in the parlance of CIA. The Sun-Tzuan General wins whatever the circumstances.

WHEN Bute joined the court of the Prince and Princess of Wales, their son George William was an emotional basket case. Bute lavished attention on the lad, won his trust and admiration, became his mentor. Indeed, Bute made himself so delightfully indispensable around Leicester House that the Prince appointed him, in 1750, to the most intimate position on his staff, Lord of the Bedchamber. Nothing happened in the life of the two heirs to the throne of England that was not privy to a man under obedience to the Unknown Superior.

But in the year following Bute's appointment, the Prince died mysteriously at the age of forty-four. Rumors that Bute was responsible circulated for a while and evaporated. However, gossip linking Bute romantically to Princess Augusta never went away, even though he was husband to a devoted wife and happy family.

George II, surprisingly desolate over the Prince's untimely death, remained an absurdly stern grandfather to George William. Until his own death in 1760, George II grew increasingly melancholic and disinterested in ruling. Parliament gained strength. Bute acted the surrogate father to the future king. Caring for the gardens at Leicester House, he inspired the boy with a lifelong interest in botany. He encouraged him to patronize the arts – the composer Handel, though blind, was still superintending performances of his works at the royal behest. However, Bute did little to allay George's tormenting fears of inadequacy. Reinforcing himself as the ideal of conduct, the Scot nourished the boy's self-distrust, which would become the most prominent feature of his maturity.

Such was the context of English power when Lorenzo Ricci tipped the stones in the Ohio valley that tumbled into a costly world war between England and France. Six years into the war, George II died at the age of seventy-seven. He left behind a disunited Parliament and a dysfunctional heir barely out of his teens. George William, now King George III, fearfully turned the British Empire over to John Stuart. Bute acted swiftly to conform to the wishes of his Unknown Superior. He began by appointing a more compliant first lord of the Treasury, the office later to be known as Prime Minister. Next, with secretly-funded grants, he purchased votes from key members of Parliament widely known as "the King's Friends." Under the noble pretext of achieving "a closer unity of the British Empire under Parliament," Bute whipped the King's Friends into passing a law to enforce writs of assistance across the Atlantic. These were revenue-raising warrants issued summarily under the royal seal requiring a law officer to take possession of lands without trial, without jury.

One does not need a doctorate in political science to know that summary expropriation is a sure way to divide an empire, not unite it. When the writs were enforced in Massachusetts, James

CHAPTER 15   THE MADNESS OF KING GEORGE III

Otis resigned his Advocate-General's post in the Court of Admiralty to preach against them "in a style of oratory," John Adams would later recall, "that I have never heard equalled in this or any other country." In July 1776, Adams would declare that the enforcement of Bute's writs of assistance in 1761 was "the commencement of this controversy between Great Britain and America."[1]

Lorenzo Ricci's War, or the Maritime War, or the French and Indian Wars, came to an end in 1763. England was the apparent victor. Bute was sent by his protege, George III, to negotiate a peace in Paris. Assisted by Robert Petty, Lord Shelburne, the notorious "Jesuit of Berkeley Square," Bute perfected the Treaty of Paris. Under its terms England won from France all of Catholic Quebec and the region east of the Mississippi, except for the island of New Orleans. This was such a great territorial windfall for the colonists that North Carolinians created Bute County in the northeastern part of the colony.[2] However, Bute restricted the windfall by ordering the infamous Royal Proclamation of 1763, which prohibited Americans from moving west of a line drawn along the crest of the Allegheny Mountains. Most colonists viewed the Proclamation as a scheme to imprison them between the Alleghenies and the Atlantic. To purchasers of western real estate prior to the Treaty, it was legalized theft. The churchgoers saw a papal advance: "With Roman Catholicism no longer actively persecuted in England, many Americans concluded that the mother country was about to return to Rome."[3]

Prior to Lorenzo Ricci's accession to the black papacy in 1758, the colonists had been blissfully loyal to the mother country. Looking back on the pre-Riccian years while testifying before the House of Commons in 1766, Benjamin Franklin recalled that "the colonists were governed by England at the expense only of a little pen, ink, and paper; they were led by a thread." Yet, with the rise of Ricci, as if in preparation for the absurdities of Bute, radical propagandists began appearing throughout the colonies - Christopher Gadsden in South Carolina, Cornelius Harnett in North Carolina, Patrick Henry and Thomas Jefferson in Virginia, and, in Pennsylvania, Charles Thomson. The dean of all these propagandists was Samuel Adams, the celebrated "Father of the American Revolution" and Freemasonry's "dominant figure in the mobilization of the Boston artisans and inland towns."[4] John Adams, in a letter dated February 9, 1819, framed his cousin Sam's political activism within *exactly* the seventeen years of Lorenzo Ricci's generalate:

> Samuel Adams, to my certain knowledge, from 1758 to 1775, that is, for seventeen years, made it his constant rule to watch the rise of every brilliant genius, to seek his acquaintance, to court his friendship, to cultivate his natural feelings in favor of his native country, to warn him against the hostile designs of Great Britain, and to fix his affections and reflections on the side of his native country.

Thus, well before the advent of much to rebel against – well before Bute's writs of assistance and the Royal Proclamation – a propaganda of American rebellion was being organized. At the same time, Dr. Franklin put together the means of disseminating it. He streamlined the colonial postal system to flow smoothly and efficiently from southern Virginia through eastern New England.

On the diplomatic front, England's future war-making capability was stunted by the Paris negotiations of Bute and Shelburne, which isolated England from any possibility of forming helpful European alliances. This, in 1763, was of negligible importance to anyone but the foreknowing and omniscient Lorenzo Ricci. When the hour came for America to revolt for independence, and no one but Ricci knew when that hour would come, England had to be friendlessly alone.

Having weakened England and stimulated the production of hostile, divisive rhetoric in America, Bute resigned from public life a very unpopular man. But the king's mentor was not yet finished. From the shadows, Bute handpicked a new Prime Minister, George Grenville. Grenville made a broad show of refusing to accept office unless the king promised never again to employ Bute in office or seek his counsel. The king promised. Pledging to give the British Empire a thorough overhauling, Grenville then proceeded (with

CHAPTER 15   THE MADNESS OF KING GEORGE III

Bute's secret counsel and more money grants from the King's Friends) to create dynamic situations that accelerated Britain and the colonies toward divorce.

Duties were increased on colonial imports, justified by the notion that the colonies should contribute their fair share to the increased expenses of running an Empire much expanded by the Treaty of Paris. Higher duties heightened smuggling activities, which in turn increased the admiralty caseload. Americans began sniffing tyranny in the breeze.

Grenville's new Sugar and Molasses Act enforced ruinous duties on foreign staples necessary for rum-making. The Act reduced imports of sugar and molasses from the French, Spanish, and Dutch West Indies, which in turn greatly reduced the meat, fish, flour, horses and lumber which the colonies could export to the islands. This caused a slump in colonial production. Large debts which colonists owed to their British creditors for furniture, clothing, ironware, pottery, jewelry, and many other articles, went unpaid. Merchants complained that Parliament was killing the goose that laid the golden egg. Parliament's strange response was to prohibit the colonies from issuing paper currency to supply their lack of gold and silver. George Grenville did, however, invite the fuming colonists to propose suggestions for how they would like to be taxed. When the colonists refused to dignify the invitation with a response, Parliament in March 1765 passed, without debate or opposition, an even more infuriating measure.

The Stamp Act required the purchasing and fixing of stamps to all colonial deeds, leases, bills of sale, pamphlets, newspapers, advertisements, mortgages, wills, and contracts. If duties on sugar and molasses could be considered part of the regulation of the Empire's trade, the Stamp Act was a tax levied by a body thousands of miles away for the sole purpose of raising a revenue. It affected all classes of colonist. Never before had Parliament dared to impose such a tax. Whereas the duty on foreign molasses or anti-smuggling measures were felt only by the great merchants in New York, Boston, Philadelphia, or Charleston, the Stamp Act affected a wider public. It added the price of a stamp to the lawyer's bill of every colonist selling a horse, making a will, or mortgaging a house. The price of every newspaper was increased by the stated value of the stamp attached to it.

In Massachusetts, "Britannus Americanus," one of Sam Adams' more than twenty pseudonyms, charged that it was as absurd for Parliament to tax the American people as it would be for an assembly of Americans to tax the people of England. In Virginia, Patrick Henry cried his slogan *"NO TAXATION WITHOUT REPRESENTATION!"* From the London Coffee House in Philadelphia, Charles Thomson led a secret club of workers, teachers, merchants and professionals in advocating the production and sales of local goods strengthened by an intercolonial agreement not to import goods from Britain.

A month before the first stamps arrived, Sam Adams agitated Massachusetts to hold a "Stamp Act Congress," which convened at New York in October. The Congress drew up a Declaration of Rights and Grievances protesting that the Act threatened "the liberties of the colonies." By the time the stamps arrived from England in November, the colonists had forced most of the stamp-distributors to resign. The merchants of Boston, New York, and Philadelphia agreed not to import English goods, causing a decline in trade with Great Britain of about twenty-five percent within a year. In an address before the House of Commons, Benjamin Franklin issued his famous warning that if troops should be sent to the colonies to enforce the Act, they "will not find a revolution there but might very well *create one.*"

Grenville's ministry suddenly fell to William Pitt and Lord Rockingham, who repealed the Stamp Act in March. The colonies rejoiced and pledged loyalty to George III. They hardly noticed that the King's Friends had accompanied the repeal with a Declaratory Act claiming "full power and authority to bind the colonies and people of America, subjects of the Crown of Great Britain, in all cases whatsoever."

Regarding Patrick Henry's objections to unfair taxation as "so much nonsense," Charles Townshend, Chancellor of the Exchequer, vowed to get "plenty of revenue from the colonies." In the

CHAPTER 15   THE MADNESS OF KING GEORGE III

summer of 1767, he and the King's Friends passed acts laying duties on glass, painters' colors, red and white lead, paper, and tea shipped to America. But the acts produced little revenue. By Townshend's own estimate, made shortly before his premature death at forty-two, the British Treasury stood to gain no more than £40,000. The real, covert, purpose of the Acts appears to have been not to get "plenty of revenue," but to stimulate the rebellious investment of colonial capital in local manufacturing.

In March of 1770, a small crowd of jeering Bostonians pelted a few British redcoats with snowballs. The angry redcoats fired into the crowd, killing four men, wounding several more. The town and surrounding countryside reacted in rage to the Boston Massacre. Samuel Adams led his disciples to the mansion of acting Governor Thomas Hutchinson and demanded the immediate deportation of the redcoats, who wisely retreated to Castle William on the harbor. When news of the Massacre reached England, the King's Friends scolded Hutchinson's "cowardly surrender to Sam Adams's regiments." Thenceforth, each anniversary of the Boston Massacre became an occasion for Adams and others to make more blistering orations against British tyranny in favor of independence.

In 1770, Lord North, the new Prime Minister, declared the Townshend Acts were costing more to collect than the revenue was returning to the Treasury. North secured the repeal of all the Townshend duties, except a tax on tea of threepence a pound to prove Parliament had authority to tax the colonies. The colonists weren't affected by this miniscule tax, since most of their tea was smuggled in from Holland anyway. Feelings toward England turned amicable once again, as colonial merchants increased orders from British firms from £1,336,122 in 1769 to £4,200,000. Sam Adams, Patrick Henry, Charles Thomson and Thomas Jefferson took advantage of the lull to agitate. Observing the first anniversary of the Boston Massacre on March 5, 1771, Adams called for action and solidarity:

> It is high time for the people of this country explicitly to declare whether they will be Freemen or Slaves. Let it be the

topic of conversation in every social Club. Let every Town assemble. Let Associations & Combinations be everywhere set up to consult and recover our just Rights.⁵

Between 1770 and 1773, about the only troublesome confrontations were those between British revenue vessels and smugglers. The colonies began producing more. Trade was so brisk that merchants, formerly the chief opponents of British rule, had little to protest. They turned their full attention back to business.

And then Lorenzo Ricci nudged his weightiest boulders to date, the Religious Right, the Protestant churchgoers. How he did this is the subject of our next chapter.

JOHN CARROLL, BISHOP OF BALTIMORE
AND FOUNDER OF GEORGETOWN UNIVERSITY.
(From the portrait by Gilbert Stuart)

Chapter 16

TWEAKING THE RELIGIOUS RIGHT

AS THE FUROR over the Stamp Act was cooling down, the Jesuits of Maryland and Pennsylvania discovered that the director of Catholic operations in the British colonies, Bishop Richard Challoner, had asked Rome to ordain an American bishop.

The American Jesuits disliked the idea. Father Ferdinand Steinmayer (alias Farmer) of New York cautioned Bishop Challoner, "It is incredible how hateful to non-Catholics in all parts of America is the very name of bishop." Still, in Challoner's view, an American bishop would establish better order in the colonies, restore discipline, and make it possible for colonial Catholics to be confirmed. Steinmayer and his American brethren strenuously opposed the idea on grounds that it would only make life among Protestants more difficult for Catholics. They collected lay support for their views and asked Challoner himself to forward the protests to Rome, which he declined to do, leaving it to the Jesuits to state their own case.[1]

Rome never replied to Challoner's petition for an American bishop. The bishop later discovered that the petition, made in a letter to Cardinal Spinelli and entered into the post in 1764, *never left England.* In Bishop Challoner's words, "it was opened, and stopt on this side of the water."[2]

Whoever opened Challoner's letter must have passed its contents on to the Church of England. For no sooner had Challoner posted his letter than the *Anglican* Bishop of London, who had thus far been content to rule his American subjects from London, asked the British cabinet to permit the *Church of England* to create an American bishop to "attend the sheperdless flock in the colonies." When word of this request reached the colonies, which were mostly Protestant but less than fifteen percent Anglican,[3] the reaction must have elated Lorenzo Ricci. The sons and daughters of immigrants who had braved wild Indians and rattlesnakes to escape religious prelates took the Bishop's petition to be the worst act of tyranny yet, the most pressing cause for alarm, the number one thing to revolt against.

The American bishop scare was whipped up in the non-Anglican Protestant church pulpit – the era's most electrifying communications medium. Presbyterian and Congregationalist preachers, representing nearly fifty percent of the churched colonists, charged that an American bishop would be "an ecclesiastical Stamp Act" which would strip Americans of all their liberties, civil as well as religious, and "if submitted to will at length grind us to powder."[4] They warned that an American bishop would dominate the colonial governors and councils, strengthen the position of the colonial oligarchy, and drive dissenters from political life with a Test Act requiring officials to state their religious preference. Having brought the colonial governments under his control, the American bishop would then establish the Church of Rome in all the colonies and impose taxes for the support of its hierarchy. A letter in the *New York Gazette or Weekly Post Boy* for March 14, 1768 charged that an American bishop would "introduce a system of episcopal palaces, of pontifical revenues, of spiritual courts and all the pomp, grandeur, luxury, and regalia of an American Lambeth" – Lambeth Palace being the residence of the Archbishop of

CHAPTER 16   TWEAKING THE RELIGIOUS RIGHT

Canterbury, head of all England after the royal family. An American bishop would transform Americans into a people "compelled to fall upon their knees in the streets and adore the papal miter as the Apostolic Tyrant rides by in his gilded equipage."

Rev. Jonathan Mayhew, Dudleian Lecturer at Harvard, inveighed against "Popish Idolatry" in a famous (and arguably prophetic) sermon by that title, saying,

> Let the bishops get their foot in the stirrup, and their beast, the laity, will prance and flounce about to no purpose. Bishops will prove to be the Trojan horse by which Popery will subjugate North America.

The American bishop scare did more to foment the colonists to revolt, and eventually raised more soldiery, than all the tyrannical writs and tax schemes combined. Immediately, it created permanent Committees of Correspondence, an intercolonial organization of churches, and a "Society of Dissenters" based in New York. These organizations brought all opposed to the Church of England into correspondence with one another, whether in America, Great Britain, or Ireland.[5] The specter of an American bishop gave the colonial patriots an almost inexhaustible fund of propaganda to employ against any form of perceived tyranny at home and abroad. It served, in Jonathan Boucher's words, "to keep the public mind in a state of ferment and effervescence; to make the people jealous and suspicious of all measures not brought forward by [popularly-approved leaders]; and above all, to train and habituate the people to opposition."[6]

The fact that Americans were trained and habituated to oppose the British Crown and the Church of England not by Roman Catholics but by Protestant churchmen is, to my mind, proof of the Sun-Tzuan ingenuity of Lorenzo Ricci. Sun-Tzu said: "The General will know how to shape at will, not only the army he is commanding but also that of his enemies." While Ricci's own army was appearing in the world's opinion markets to be a band of vicious dolts slipping down into their well-deserved oblivion, a small elite corps of indispensibles, some neither knowing nor caring who their true boss was, were facilitating English-speaking Protestant churchgoers in systematically annihilating one another! Lorenzo Ricci's orchestration had reached such fullness that he could now soliloquize Iago's boast in *Othello:* "Now, whether he kill Cassio or Cassio him, or each do kill the other, every way makes my gain."

Back in the nineteen-sixties and seventies, Central American Jesuits designed posters to motivate campesinos to overthrow corrupt politicians. The posters for this Bellarminian liberation theology depicted an angry Jesus Christ in the image of Che Guevara, swathed in fatigues, draped in bullet-belts, holding a submachine gun at the ready, a Rambo Jesus, a Jesus whose Sacred Heart called for social action that included killing. The American bishop scare aroused the same dynamic in the 1770's. What was considered by many to be the most influential sermon on the subject was preached to Boston's Ancient and Honorable Artillery Company by Rev. Jonathan Mayhew's successor at Harvard, Rev. Simeon Howard. Simeon Howard received his early preaching experience in Nova Scotia – or Acadia, as the French settlers called it. He experienced first-hand the uprooting and expulsion, by British soldiers, of some three thousand French Catholic Acadians, along with their Jesuit priests. Cruelly, often violently, the Acadians were forced to emigrate to various American colonies, with no compensation for property or livestock. (Longfellow memorialized the event in *Evangeline).*

With a casuistry that would have delighted Cardinal Bellarmine, Rev. Howard's famous Artillery Company sermon openly advocated the use of violence against a political tyrant. Our duty to defend personal liberty and property, he argued, is stated in Scripture at Galatians 5:1 – "Stand fast therefore in the liberty wherewith Christ hath made us free." True, Rev. Howard admitted, Christ requires us to "resist not evil – love your enemies, do good to them that hate you" (Matthew 5), and "recompense to no man evil for evil – avenge not yourselves" (Romans 12, 17, 19). But these precepts apply only to cases of "small injuries," Howard said, not large ones, such as tyranny.

CHAPTER 16   TWEAKING THE RELIGIOUS RIGHT

Nor, said Rev. Howard, should we fully accept Christ's commandments on property. "Love not the world, nor the things that are in the world" (John 2:5), and "Lay not up for yourselves treasure on earth" (Matthew 6:19), and "Give to him that asketh thee, and from him that would borrow of thee, turn not thou away" (Matthew 5:42) – such precepts as these, Rev. Howard said, are "indefinite expressions" which "we have a right to limit."

Now, the defensive application of lethal force is reasonable, and noble, and patriotic. But it is not recommended by Jesus Christ. The Jesus of the Scriptures cautions that life by the sword means death by the sword. It is Rome, not Jesus, that commands the use of lethal force – Rome, whose natural-law society was built on the willingness of the individual to risk his own life in killing to preserve the Religious State. And it was Rome that Simeon Howard beseeched his audience to emulate: "Rome, who rose to be mistress of the world by an army composed of men of property and worth."

A decade after the American bishop scare had broken out, thousands of American Protestant and Catholic churchgoers began killing and being killed to win The War That Would Keep Anglican Bishops Out of America. And they won this war. But the utterly stupefying outcome of their victory was that no bishops were kept *out* of America: two bishops were brought *into* America, an Anglican and a Roman Catholic!

The Roman Catholic, of course, was John Carroll. This Jesuit son of Maryland was consecrated Bishop of Baltimore on August 15, 1790, in the chapel of Lulworth, a castle set high on the Dorset coast of England owned by the Welds, a prominent Roman Catholic family. Lulworth's upper "Red Room" looks to the east upon a commanding view of the estate's long entrance meadow and to the south upon a famous smugglers' cove in the distance. A frequent visitor to Lulworth Castle, and honored guest in its Red Room, I am told, was King George III.

Bishop Carroll became the Holy See's direct representative not just in Baltimore but throughout the U.S. This fact was validated in 1798 by Judge Addison, President of the Court of Common

Pleas of the Fifth Circuit of Pennsylvania in the case of Fromm vs. Carroll. Fromm was a recalcitrant German Franciscan who wanted to establish his own German-speaking, laity-owned parish. Addison ruled that "the Bishop of Baltimore has sole episcopal authority over the Catholic Church of the United States, and without authority from him no Catholic priest can exercise any pastoral function over any congregation within the United States." Fromm was excommunicated and held up as an example of what happens to rebels against wholesome Church authority. Addison's use of the term "Catholic Church of the United States" is an interesting judicial notice that Carroll's ordination instituted, for all practical purposes, a secular church ruled by the black papacy. Eminent Catholic historian Thomas O'Gorman concurred in 1895, observing that American Catholicism was, "in its inception, wholly a Jesuit affair and [has] largely remained so."[7]

America's first Anglican bishop, ordained in 1784, was Rev. Samuel Seabury of Connecticut. Rev. Seabury was both a High Churchman and a Freemason.[8] To avoid the political repercussions of swearing allegiance to the Church of England so soon after 1776, Seabury was consecrated in November 1784 at Aberdeen, Scotland. Of critical importance to Rome was that the three bishops consecrating Seabury were all "nonjuring" bishops. "Nonjuring" described the class of Catholic bishops that stood in the succession of "Jacobite" clergy who, remaining loyal to King James II after his abdication in 1689, had refused to take a loyalty oath to James' successors – his daughter, Mary Stuart, and son-in-law, William of Orange, both Protestants.[9] America's first Protestant bishop, like his Roman Catholic counterpart, owed allegiance to Rome.

This obscure fact is commemorated in one of London's most heavily-trafficked and world-famous locations. The spacious grassy lawns on either side of the great stairway leading up to the National Portrait Gallery facing Trafalgar Square are identical except for their bronze statuary, one piece alone placed at the center of each lawn. On the north lawn stands James II, crowned with imperial laurel, wearing the armor of Julius Caesar. (An elderly British Je-

CHAPTER 16 TWEAKING THE RELIGIOUS RIGHT

suit with a passion for offbeat historical detail confided to me that James loved to go in Caesarean drag.) On the south lawn stands the celebrated Houdon figure of... *George Washington,* garbed in period attire, leaning for support upon a huge bundle of rods from which projects the head of an axe – the *fasces,* ancient emblem of Roman legal authority! When Bishop Seabury united his episcopate with the other two Anglican communions in America in 1789, the Protestant Episcopal Church in the United States was born. George Washington was a member of this Church. The London statuary are explaining the little-known historical fact that James II's Roman Catholic rulership of the English-speaking people was resumed in the First President of the Constitutional United States of America. It is a tribute to the phenomenal generalate of Lorenzo Ricci.

John Carroll spent his final years in Europe helping to develop Lorenzo Ricci's vision of rebellion in America. He moved cautiously, and often incognito. What few traces he left behind are quite revealing.

ARCHBISHOP NIKOLAUS VON HONTHEIM (JUSTINIUS FEBRONIUS)
(From a painting in Trier)

Chapter 17

A TIMELY GRAND TOUR

AMONG THE MANY British visitors to Rome during Clement XIV's sweetening toward England in the early 1770's was a young member of an ancient ruling family of Dorset and Somerset counties named Charles Philippe Stourton.[1] Charles Philippe was nephew to the Dukes of Norfolk. We remember the Norfolks, Thomas and Edward Howard, for their significant contributions to American independence – Thomas, originator of colonial Freemasonry; Edward, coupler of Lord Bute to the future George III.

Arriving in Rome with Charles Philippe was his professor at the Jesuit college in the medieval Flemish (now Belgian) city of Bruges, John Carroll. The pair were enjoying a Grand Tour of Europe which had begun in the summer of 1771.

From Bruges they had proceeded by carriage down through Alsace-Lorraine to Strasbourg, across the Rhine to Baden-Baden, then upstream to Carlsruhe, Bruschal, Heidelberg, Mannheim,

Worms, and Mainz. From Mainz they made a curious detour over to Trier, back to Mannheim, through Swabia to Augsburg, then to Munich, Innsbruch, across the Italian border to Trent, along the Adige River to Roveredo, Verona, Mantua, Modena, and Bologna. They reached Rome in the autumn of 1772.

In Rome, Lorenzo Ricci appointed Carroll to the position of Prefect of the Sodality. This title designates, according to the New Catholic Encyclopedia, "a chief organizer of laymen for the promotion of some form of social action." For the promotion of what social action, I wonder, might Ricci have ordained Carroll to organize, if not the American Revolution?

While John was in Rome with Lorenzo Ricci, his cousin Charles Carroll, now in his mid-thirties, pulled off a clever media ruse in Maryland. It won him tremendous popularity and established him as an important civic leader. In January 1773, a letter in the Maryland *Gazette* attacked the administration of Maryland Governor Robert Edens. The letter was signed "First Citizen." In a subsequent *Gazette,* the attack was demolished by the eloquent arguments of a "Second Citizen." But in February, "First Citizen" demolished "Second Citizen." As the duel continued on into the summer, "First Citizen" was revealed to be Charles Carroll. Whereupon "Second Citizen" nastily *slandered* Carroll, putting him down as a "disfranchised Catholic." Suddenly now, Carroll was an underdog – just like his fellow Americans in relation to the British Crown. Although Charles was a super-rich lawyer-landowner educated at the best Jesuit colleges in Europe, the people lavished him with sympathy. They despised "Second Citizen" for his bigotry. Maryland and America now had a new hero, a preeminent champion of religious liberties, a Roman Catholic First Citizen advocating a new political order. Loathsome Second Citizen made the status quo seem distasteful and undesirable – which, of course, was his assignment in the ruse. Second Citizen turned out to be the acknowledged head of the American bar, a Mr. Dulany....

CHAPTER 17   A TIMELY GRAND TOUR

MEANWHILE, with the coming of spring, Carroll and Stourton left Rome for Florence, Genoa, Lyons, Paris, Liège, arriving back in Bruges just a few weeks before Ganganelli, Clement XIV, disestablished the Jesuits. Carroll kept a journal of their tour.[2] Partly a study-guide for Charles Philippe, partly a travelog, it's a "fragmentary and circumspect" document, as one historian gingerly put it. Here and there, one finds snatches of informal political opinion. Although Carroll's opinions are interesting, it's his circumspection that intrigues us most, it's what his journal *doesn't* say. Traveling with a student appears ordinary enough, but Charles Philippe Stourton was no ordinary collegian. He was a student of casuistry, equivocation, and Bellarminian liberation theology taught by professionals sworn to expand Roman Catholicism and extirpate Protestantism. He had been indoctrinated to obedience through the Spiritual Exercises, was a member of England's premier Catholic and Masonic family, and was about the age of Alexander Hamilton (who by then was already turning out anonymous revolutionary pamphlets at King's College in New York). Nor were Carroll and Stourton merely sight-seeing. They were up to something big. Carroll's journal alludes to meetings with high-ranking officials in church and state, but gives no specific names. Writing to an English Jesuit colleague, he confided "I keep a close incognito during this time."[3]

Despite Carroll's circumspection, his itinerary reveals certain clues. Consider that odd detour to Trier from the route between Mainz and Mannheim. Trier is more than two hundred kilometers out of the way, quite a long day's journey. What might warrant such a deviation? There appeared in 1763 a highly controversial book by an obviously pseudonymous person, "Justinius Febronius." The pseudonym belonged to Bishop Nikolaus von Hontheim, Chancellor of the University of Trier. In John Carroll's day, Trier University had been run by Jesuits for more than a century. The book, of which there is apparently no published English translation out of its original Latin, is entitled *On the State of the Church and the Legitimate Power of the Roman Pontiff.*

The gist of State *of the Church* suggests why Carroll had to visit

Trier: "Febronianism," the philosophy of von Hontheim's book, contains the formula for administering Protestant America as a Bellarminian commonwealth! Febronianism calls for decentralizing the Roman Catholic Church into independent *national* churches modeled on the Church of England. Because they are ruled directly by kings and princes, these churches are more correctly called "States." The Pope may be successor to Peter, Prince of the Apostles, but under Febronianism he has no legal jurisdiction. He is merely a principle of unity, a spiritual unifier obligated to abide by the decrees of general councils under the leadership of bishops and their properly enlightened laymen.

Crucial to Febronianism's application is "thorough popular education." Once laymen, bishops, and councils are "properly enlightened" they will be empowered to resist any attempts of the papacy to exert monarchial control over the Church. Febronius emphasized that his system would succeed only in a milieu of popular enlightenment. His context presumes an enlightenment

CHAPTER 17 A TIMELY GRAND TOUR

wherein the public is indoctrinated with the Jesuit *ratio studiorum's* full humanist diet, of course. It cannot operate where Scripture reigns supreme. Once the milieu's understanding, its *mentality*, has been shaped by the Superior General of the Society of Jesus, it will respond with unquestioning obedience to the will of the man whose fundamental duty is the expansion of Roman Catholicism and the extirpation of Protestantism. Thus will unfold a perfect secular political state within the Roman Catholic Church, an autocracy ruled by a monarch invisible to all but the few who, by the grace of God, cannot be deceived.⁴

Febronianism was the secret formula for returning the non-Catholic world to the bosom of the Church. To mask this fact, the Vatican dramatically condemned the book. The jesuited Clement XIII had banned it from colleges and universities. In a rather quaint example of academic "blown cover as cover," Bishop von Hontheim, whom few realized was Febronius, even banned it from his own classes at the University!

On the State of the Church is arguably Lorenzo Ricci's "American Manifesto," the social blueprint for how the General intended to realize Bellarminian liberation in a Protestant monarchy. The full title page of the first edition copy of the book says it all:

> *On the State of the Church and the Legitimate Power of the Roman Pontiff: A Singular Book On the Properly-Ordered Reunification with Dissidents in the Christian Religion.*

Here one beholds a description of the momentous social change that the American Revolution would indeed produce – neither monarchial overthrow, nor democracy, nor republicanism, but a "properly-ordered reunification with dissidents in the Christian religion," that is, the reunification of Roman Catholics with Protestants under a secularized religion whose values – long on humanism, short on Scripture – are taught through public schools following the Jesuit *ratio studiorum*. "Reunification" means that Protestantism has been *reabsorbed* into Rome. This, in the eyes of the black papacy, to the Sun-Tzuan mind, and to common sense, equals the practical extirpation of Protestantism.

ALTHOUGH Bishop von Hontheim lived in Trier, he was Archbishop of Mainz. His jurisdiction extended to the Mainz principality of Hesse-Hanover. Von Hontheim was thus the spiritual counterpart of the ruler of Hesse-Hanover, Frederick II (not to be confused with the King of Prussia, Frederick the Great, who was also a Frederick II.) Frederick II of Hesse was married to the aunt of the King of England, which made him George III's uncle. Born a Protestant, Frederick subscribed to the Rosicrucian style of Freemasonry. Although Jesuits converted him to Roman Catholicism, he nevertheless remained a Rosicrucian secretly active.

Frederick of Hesse was one of Europe's richest rulers. Much of his business was handled by his son, Prince William, also a Rosicrucian Freemason. William's specialty was facilitating war. He drafted able-bodied male Hessians, outfitted and trained them for battle, and then sold them to his English cousin George, who used them to fight alongside his own redcoats. Every time a Hessian was killed, William received a reparation in the form of extra compensation. As casualties mounted, so did his profits, which he loaned out at interest.

In September 1769, Prince William appointed Meyer Amschel Rothschild of nearby Frankfurt to transact some of his financial affairs in the capacity of Crown Agent. Aware that the Rothschilds are an important Jewish family, I looked them up in *Encyclopedia Judaica* and discovered that they bear the title "Guardians of the Vatican Treasury." The Vatican Treasury, of course, holds the imperial wealth of Rome. Imperial wealth grows in proportion to its victories in war – as the Jesuit empowerment *Regimini militantis ecclesiae* implies, the Church-at-War is more necessary than the Church-at-Peace. According to H. Russell Robinson's illustrated *Armour of Imperial Rome*, Caesarean soldiers protected themselves in battle with shields painted red. Since the soldiery is the State's most valuable resource (the Council of Trent admitted this in preferring the Jesuits to all other religious orders), it is easy to understand why the red shield was identified with the very life of the Church. Hence, the appropriateness of the name *Rothschild*, German for "red shield." The appointment of Rothschild gave the

CHAPTER 17 A TIMELY GRAND TOUR

black papacy absolute financial privacy and secrecy. Who would ever search a family of orthodox Jews for the key to the wealth of the Roman Catholic Church? I believe this appointment explains why the House of Rothschild is famous for helping nations go to war. It is fascinating that, as Meyer Rothschild's sons grew into the family business, the firm took on the title *Meyer Amschel Rothschild und Söhne,* which gives us the notariqon MARS. Isn't Mars the Roman God of War, whose heavenly manifestation is "the red planet"? There is powerful cabalah here, and there's hardly an acre of inhabitable earth that hasn't been affected by it in some way.

It may never be known if John Carroll and Charles Philippe Stourton paid a call on the offices of Meyer Rothschild during their Grand Tour. Carroll was not permitted to keep a record, and the Rothschild name is synonymous with secrecy. But a call, keeping a "close incognito," at the House of Rothschild would not be inconsistent with outcome. The newly-designed Prefect of the Sodality, chief organizer of laymen for social action, would have a legitimate need to talk finances with the Church's most secret trustee. As things were developing, General Ricci needed an American financial crisis to provoke the colonists into resolving the utter necessity of war.

Carroll's journal reflects that he and Stourton did enter the Frankfurt-Mainz area, which is Rothschild country, in early spring 1772. If we suppose they talked financial crisis with the Rothschilds, the outcome of their talks actually did occur several months later. During July, in fact, the British banking system underwent a severe credit reduction. This consequently threw American merchants into an extreme financial distress that did not end until the Revolutionary War itself produced a business boom in 1776. Rothschild, with his access to Hesse-Hanover's vast wealth, and conceivably that of the Jesuits as well, had power to affect a credit reduction in British banking. And Rothschild's profiting from the Revolutionary War is well known. If, during the spring of 1772, the circumspect young Jesuit professor conveyed to the powerful young Jewish banker Lorenzo Ricci's need for a financial disturbance in England and America, didn't John Carroll admirably serve his Superior General, his Church, and his country? And didn't Rothschild do his client likewise?

Even as Carroll and Stourton were networking (according to my surmise) with Ricci and the bankers of war, Amiot's Sun-Tzu was published. Carroll's circumspection bars us ever from knowing whether he and Stourton came upon a copy and read it. Did Rothschild know the book? Even if they knew it well, the experience could not possibly have been for them the adventure in irony it is for us now. We open *The Thirteen Articles* and hear the gentle voice of the man in charge of the papacy's most important business, the man who decided everything, who was in the process of gaining advantage from dangerous and critical circumstances, whose intentions were unguessable, whose decisions were shaping both his own army and the armies of his English-speaking Protestant enemies, the man who through cleverness and ruse had already secured the obedience of his enemies in London and Boston and Paris and Philadelphia although they believed him and his army to be far away and slumped in rest from sustained losses, the man who would win the most important War in modern times without giving battle or drawing a sword, who uniquely knew the day, the hour, the moment of battle-less, sword-less combat. Lorenzo Ricci's voice whispers to us across the centuries between the lines in passages such as these:[5]

> A State's most important business is its army. It is the General who decides everything. If he is clever, he will gain an advantage from even the most dangerous & critical circumstances. He will know how to shape at will, not only the army he is commanding but also that of his enemies.
>
> Try to be victorious without giving battle. Without giving battle, without spilling a drop of blood, without even drawing a sword, the clever General succeeds in capturing cities. Without setting foot in a foreign Kingdom, he finds the means to conquer them. He acts in such a way that those who are inferior to him can never guess his intentions. He has them change location, even taking them to rather difficult places where they must work & suffer.
>
> Do not disdain the use of artifice. Begin by learning every-

CHAPTER 17   A TIMELY GRAND TOUR

thing there is to know about your enemies. Know exactly what relationships they have, their reciprocal liaisons & interests. Do not spare large amounts of money. Have spies everywhere, be informed of everything.

Overlook nothing to corrupt what is best on the enemy's side: offers, presents, caresses, let nothing be omitted. Maintain secret liaisons with those amongst the enemy who are the most depraved. Use them for your own ends, along with other depraved individuals. Cross through their government, sowing dissension amongst their Chiefs. Ceaselessly give them false alarms & bad advice. Engage the Governors of their Provinces in your interests. That is approximately what you must do, if you wish to fool them by cleverness & ruse.

When a clever General goes into action, the enemy is already defeated. When he fights, he alone must do more than his entire army, not through the strength of his arm but through his prudence, his manner of commanding, & above all his ruses. The great secret of solving all problems consists of the art of knowing how to create division when necessary.

What is far must be brought near, advantage must be drawn even from losses, and slowness must be turned into diligence. You must be near when the enemy believes you to be far, have a real advantage when the enemy believes you have sustained some losses, be occupied by useful work when he believes you are slumped in rest, and use all sorts of diligence when he only perceives you to be moving slowly. Thus, by throwing him off track, you will lull him to sleep in order to attack him when he expects it the least & without him having the time to prepare for it.

As it is essential for you to be completely familiar with the place where you must fight, it is no less important for you to know the day, the hour, even the moment of combat. That is a calculation which you must not neglect.

You, therefore, who are at the head of an army must overlook nothing to render yourself worthy of the position you hold. Throw your gaze upon the measurements of quantities & the measurements of dimensions. Remember the rules of calculus. Consider the effects of balance. Examine what victory really is. Think about all of this deeply & you will have everything you need in order to never be defeated by your enemies.

They who possess the true art of governing troops well are

those who have known & who know how to make their power formidable, who have acquired unlimited authority, who are not brought low by any event no matter how vexing, who do nothing with precipitation, who conduct themselves as calmly when they are surprised as they do when their actions have been planned long in advance, and who always act in everything they do with that promptness which is in fact the fruit of cleverness combined with great experience.

The strength of this sort of warrior is like that of those great bows which can only be stretched with the help of some machine. Their authority has the effect of those terrible weapons which are shot from bows which are thus stretched. Everything succumbs to their blows, everything is laid low....

If you do exactly as I have indicated, success will accompany all your steps. Everywhere you will be a conqueror, you will spare the lives of your soldiers, you will affirm your country in its former possessions and procure new ones, you will augment the splendor & glory of the State, and the Prince as well as his subjects will be indebted to you for the sweet tranquility in which they will henceforth live their lives. What objects can be more worthy of your attention & all your efforts?

CHARLES Philippe Stourton and John Carroll departed Rome for Flanders in March 1773. The journey took them four months. They passed through Florence, Genoa, Lyons, and Paris, arriving at Liège in early July. John returned Charles Philippe to his father, Lord Stourton, and proceeded alone to the Jesuit College at Bruges.

Meanwhile, in London, during the month of April, the British East India Company presented the King's Friends a scheme which, if measured by the way it would anger American merchants and point them inexorably toward rebellion, could only have sprung from the Sun-Tzuan intellect of Lorenzo Ricci – "*I demand the art of making enemies move as one wishes.*" That scheme, a plan to glut New England with cheap tea, is the subject of our next chapter.

KING GEORGE III

Chapter 18

THE STIMULATING EFFECTS OF TEA

THE EAST INDIA COMPANY was a major subsidizer of the Jesuit mission to Beijing. The Jesuits, in turn, interceded with oriental monarchs to secure lucrative commercial favors for the Company, including monopolies on tea, spices, saltpeter (for explosives), silks, and the world's opium trade. Indeed, according to Reid's *Commerce and Conquest: The Story of the Honourable East India Company,* the Company appears to owe its very existence to the Society of Jesus. How this came to be is worth a digression.

Briefly, in 1583, four young commercial travelers – Fitch, Newbery, Leeds, and Storey – set out from London with letters of introduction from Queen Elizabeth to the Emperor of China. Somewhere east of the Persian Gulf, they were arrested by the Portuguese for illegally crossing the "line of demarcation." Pope Alessandro VI (whose mistress, we recall, was Giulia Farnese, Paul III's beautiful sister) had drawn the line in 1493 from the North

Pole through the Azores to the South Pole. All lands west of the line he granted to Spain and those east to Portugal.

The four violators were sent in chains to the Portuguese colony of Goa on the western coast of India. In Goa, they were rescued by a fellow countryman, Thomas Stevens. Stevens had influence. He was Rector of the University of Goa, and he was a Jesuit priest. Father Stevens arranged their release, but apparently not without certain conditions. Storey joined the Society of Jesus. Newbery and Leedes accepted posts in the Goan colonial government. Ralph Fitch proceeded on to China, evidently under an Ignatian oath, otherwise the Portuguese Viceroy would not have permitted him to carry on.

In 1591, Fitch returned to England and, like Marco Polo before him, tantalized adventurers with the lucrative possibilities of transporting to the western hemisphere all the oriental splendors he'd seen. Eight years later, on September 24, 1599, with a subscription of a little more than £30, Fitch and several others formed the East India Company.

And now, in 1773, the East India Company was governed by Freemasons, whose Grand Master since 1772 was the ninth Lord Petre (his mastery would continue until 1777). Related to the Stourtons, Norfolks, and Arundells, the Petre family (pronounced "Peter") was highly esteemed by the Society of Jesus. It was the Petres who, back in the sixteenth century, bankrolled the original Jesuit missions to England.

The East India Company's most powerful political attaché was Robert Petty, Lord Shelburne. We recall Shelburne as "The Jesuit of Berkeley Square" who worked in 1763 with Lord Bute to conclude the French and Indian Wars with the Treaty of Paris, which isolated England from European alliances and angered the Americans over the western lands. Acting on East India Company's behalf, Shelburne colluded with the King's Friends on a scheme designed to disturb the relative peace which had existed between American merchants and England since the repeal of the Townshend Acts in 1770. It went like this.

Stored in the Company's dockside British warehouses were

CHAPTER 18   THE STIMULATING EFFECTS OF TEA

seventeen million pounds of surplus tea. This tea could not be released for sale until a duty of one shilling per pound was paid to the Crown. If the King would exempt the Company from paying the shilling duty, the Company would sell the tea through special consignees to Americans at prices lower than the colonists were paying for either the dutied English tea or the smuggled Dutch tea. Everyone would win. The American tea-drinkers, still suffering from the depressive effects of the British banking crisis of July 1772, would win. East India Company would win. And with a windfall duty of not one but *three* shillings a pound, the Crown would win. The only loser would be the colonial tea merchants, who had been enjoying nice profits on both dutied and smuggled tea. The King's Friends directed Parliament to put the scheme into law, and on May 10, 1773, the "Tea Act" went into effect.

Predictably, the tea merchants reacted in fury. Over the next six months, they pressed the intercolonial network of dissident propagandists to help them mount a protest. What began as an injustice against tea merchants was amplified by the propagandists into a widely-felt injustice against the colonies generally....

THEN, on July 21, 1773, Ganganelli, Clement XIV, abolished the Jesuits "for all eternity." His brief of disestablishment is entitled *Dominus ac Redemptor noster,* which is usually translated "God and Our Redeemer." We should note that *"redemptor"* also means "revenue agent." Considering that the brief's real effect in the long term was a dramatic increase in papal revenues from a new Febronian America, perhaps "God and Our Revenue Agent" would be a more appropriate translation, if not the intended one.

Although Catholic history calls the Disestablishment "a supreme tragedy," John Carroll more accurately appraised it as the "secularisation" of the Society of Jesus. Thousands of Jesuits now rose to secular prominence throughout the western world, in the arts, sciences, and government. Raimondo Ximenes became a radical Freemason. Alessandro Zorzi from Venice joined the editors of the Italian *Encyclopedia.* Dr. Boscovich arrived in Paris where his scientific reputation secured him the post of Director of Optics of the French Navy. Esteban Arteaga became a music critic and published a book in Paris entitled *The Revolution in the Italian Musical Theatre*. We've already seen how Professor Joseph-Ignace Guillotin of the Bordeaux College became the physician who gave France the beheading machine named after him. Adam Weishaupt, dismissed from the Jesuit college at Ingolstadt, attracted the fiercer elements of European Rosicrucian Freemasonry into a new secret cult in Bavaria. His "Illuminati," whose cover was eventually blown in order to convince public opinion that *evil* secret societies were being diligently unmasked when in fact they were not – was another instance of "blown cover as cover." Countless other members of the greatest clandestine intelligence agency the world has ever known, now secularized with the jeering approval of its enemies, crossed the Atlantic to help guide Americans through the pains of becoming the first nation expressly designed to be a Febronian, Bellarminian democratic republican Church-State. What an amazing production, all the more impressive for the complete invisibility of its means!

We've seen how the Brief of Disestablishment was served upon Lorenzo Ricci in mid-August, and how the General was removed to the English College a few blocks away, where he remained for five weeks, until late September. Interestingly, the Dean of the English College at that time was a thirty-two-year-old Jesuit professor of controversial theology named John Mattingly. Mattingly was an American, said to be the lone American Jesuit in Rome. He was a native of Maryland, a graduate of St. Omer's, and a dear friend of John Carroll, who (as we know) had departed Rome five months before Ricci's arrest. Within fifteen years, Carroll would invite Mattingly to become the first president of Georgetown University, an offer Mattingly would decline.

What might Lorenzo Ricci be likely to discuss for five weeks (a) under a British roof, (b) in the custody of a young American Jesuit, (c) at a time when American merchants were incensed at being cheated out of their tea profits by a new law (d) sponsored by British Freemasons, (e) whose Grand Master happened to be Ricci's secret servant?

CHAPTER 18   THE STIMULATING EFFECTS OF TEA

Might the General have been conferring with members of the British East India Company, one of the English College's major patrons? Might their discussions have involved to which American ports their tea might be most advantageously shipped, and when? Apparently so, for while Ricci was residing at the English College, Parliament authorized the East India Company to ship half a million pounds of tea to Boston, New York, Philadelphia, and Charleston, consigned to a group of specially-chosen merchants.

Might Ricci have been formulating with Carroll's friend Mattingly plans for a demonstration intended to climax the agitations that had been fomented in the colonies since the beginning of his generalate, in 1758? Might he have suggested a spectacular event to occur in, say, Boston Harbor, symbolizing the colonists' frustrations with England? And might not Parliament respond to this event with vengeful measures designed to push the colonists over the brink of rebellion? Aren't five weeks sufficient time to script such a "Boston Tea Party," along with the harsh legal measures with which it might be punished? As well as how the colonists' violent reaction to the punishment might be coordinated? Outcome suggests that Ricci did more in his five weeks at the English College than languish in custody.

We have seen how the General was taken from the English College to Castel Sant'Angelo, with its secret tunnel to the papal apartments in the Vatican. For many months after his "imprisonment," Lorenzo Ricci was "questioned by the Inquisition," according to traditional Church history. But the Inquisition had been administered by Jesuits since 1542. Not surprisingly, the inquisitors pried absolutely no useful information out of Lorenzo Ricci....

IN October of 1773, Austrian officials with drawn bayonets descended upon the Jesuit College in Bruges – the officials were Austrian because Bruges was under the jurisdiction of the Austrian government. They arrested John Carroll and the rest of the college faculty and students. Stripped of his possessions and papers, Carroll was spared further humiliation by the timely intercession of his erstwhile traveling companion Charles Philippe Stourton's cousin, Henry Howard, Lord Arundell of Wiltshire. The Catholic nobleman escorted Carroll across the English Channel to Wiltshire's lushly rolling hills. On his family estate near Tisbury, Howard had been constructing a Palladian mansion, New Wardour Castle. One of Carroll's duties was to write his version of the closing of Bruges College in order to help Henry Howard and other English sponsors of the college win damages from the Austrian government. His principal chore, however, was to administer the Chapel occupying New Wardour Castle's west wing. In this way Carroll established a connection with Henry Howard's art agent in Rome, a Jesuit named Francis Thorpe.[2] Thorpe was a renowned intelligence-broker, a man whose knowledge of Rome, its happenings and resources, was legendary. His apartment was a favorite meeting place for visiting English nobility, and his favorite English nobleman was Henry Howard.[3] Howard had put Father Thorpe in charge of "every detail, every aspect of the Chapel's design." Father Thorpe and John Carroll needed no introduction to one another. From the editor's notes to Carroll's letters, we learn that Thorpe taught at St. Omer's during the years John was a student there. Moreover, he was *Carroll's favorite instructor*.

These remarkable facts suggest interesting probabilities. From Tisbury, in less than a day, Carroll could reach Benjamin Franklin's residence in London by stagecoach. Franklin, for his scientific achievements and enlightened egalitarianism, had long been the toast of Europe, a darling of Jesuit intellectuals. He was the exclusive colonial agent now, representing the commercial interests of all thirteen colonies before the Crown. Franklin knew more about America than anyone else living in England, and more about England than any other American. Francis Thorpe knew more about England than anyone else living in Rome, and more about Rome than any other Englishman.

And both men knew John Carroll well.

And there Carroll was, for the six months during which time the Tea Act erupted into the most explosive scandal of the revolutionary epoch, poised in Tisbury to facilitate information

CHAPTER 18 THE STIMULATING EFFECTS OF TEA

between these two personal friends of his, geniuses, *institutions*. But where is the evidence that anything bearing on the American Revolution transpired between Ricci and Thorpe and Carroll and Franklin and Howard and the entire Anglo-American Masonic system? We are left with nothing but clues and outcome, which nonetheless emphatically point to a fruitful collaboration.

During the night of December 16, 1773, a gang of Indians climbed aboard certain ships in Boston Harbor, ripped open three hundred forty-two of the East India Company's tea-chests and threw overboard their contents, valued at $90,000. Well, they *looked* like Indians, and witnesses *thought* they were Indians, but the big open secret was that they were Freemasons in disguise. Perhaps the most succinct statement on the subject appears in respected Masonic historian Arthur Edward Waite's *New Encyclopedia of Freemasonry:* "The Boston Tea Party was entirely Masonic, carried out by members of the St. John's Lodge during an adjourned meeting."

Parliament reacted to the Boston Tea Party in a way calculated to increase dozens of rolling boulders into a devastating landslide. Without seriously inquiring into who was responsible, and wholly disregarding the offer of more than a hundred Boston merchants to make restitution, Parliament rushed into law a mass of unreasonably punitive legislation – closing the port of Boston to trade, forbidding town meetings without the consent of the governor, denying the Massachusetts legislature the right to choose the governor's council, providing for the quartering of British and Hessian troops in the colony, and ordering that any officer or soldier of the Crown accused of an act of violence in the performance of his duty should be sent to another colony or to England for what would surely be a sweetheart trial.

To complete the overkill, Parliament passed the Quebec Act, which cut off the claims of Massachusetts, Connecticut, Virginia, and New York to their western lands, and placed these lands, to add insult to injury, under the French Catholic jurisdiction of Quebec.

So exaggeratedly out of proportion to the offense they were framed to punish, these notorious "Intolerable Acts" caused every class of American to sympathize with the Tea Partyers. Suddenly, independence was no longer a radical alternative. The Intolerables rendered independence the subject of sensible, serious conversation as never before.

Governor Hutchinson was recalled to England and was replaced by General Thomas Gage, who brought an army of four thousand men to quarter in Boston. Gage vowed severe discipline. The colonists vowed severe resistance. "The die is cast," George III wrote to Lord North. "The colonies must either triumph or submit."

JOHN Carroll left Wardour Castle in May 1774 and sailed for Maryland to reunite with his aged and widowed mother, the former Eleanor Darnall, whom he had not seen in twenty-five years. The history of Eleanor Darnall is the history of Maryland, which bears some reflection here.

In 1625, at about the time young Charles Stuart was inheriting the throne of England from his father, King James I, the Jesuits converted a high government official to Roman Catholicism. That official was Secretary of State George Calvert, the first Lord Baltimore. For the sake of appearances – it was deemed inappropriate for a Catholic to serve a Calvinist monarch – Baltimore resigned his post. Meanwhile, behind the scenes the Jesuits perfected an audacious marriage arrangement between Charles, now King Charles I, and a Roman Catholic princess, Henriette-Marie, sister of Louis XIII of France. The marriage purported to be good for Charles' economic interests. He went out of his way to accommodate the Jesuits. Although a Scottish Calvinist, Charles conducted his monarchy in many respects as though it were Roman Catholic. He systematically weakened England's foreign policy toward Catholic France, the country of his Queen. He promoted to the highest levels in the Church of England members of the High Church Party, clergymen sympathetic with Roman Catholic ritual and traditions. And he squandered England's resources in a pointless, Jesuit-engineered war with Spain.

CHAPTER 18   THE STIMULATING EFFECTS OF TEA

Seven years into his marriage with Henriette-Marie, Charles found himself stuck between personal indebtedness to Ignatian creditors and a stingy Parliament. In hopes of generating tax revenues abroad, he carved a feudal barony out of northern Virginia and granted it to Lord Baltimore. But Baltimore died before developing the grant. The charter passed down to his son, Cecilius Calvert.

Calvert, the new Lord Baltimore, called persecuted emigrants desiring religious and tax freedom to participate in a voyage to a place bearing a name dear to Catholics "Maryland," after the Blessed Virgin. Baltimore did not neglect appealing to the irreligious niche as well. A number of his advertisements spoke of the limitless opportunities from settling in "Merrie Land."

On November 22, 1633, two ships, the *Ark* and the *Dove,* set sail from London. The passenger list included three Jesuits, sixteen to twenty Roman Catholic gentlemen, several hundred predominantly Protestant slaves and laborers, and Cecilius Calvert's brother Leonard. Leonard Calvert had been appointed Maryland's first governor. The voyage of the *Ark* and the *Dove* was spiritually directed by a Jesuit priest named Andrew White. Educated at both St. Omer's and Douai, a professor for twenty years in Portugal, Spain, and Flanders, Andrew White is remembered by the Church as "the Apostle to Maryland."

Choosing an *Andrew* for the task was good liturgical cabalah on the part of the Gesu. Andrew was the brother of the apostle Peter, the first Pope, the Rock upon whom Roman Catholicism claims to be established. Andrew is the Patron Saint of Scotland; King Charles I was a Scot. A personal representative of the king's brotherly attitude toward Rome could not be more eloquently identified than by the simple name "Andrew." Andrew White consecrated the Maryland voyage to two Catholic saints: the Virgin Mary, Protectress of the Jesuits, and Ignatius Loyola, only recently decreed Patron Saint of Maryland by Urban VIII, the second pupil of Jesuits to be elected Pope.

The ships were at sea nearly four months. Finally, one hundred twenty-three days from England, on March 25, 1634, the parties reached St. Clements Island in the mouth of the Potomac River.

It was an auspicious day. Not only was March 25 the first day of spring, but also it was the first day of the Julian calendar. (In 1752 the colonies would adopt the Gregorian calendar, which we follow today.) On March 25, Andrew White read the first Roman Mass ever held in any of the original thirteen colonies. Then he formally took possession of the land "for our Saviour and for our Sovereign Lord King of England."

Maryland historians trace the juridical origins of the Roman Catholic Church in the United States to a Patuxent Indian chieftain's wigwam, which Andrew White denoted in his diary "the first chapel of Maryland." White introduced Roman Catholicism to the Patuxents, Anacostics, and Piscataways on real estate that today comprises the District of Columbia. It's quite probable that the District of Columbia's executive mansion was termed "White House" less because of a color of exterior paint than out of reverence for the Apostle to Maryland. Every utterance of "White House" should fill the historically knowledgeable Jesuit with pride in his Society's achievements.

Conversions among the Indians ran high, but the Society enjoyed greater profits evangelizing Protestants. For every Protestant settler converted, the Jesuits won a land grant from Cecilius Calvert. Other lands Calvert retained and passed on to his descendants. Over the generations, Rock Creek Farm with its "Rome," on which the U.S. Capitol was erected, devolved to the Calvert heiress Eleanor Darnall and her husband, an Irish immigrant whose marriage and abilities had earned enough money to make him a prosperous merchant-planter. It was to this couple, and on this land, that the first American bishop was born in 1735.

Like his older brother Daniel, Jacky Carroll did his earliest schooling at Bohemia Manor, a secret Jesuit academy just down the road. Bohemia Manor had to be run secretly because of anti-Catholic laws resulting from the abdication of Catholic James II and the succession of Protestants William and Mary to the British throne in 1689. The Penal Period in Maryland, which would extend up to the American Revolution, served the black papacy well by inclining affluent Catholic families to send their sons across the

CHAPTER 18 THE STIMULATING EFFECTS OF TEA

Atlantic to take the Jesuit *ratio studiorum* at St. Omer's. Indeed, more Americans went to St. Omer's College in the eighteenth century than to Oxford and Cambridge combined.[4]

At the tender age of thirteen, Jacky sailed to Europe with his even younger cousin, Charles Carroll, for schooling at St. Omer's. Daniel returned home from there to help manage the family interests he stood to inherit. In 1753, Jacky entered the novitiate of the Jesuits at Watten in the Netherlands. Charles went on to study pre-law at Voltaire's alma mater, the Collège Louis-le-Grand in Paris. In 1758, Jacky returned to St. Omer's to teach, while Charles crossed the Channel to England, enrolling in London's premier school for barristers, the Inner Temple, founded in the fourteenth century by the Knights Templar.[5]

Jacky was ordained to the Jesuit priesthood in 1761. When he learned that St. Omer's was about to be seized by the French government in preparation for the royal edict suppressing the Jesuits in France, he with other teachers and their pupils moved to Bruges. In 1769, he renounced his Calvert inheritance, sloughed off his nickname, took the extreme Jesuit vow of papal obedience, and began teaching philosophy and theology at the English college in Liège. It was here that he befriended Charles Philippe Stourton, his Grand Tour companion.

JOHN Carroll's arrival at his mother's home in Maryland coincided with Paul Revere's ride to Philadelphia bearing letters from the Boston Committee of Correspondence seeking aid from Charles Thomson's group in protesting the closing of Boston Harbor. From his mother's estate at Rock Creek, Carroll dealt with the aftermath of the Tea Act by exercising his "secularised" priestly authority as Prefect of the Sodality. He integrated the Catholics of Maryland, Pennsylvania, and northern Virginia into the movement for independence.

Charles Thomson's Philadelphia committee sent Boston a letter of support. The committee additionally proposed a congress of deputies from the colonies to (a) consider measures to restore harmony with Great Britain and (b) prevent the dispute from advancing to "an undesirable end." Thomson then notified all the colonies south of Pennsylvania of his committee's action. He suggested the necessity of calling a general congress to consider the problem. Combined with a similar call from the Virginia House of Burgesses, his suggestion was approved throughout the colonies. Plans were laid for the First Continental Congress to meet at Philadelphia in September.

On June 1, 1774, the bill closing Boston Harbor went into effect. Thomson's radicals led Philadelphia in observing a day of mourning. Shops closed, churches held services, the people remained quietly in their homes. On June 8, Thomson and more than nine hundred freeholders petitioned Governor Richard Penn to convene the Pennsylvania Assembly so that it might consider sending delegates to an all-colony congress to explore ways of restoring harmony and peace to the British Empire. The Governor refused their request, which justified Thomson's taking action outside the established order.

Thomson called for a town meeting to be held on June 18. Nearly 8,000 Philadelphians attended. Boisterously, they resolved that the closing of Boston Harbor was tyrannical, and that a Continental Congress to secure the rights and liberties of the colonies must be convened in Philadelphia.

In July, the Pennsylvania Assembly yielded to Thomson's popular pressure and agreed to name a delegation to this First Continental Congress. Thomson, however, was not named.

Thanks to the publicity from his "First Citizen/Second Citizen" media production during the first half of 1773, Charles Carroll was named by the Annapolis Committee of Correspondence to be a delegate to the First Continental Congress. But he declined the nomination. He said that his usefulness might be restricted by anti-Catholic sentiment engendered by the Quebec Act (with which Parliament had avenged the Boston Tea Party by giving the western lands of Massachusetts, Connecticut, Virginia, and New York to Catholic Quebec). He attended the Congress, however, but as an "unofficial consultant" to the Marylanders. Charles Thomson accompanied the Pennsylvanians in the same capacity.

CHAPTER 18   THE STIMULATING EFFECTS OF TEA

To prepare for the September 5th opening session, delegates began arriving in Philadelphia in late August. They congregated at a well-known radical meeting-place, the elegant mansion of Thomas Mifflin. Mifflin had studied classics under Charles Thomson at Benjamin Franklin's Academy (later to become University of Pennsylvania). They were close friends. As Mifflin's houseguest, Thomson was on hand round the clock to greet and confer with the arriving leaders, most of whom already knew him by name. John Adams' diary entry for August 30th speaks of "much conversation" he and his fellow delegates had with the learned Thomson. He called Thomson "the Sam Adams of Philadelphia," and "the life of the cause of liberty."

Thomson and the Carrolls – Charles, Daniel, and John – spent these critical preliminary days lobbying for the inevitability of war. Thomson was already heavily invested in New Jersey's Batso Furnace. Batso would furnish cannon balls, shot, kettles, spikes and nails to the army through the War Commissioner, who controlled all the executive duties of the military department. The War Commissioner was just the man Lorenzo Ricci needed for the job: *Charles Carroll.*

Thomson was elected Secretary of the First Continental Congress, an office he held under the title "Perpetual Secretary" until the United States Constitution was ratified in 1789. He led the delegates through an itemized statement of the American theory of rebellion that culminated in the critical Declaration and Resolves of October 14, 1774.

IT was while the First Continental Congress was deliberating America's future under British tyranny that Ganganelli, Pope Clement XIV, died his agonizing death (September 22, 1774). When the papacy is vacant, says *New Catholic Encyclopedia,* the administration and guardianship of the Holy See's temporal rights – that is, its business affairs – are routinely taken over by the Treasurer of the Apostolic Chamber. The Apostolic Treasurer on the day of Ganganelli's passing was Cardinal Giovanni Braschi. A fifty-seven-year-old aristocrat of impoverished parentage, Cardinal

Braschi was a sterling product of the Jesuit colleges. The *ratio studiorum* had made of him a distinguished lawyer and diplomat. He had been Apostolic Treasurer when Rothschild began serving the Catholic principality of Hesse-Hanover in 1769. This interesting fact awakens the possibility that the Cardinal and Rothschild had been involved in Ricci's American project for years. But that is only conjecture. What is beyond conjecture, however, is that until a new pope could be elected, the whole fiscal wealth of the Roman Catholic Church belonged to Braschi and to no one else. Although lacking formal entitlement, Cardinal Braschi would rule as a kind of "virtual" *Pontifex Maximus* for one of the longest periods of papal vacancy on record.

Day after day after day, the conclave haggled over a single issue – What would the candidates do about the Jesuits? Should Ganganelli's brief of Disestablishment continue to be enforced or not?

Although Lorenzo Ricci was in detention at Castel Sant'Angelo, we know he could easily hop a tunnel carriage to the Vatican for covert meetings with the Virtual Pope. In a very real way, Braschi was a creation of Ricci's. Braschi had been made a Cardinal under the sponsorship of Ganganelli, whose own cardinalate was sponsored, as we recall, by Ricci. These two most powerful men on earth, Ricci and Braschi, had been secretly allied for years. And now the turn of events had made them invisible and inaudible. These last precious days in the final bursting-forth of Ricci's grand strategy afforded ideal conditions for Braschi and Ricci to determine face-to-face with the Rothschild emissaries, out of public sight and mind, how the Vatican's immense resources – money, men, supplies – would be deployed in the coming months and years. (In October 1774, for example, colonial agent Benjamin Franklin sent England's most enlightened copywriter, Tom Paine, to beef up the pamphleteers in Philadelphia.)

The days of papal vacancy wore on – thirty, fifty, sixty, seventy-five, a hundred days, a hundred and ten. Finally, after nearly five months of confusion, on February 15, 1775, the one hundred thirty-fourth day, it was announced that Rome had a new Pope. The

CHAPTER 18   THE STIMULATING EFFECTS OF TEA

new pope was a man acceptable to both sides of the Jesuit question. He had tacitly assured the anti-Jesuits that he would continue to enforce Disestablishment, yet the pro-Jesuits knew he would enforce it *tenderly* because of the great intellectual, political, and spiritual debts he owed the Society. The new pope was best qualified for the papacy because he'd been running the Holy See with Lorenzo Ricci for the past hundred thirty-four days – *Giovanni Braschi!* Braschi took the papal name Pius VI.

And now plummeted the great avalanche.

ON February 9, 1775 the British Parliament declared Massachusetts to be "in a state of rebellion."

On March 23, Patrick Henry delivered his famous *"GIVE ME LIBERTY OR GIVE ME DEATH"* oration.

On April 19, at a tense daybreak confrontation on Lexington Green between a group of angry colonists and some eight hundred redcoats, an unseen and unidentified shootist fired on the redcoats from behind a nearby meeting-house. This was the "shot heard 'round the world" – although Ralph Waldo Emerson coined that phrase in his *Concord Hymn* (1836) to describe a skirmish at Concord Bridge, seven miles away and a few hours later. The air on Lexington Green crackled with exploding gunpowder, and when the smoke cleared, eight colonists lay dead.[6]

As the redcoats returned to Boston, they were attacked by ever-increasing colonial militiamen. The Massachusetts Provincial Congress mobilized 13,600 colonial soldiers and placed Boston under a siege that lasted for almost a year.

To prevent the spread of the Boston carnage to the Quaker province, the Pennsylvania Assembly named Charles Thomson and twelve others to a committee to purchase explosives and munitions – the leading manufacturers of which happened to be Thomson and Charles Carroll.

On May 10, the Second Continental Congress convened in Philadelphia and named George Washington commander-in-chief of the Continental Army.

On June 22, Congress voted to issue a continental currency –

two million dollars in unsecured bills of credit – to be used in paying the costs of war.

On July 3, George Washington formally assumed command of the Continental Army, about seventeen thousand men gathered in Cambridge, Massachusetts.

On July 5, Congress adopted its last humble plea for peace with England, the "Olive Branch Petition," written by Charles Thomson and John Dickinson. Governor Penn of Pennsylvania personally delivered the Petition to London, but the King's Friends prevented George III from seeing Penn or even acknowledging the Petition.

On July 6, Congress adopted the Declaration of the Causes and Necessities of Taking Up Arms, which fell short of asserting independence, but vowed a holy war of liberation from slavery.

On August 23, George III issued a proclamation declaring that all thirteen American colonies were in a state of open rebellion. Two months later, in October, British forces burned Falmouth, what is presently Portland, Maine.

The war was on. But from Lorenzo Ricci's vantage point, the war was *won*. There remained only opportunities now for his enemies, the British Crown and the American colonials, to engage in blood-letting hostilities that would eventually separate and exhaust them both. *Divide et impera,* divide and conquer. What to the British was "the War of American Rebellion," and to the Americans "the War for Independence," was to General Ricci "the War of Reunification with Protestant Dissidents." From it would rise the first Febronian government on earth, a constellation of secular churches called states led by an electorate of laymen properly enlightened by the *ratio studiorum* and *united* under the spiritual guidance of *Pontifex Maximus,* and paying tribute to Rome for the privilege. *United ... States.*

The *real* war over, there began now the unraveling, which was the *historical* war, the *theatrical* war. This would consist of a series of bloody battles mounted by Congress and Crown for the people's participation, observation, and commemoration. These events would produce Caesarean Rome's essential emotional cornerstone.

CHAPTER 18 THE STIMULATING EFFECTS OF TEA

Like Virgil's *Aeneid,* epic national heroes would forge a fictitious national legacy. We must not forget Charles Thomson's candid assessment that the Revolution's leaders were largely deceptions, men of "supposed wisdom and valor" who were far inferior to "the qualities that have been ascribed to them."

And there is evidence – admittedly the faintest hint of evidence (as is so often the case with clandestine warriors) – that Lorenzo Ricci communed with these American heroes, and gave them instruction, on their own soil. This evidence is presented in our next chapter.

THE GENERALATE OF LORENZO RICCI — 1750-1775
A Brief Summary of Events

	EUROWORLD	ENGLAND	AMERICA
1758	LORENZO RICCI elected Black Pope, CLEMENT XIII elected Pope. JOHN CARROLL begins teaching at ST. OMER'S. POMBAL denounces Jesuits in PORTUGAL.	BENJ. FRANKLIN in LONDON seeking greater British presence in Pennsylvania. KING GEORGE II obliges by plunging England into the French & Indian Wars. CHAS. CARROLL graduates in civil law from Jesuit college in PARIS, arrives in London for more legal studies at the MIDDLE TEMPLE.	Colonies happy, seeking greater British presence, yet SAM ADAMS begins organizing against Great Britain. Gadsden in S.C., Harnett in N.C., Patrick Henry and Jefferson in Virginia, and Chas. Thomson in Phila. follow suit.
1759	Jesuits expelled from PORTUGAL, VOLTAIRE bashes Jesuits in two hit plays in Paris, GANGANELLI becomes cardinal, under RICCI'S sponsorship.	GEORGE II'S grandson, the PRINCE OF WALES, matures under the spiritual direction of LORD BUTE.	CHAS. THOMSON formalizes "YOUNG JUNTO," a secret club for young men interested in useful arts and sciences cloned from FRANKLIN'S "JUNTO," and akin to SAM ADAMS' "CAUCUS CLUB" in Boston.
1760	Jesuits under attack in SPAIN.	GEORGE III takes throne upon Grandfather's death, BUTE runs Parliament through "KING'S FRIENDS."	Happy to be English subjects, COLONISTS are peacefully "ruled by a little pen, ink, and paper-led by a thread."
1761	Jesuits condemned in SPAIN.	BUTE, virtual head of British government, chooses mate for GEORGE III, Queen CHARLOTTE of Mecklenburg.	WRITS OF ASSISTANCE imposed on colonists by KING'S FRIENDS. JOHN ADAMS considers this the "COMMENCEMENT OF THE CONTROVERSY."
1762	Jesuits condemned by FRENCH parlement. JOHN CARROLL transfers to BRUGES.		BENJ. FRANKLIN returns to install POSTAL SYSTEM connecting southern Virginia with eastern New England
1763	FEBRONIUS publishes STATE OF THE-'. CHURCH, calling for reunification of Protestants with Catholics in states under the papacy's spiritual direction.	ENGLAND wins FRENCH & INDIAN WARS, but under terms of the PEACE OF PARIS, negotiated by LORD BUTE, is cut off from any European alliances and made object of colonial resentment. BUTE forced to resign.	Colonists resent ENGLAND'S grant of lands to FRANCE under the PEACE OF PARIS. The secret clubs agitate against England.
1764	Pope CLEMENT XIII bans FEBRONIUS' book. LOUIS XV suppresses Jesuits by royal edict in FRANCE.	BUTE picks GRENVILLE new Prime Minister. GRENVILLE increases duties on colonial imports. CHAS. CARROLL leaves England for MARYLAND.	FRANKLIN returns to England to lobby for Pennsylvania's becoming a royal colony. Colonists resent GRENVILLE'S measures, smuggling increases, GRENVILLE brings ADMIRALTY COURTS inland
1765	CLEMENT XIII authorizes office of SACRED HEART, a Jesuit cult which holds believers responsible for reparations for the sins of the world, payable through prayers, penances, masses and SOCIAL ACTION.	GRENVILLE passes STAMP ACT. ANGLICAN CHURCH requests British cabinet to establish an AMERICAN BISHOP.	CHAS. CARROLL arrives in MARYLAND. The AMERICAN BISHOP SCARE "trains and habituates the colonists to opposition." PATRICK HENRY, furious at STAMP ACT, cries "No taxation without representation!" SAM ADAMS convenes STAMP ACT CONGRESS in NEW YORK.
1766	CLEMENT XIII appoints Jesuited GIOV. BRASCHI Treasurer of the Apostolic Chamber.	GRENVILLE falls. STAMP ACT repealed, with rider that PARLIAMENT has "full power" to bind colonies, CHAS. TOWNSHEND takes over as Prime Minister.	Colonies exuberant over STAMP ACT repeal.
1767	KING CHARLES III expels Jesuits from SPAIN.	TOWNSHEND ACTS place high duties on goods received in America.	TOWNSHEND ACTS stimulate colonial productivity.

CHAPTER 18   THE STIMULATING EFFECTS OF TEA

	EUROWORLD	ENGLAND	AMERICA
1768	Jesuits expelled from other Catholic countries.	First *ENCYCLOPEDIA BRITTANICA* published.	Productivity and self-support help raise comfort level of **SEPARATION** and **INDEPENDENCE** among colonists.
1768	Day before meeting with European powers to discuss **DISSOLUTION OF JESUITS**, Pope **CLEMENT XIII** dies suddenly. **GANGANELLI** elected **CLEMENT XIV**. **ROTHSCHILD** appointed guardian of Vatican treasury. **JOHN CARROLL** ordained a Jesuit.	**TOWNSHEND ACTS** costing more to enforce than revenue returns. **BENJ. FRANKLIN** now representing **PENNSYLVANIA, GEORGIA**, and **NEW JERSEY** in **LONDON**.	**CHAS. THOMSON** opens a rum distillery near **PHILADELPHIA**.
1770		**FRANKLIN** adds **MASSACHUSETTS** to list, making him chief spokesmen for American interests in England. **TOWNSHEND ACTS** repealed	**REDCOATS** fire into an angry Boston crowd. **BOSTON MASSACRE** becomes the symbol of British tyranny.
1771	**JOHN CARROLL** begins tour of Europe with **CHARLES STOURTON**.		On anniversary of **BOSTON MASSACRE**, **SAM ADAMS** calls for **ACTION AND SOLIDARITY** against England.
1772	**RICCI** causes *AMIOT'S SUN-TZU* to be published in **PARIS**, disclosing his strategy for bringing America under Rome's dominion.		
1773	After making **GIOV. BRASCHI** cardinal, **CLEMENT XIV** dissolves Jesuits on July 21. On August 17, **LORENZO RICCI** is taken to **ENGLISH COLLEGE** for meetings with **JOHN MATTINGLY** of **MARYLAND, BRASCHI**, and others, perhaps including **EAST INDIA COMPANY**. Sept. 22, **RICCI** taken to **CASTEL SANT'ANGELO**, as Tea Act product heads for Boston.	In May, **PARLIAMENT** passes the **TEA ACT**, proposed by **EAST INDIA COMPANY**. **JOHN CARROLL** arrives at **WARDOUR CASTLE** in Wiltshire, England, to serve as Chaplain to the **ARUNDELLS**.	**CHAS. CARROLL** runs his *"FIRST CITIZEN"* opinion shaper. **CHAS. THOMSON'S** group turns back Tea Act product meant for Philadelphia. **DISGUISED FREEMASONS** stage the **BOSTON TEA PARTY**, Dec. 16
1774	Pope **CLEMENT XIV** dies. Church gives appearance of serious disability. **RICCI** accesses **VATICAN** via tunnel from **SANT'ANGELO** for meetings with **CARDINAL BRASCHI**, who runs Holy See during long conclave to elect successor.	**PARLIAMENT** enacts the **INTOLERABLE ACTS**, ostensibly to punish the colonies for **TEA PARTY** offense, but meant to drive them to **SEPARATION**. **GEORGE III** writes **LORD NORTH**: "The die is cast; the colonies must either triumph or submit." **TOM PAINE** boards ship for America with letter of introduction from **BENJ. FRANKLIN**. **JOHN CARROLL** also departs for America	Efforts of **CHAS. THOMSON** result in **FIRST CONTINENTAL CONGRESS** at Philadelphia in Sept., with **THOMSON** serving as *"PERPETUAL SECRETARY"* for the next fifteen years. **CHAS. CARROLL** attends first **CONGRESS** as "unofficial consultant" to Maryland delegation. **THOS. MIFFLIN'S** house scene of secret meetings between **CARROLLS** and patriot leaders. **CHAS. CARROLL** and **CHAS. THOMSON** manufacture explosives and weaponry.
1775	Long conclave (143 days) elects **GIOV. BRASCHI** pope, who takes name **PIUS VI**. **LORENZO RICCI** "dies" in **CASTEL SANT'ANGELO** Nov 24.	**GEORGE III** ignores *"OLIVE BRANCH PETITION"* offered by Congress.	On Apr. 19, **REDCOATS** fire on Americans in response to an unseen shootist at **LEXINGTON GREEN**, near Concord Bridge
1776	**JOHN AND CHAS. CARROLL** join Congressional **MISSION TO CANADA** and secure **QUEBEC'S NEUTRALITY** in the coming War		**PAINE'S** *COMMON SENSE* published. **DECLARATION OF INDEPENDENCE** resolved JULY 2, MDCCLXXVI.

THE NEW REPUBLIC'S FIRST FLAG: THE FLAG OF
THE EAST INDIA COMPANY

Chapter 19

THE DEATH & RESURRECTION OF LORENZO RICCI

O N NOVEMBER 19, 1775 officials at Castel Sant'Angelo were presented the following deposition, given under oath and signed by Lorenzo Ricci: "The Society of Jesus that is dissolved offered no reason or pretext whatsoever for its dissolution."

This, Ricci's last official statement, is a masterpiece of mental reservation, for indeed the Society had not offered a pretext or reason for its dissolution, and indeed Lorenzo Ricci had not furnished a pretext or reason for his incarceration. The Jesuits had been dissolved and Ricci imprisoned *for no offered reasons whatsoever;* ergo, their dissolution for all eternity was null and void. Outcome would prove this fact: the Society of Jesus would be officially restored in 1814. Since the Disestablishment was a nullity from the beginning, it must follow that the Jesuits were still technically alive as the world's largest clandestine *milice du Christ*. Legally, thousands of Jesuits were still bound to their oath of obedience to the black papacy. They were free now to expand Roman Catholicism with perfect invisibility, end justifying means, dedicating their encyclopedic skills in the useful arts, law, religion, medicine, philosophy, the humanities, finance, commerce, communications, diplomacy, banking, finance, espionage, and intrigue – dedicating all to both sides of the self-extirpating Protestant belligerents. *"Now, whether he kill Cassio or Cassio him, or each do kill the other, every way makes my gain!"*

If the Society of Jesus could conquer though believed dead, could not its Superior General do the same? When Lorenzo Ricci "died" in his cell at Castel Sant'Angelo on November 24, 1775, what if his "death" was no more physical than the supposed disestablishment of his army? Lesser mystics than Ricci, who secretly commanded the Rosicrucians, were known to die and resurrect at the threshold of important endeavors:

> According to material available, the supreme council of the Fraternity of the Rose Croix [Rosicrucians] was composed of a certain number of individuals who had died what is known as the "philosophic death." When the time came for an initiate to enter upon his labors for the Order, he conveniently "died" under somewhat mysterious circumstances. In reality he changed his name and place of residence, and a box of rocks or a body secured for the purpose was buried in his stead. It is believed that this happened in the case of Sir Francis Bacon who, like all servants of the Mysteries, renounced all personal credit and permitted others to be considered as the authors of the documents which he wrote or inspired.[1]

Was it really Ricci's body lying in state at the cathedral of San Giovanni d'Fiorentini during the elaborate funeral mass that Pius VI arranged for him? Was it really Lorenzo Ricci who was entombed beneath the Church of the Gesu a week later, in the vault reserved for Generals of the Society? Or was it a wax effigy sculpted by artisans upon a corpse of Ricci's dimensions under the direction of John Carroll's collaborator, man-about-Rome and art agent *extraordinaire* Francis Thorpe?

Of course, Lorenzo Ricci would have covered his tracks in sub-

CHAPTER 19 THE DEATH & RESURRECTION OF LORENZO RICCI

limely Sun-Tzuan fashion, so we can never be sure. But is it not consistent with his authority, resources, motives, and modus operandi, as well as the verifiable outcome of American Independence, that the General would feign death at precisely this opportunity and sail to America in order to conduct his orchestrations personally? Reflect on his counsel in *The Thirteen Articles* of Sun-Tzu, particularly –

> The great art of a General is to arrange for the enemy never to know the place where he will have to fight & to carefully withhold from him knowledge of which posts he must guard. If he manages that & can also hide the slightest of his movements, then he is not only a clever General, he is an extraordinary man, a prodigy. Without being seen, he sees. He hears without being heard.
>
> Go to places where the enemy would never suspect that you intended to go.... Do not think of gathering the fruits of your victory until his entire defeat has put you in a position where you can yourself reconnoitre surely, tranquilly & with leisure.

If the General did sail to America rather than lie in state, he would arrive not as a conquering hero but as a gentle, harmless, nameless, scholarly old man who spent most of his time reading. And during the course of his stay, inevitably, someone would observe his subtle power over great patriots and write about it. Just such a person was observed and written about.

D URING the fall of 1775, Congress authorized a committee made up of Benjamin Franklin, Thomas Lynch, Benjamin Harrison and George Washington to consider and recommend a design for the first united colonial flag. The so-called "Flag Committee" traveled to Cambridge, Massachusetts. There, according to the only known account of its proceedings, given in Robert Allen Campbell's book, *Our Flag* (Chicago, 1890), the Committee mysteriously shared its authority with a total stranger. This stranger was an elderly European transient known only as "the Professor."

He had arrived from parts unknown at summer's end. (The prisoner of Castel Sant'Angelo had not been publicly seen in two years – ample time to manage Braschi's election to the papacy, relax, pack important things, die the philosopher's death, and take a three-month voyage to Boston Harbor). Since his arrival, the Professor had occupied a guestroom in a private Cambridge home whose hostess, "one of his earnest and intelligent disciples," would remember him in her diary (cited in Campbell's book) as "a quiet and very interesting member of the family."

What the hostess records about the Professor matches remarkably what is known about the character of Lorenzo Ricci. For example, the Professor is perceived to be "more than three-score and ten" years of age; Lorenzo Ricci was seventy-two. The Professor spoke many languages fluently, displayed an encyclopedic knowledge of history, and was "seemingly at home upon any and every topic coming up in conversation." We might expect the very same of Lorenzo Ricci, a distinguished professor of literature, philosophy and theology at the Roman College and a well-established confidant of Europe's leading intellectuals, *philosophes,* and mystics. The Professor kept "locked away in a large, old fashioned, cubically shaped, iron bound, heavy, oaken chest, a number of very rare old books and ancient manuscripts," which he spent much of his time "deciphering, translating, or rewriting." We might expect as much of Lorenzo Ricci, the voracious scholar and publisher of oriental masterworks.

On the morning of December 13, 1775, the committeemen arrived in Cambridge for a midday feast. The Professor greeted them as we might expect Lorenzo Ricci would, "with an ease, grace and dignity [evidencing] his superior ability, experience and attainments, and ... with a courtly bow that left no room to doubt that he had habitually associated with those in acknowledged authority." When Benjamin Franklin was presented to him, the hostess watched the patriarchal Doctor lock hands with the patriarchal Professor, "and as fingers closed upon fingers, their eyes also met, and there was an instantaneous, a very apparent and a mutually gratified recognition." What had the woman witnessed? The

CHAPTER 19   THE DEATH & RESURRECTION OF LORENZO RICCI

Ultimate Summit? Unknown Superior revealing himself to America's Grandest Freemason?

The table talk soon focused on subjects that had occupied Lorenzo Ricci's attention since the beginning of his generalate. The hostess witnessed them discussing "the relation of the Colonies to each other and to the Mother Country." She saw them discuss "the related question of one's duty to the Colony, as related to his allegiance to Great Britain." She saw the Professor take "a noticeable, though not at all an obtrusive, part in the conversation, himself possessed of a wonderful fund of varied and accurate information concerning the Colonies, an understanding of their progress, condition and needs, and a familiarity with the principles and operations of British and European statesmanship." Wouldn't we expect as much from the Superior General of the world's best intelligence agency?

After lunch, General Washington and the committeemen held a "brief, undertone conversation." Then Dr. Franklin rose and stated: "As the chairman of this committee, speaking for my associates, with their consent, and with the approval of General Washington, I respectfully invite the Professor to meet with the Committee as one of its members; and we, each one, personally and urgently, request him to accept the responsibility, and to give us, and the American Colonies, the benefit of his counsel."

Taking the floor, the Professor accepted the responsibility. Then, startlingly, he proposed that his disciple, the hostess, be placed on the committee "because she is our hostess, because she is a woman, and above all, because she is a superior woman." (The committee considered this an innovation; yet the Jesuits had been employing female coadjutors for centuries.) The proposal was "immediately and unanimously adopted." Luncheon was adjourned. The committee would reconvene at seven in the evening, "in the guest chamber usually occupied by the Professor."

Franklin and the Professor spent the afternoon together walking about Cambridge. When they returned, the hostess noted that "both of them wore the relieved and confident look of earnest and determined men who had, in a satisfactory way, solved a perplexing problem, and of victors who had successfully mastered a difficult and dangerous situation."

At the evening session, Franklin turned the meeting over to "his new-found and abundantly honored friend." The subject was a flag. Addressing the committee as "Comrade Americans," the Professor explained that, since the colonies were still dependent upon Great Britain, "we are not expected to design or recommend a flag which will represent a new government or an independent nation," but instead one "that will testify our present loyalty as English Subjects," a flag that was "already in use," a flag that had been recognized by the British government for "half a century," a flag having a field of alternate horizontal red and white stripes with the Grand Union Flag of Great Britain in the upper left corner.

"I refer," he said, "to the *flag of the East India Company.*"

To hide the fact that Americans would be fighting under the private flag of an international mercantile corporation controlled by Jesuits, the Professor provided a plausible cover whereby the flag could be "explained to the masses:"

> "The Union Flag of the Mother Country is retained as the union [upper left corner] of our new flag to announce that the Colonies are loyal to the just and legitimate sovereignty of the British Government. The thirteen stripes will at once be understood to represent the thirteen Colonies; their equal width will type the equal rank, rights and responsibilities of the Colonies. The union of the stripes in the field of our flag will announce the unity of interests and the cooperative union of efforts, which the Colonies recognize and put forth in their common cause. The white stripes will signify that we consider our demands just and reasonable; and that we will seek to secure our rights through peaceable, intelligent and statesmanlike means – if they prove at all possible; and the red stripes at the top and bottom of our flag will declare that first and last – and always – we have the determination, the enthusiasm, and the power to use force – whenever we deem force necessary. The alternation of the red and white stripes will suggest that our reasons for all demands will be intelligent and forcible, and that our force in securing our rights will be just and reasonable."

CHAPTER 19   THE DEATH & RESURRECTION OF LORENZO RICCI

The Professor reminded the committee that "the masses of the people, and a large majority of the leaders of public opinion, desire a removal of grievances, and a rectification of wrongs, through a fuller recognition of their rights as British Subjects; and few of them desire and very few of them expect – at this time – any complete severance of their present political and dependent relations with the English Government." That severance would occur "before the sun in its next summer's strength" – indicating that the Professor foreknew, as Lorenzo Ricci would have foreknown, a July declaration of independence. At that time, the East India Company flag could be "easily modified" by replacing the Union Jack with stars against a blue background, "to make it announce and represent the new and independent nation."

Washington and Franklin lavished the Professor's idea with "especial approval and unstinted praise." The committee formally and unanimously adopted the East India Company's banner, known as "The Thirteen Stripes," as the "general flag and recognized standard of the Colonial Army and Navy." Just before midnight, they adjourned.

On January 2, 1776, at a formal ceremony attended by the Flag Committee, George Washington personally hoisted the East India Company flag "upon a towering and specially raised pine tree liberty pole," unfurling it to the breeze and displaying it for the first time "to his army, the citizens of the vicinity, and the British forces in Boston." The British officers at Charlestown Heights perceived the event to mean that General Washington had thus announced his surrender to them. At once, they saluted "The Thirteen Stripes" with thirteen hearty cheers. They immediately followed this spontaneous outburst of British Enthusiasm with the grander and more dignified official salute of thirteen guns, the thirteen-gun salute being the highest compliment in gunpowder, the military "God speed you."

By so colorfully equivocating both his enemies, the Professor had made himself God of Confusion. The redcoats were toasting the good health of the rebels, who in turn were fighting for the East India Company. One of the few places in the world where such ludicrous phenomena are considered standard and routine is in the pages of Lorenzo Ricci's *Thirteen Articles:* "The General decides everything; he knows how to shape, at will, not only the army he is commanding but also that of his enemies."

LORENZO Ricci's post-mortem attendance in America is strongly suggested in yet another pivotal episode, the famous "mission to Canada." This strange exercise is normally regarded by historians as a colossal failure. It began on February 15, 1776, when the Second Continental Congress resolved to send Benjamin Franklin, Samuel Chase, and Charles Carroll to Montreal with full authority "to promote or form a union" with Canada against England.

Just before the committee left Philadelphia, John Adams proposed a curious last-minute resolution. On the record, he requested "that Charles Carroll *prevail on Mr. John Carroll to accompany the committee to Canada,* to assist them in such matters as they shall think useful." Congress adopted the resolution.

How might a priest have assisted the committee in promoting or forming a union with Canada? The answer lies in demographics. Canada then was largely Quebec, and Quebec, though ruled despotically by the British since 1763, was mostly Roman Catholic. A Jesuit priest, armed with the right Vatican paperwork or password, could exert powerful influence on Canadian foreign policy. The same priest, if accompanied by the combined head of the black papacy and international Freemasonry, could *make* that policy.

The mission arrived in Montreal only to learn that Bishop Briand of Quebec had ordered Pierre Floquet, the Jesuit superior in Montreal, to consider John Carroll *persona non grata.* Floquet, however, defied his bishop and invited Carroll to say a mass in his home anyway, for which Floquet was immediately suspended from his priestly functions. The incident colored the mission with disaster (although Floquet was restored, according to Walsh's *Ameri-*

CHAPTER 19   THE DEATH & RESURRECTION OF LORENZO RICCI

can Jesuits, after a simple apology). Disaster was verified when the committee returned to Philadelphia with no prospect for any union whatsoever with Canada. Congress lamented that America's first diplomatic legation had failed.

But America's first diplomatic legation was Sun-Tzuan and Jesuitic, and Jesuit diplomacy can be expected to conceal victory behind mishap. As the *Thirteen Articles* put it, "You must have a real advantage when the enemy believes you have sustained some losses." So we examine the Canadian mishap for a real advantage and discover something far more valuable than the originally-sought union. While Bishop Briand was outwardly demeaning John Carroll, the mission was obtaining from Canada a position of *neutrality.* This was a significant achievement, considering Canada's good relationship with Great Britain on the one hand and two centuries of hostilities toward New England on the other. For the colonists, Canadian neutrality removed the threat of a powerful northwestern enemy and cleared the way for a declaration of independence. At Montreal, as at Cambridge, I sense the presence of someone infinitely more commanding than mere committeemen appointed by Congress. I sense the presence of the "honorary" committeeman unlisted in any record – the Professor, the fugitive Vicar of Christ.

Returning from Canada, Benjamin Franklin fell ill. It was John Carroll who escorted him to Philadelphia. At Franklin's invitation, Carroll moved into his home. Franklin acknowledged the fact in a letter dated May 27, 1776, mentioning "Mr. Carroll's friendly assistance and tender care of me." These were critical weeks of countdown to the Declaration of Independence. I wonder who else might have been found under the Franklin roof? Perhaps the Professor, with his dynamic oaken chest?

Philadelphia was crawling just now with social activists from all over, the very people Lorenzo Ricci had appointed John Carroll, as Prefect of the Sodality, to organize. The home of America's pre-eminent Freemason, with Carroll and perhaps even Ricci in residence, would have become the main clearing-house for sub rosa congressional business.

ON July 3, 1776, John Adams took pen in hand and dashed off a letter to his wife Abigail. Adams was a writer of Mozartean facility, concentration, and confidence. Everything he ever wrote was first-draft and good. He never struck through words, never edited. His moving hand, having writ, just moved on. "Yesterday," he scribbled,

> the greatest question was decided which ever was debated in America, and a greater, perhaps, never was nor will be decided among men. A resolution was passed without one dissenting colony, that these United Colonies are, and of right ought to have, full power to make war, conclude peace, establish commerce, and to do all other acts and things which other States may rightfully do. The *second day of July 1776* will be the most memorable date in the history of America. I am apt to believe that it will be celebrated by succeeding generations as the great anniversary festival. It ought to be commemorated as the day of deliverance, by solemn acts of devotion to God Almighty. It ought to be solemnized with pomp and parade, with shows, games, sports, guns, bells, bonfires, and illuminations, from one end of this continent to the other, from this time forward, forevermore.

If the black papacy truly had orchestrated America's breakaway from England, we would expect to find the second day of July to be rich in cabalah and in Roman Catholic liturgical color. The Liturgical Calendar is a process, authorized nowhere in the Bible, through which faithful Catholics may plead with Almighty God for favors through the merits of ascended saints on special feast days. Supposedly, the prayerful performance of an act on a date the Church has consecrated to a saint endows the act with the mystique of the saint as well as the saint's intercessory prayers to God for success.

Maryland history, for example, is grounded in the Liturgical Calendar. We recall how the original settlers of Maryland, many of whom were Roman Catholics, set sail from England, under the spiritual direction of Jesuit father Andrew White, on November 22, 1633. November 22 is the Feast Day of St. Cecilia, a third cen-

CHAPTER 19   THE DEATH & RESURRECTION OF LORENZO RICCI

tury Roman martyr and traditional patroness of musicians. Did Cecilia's spirit bless the voyage with musicality to cheer up an otherwise oppressive boredom? The voyagers reached landfall the following year on March 25, Annunciation Day, feast of the angel Gabriel's announcement to the Virgin Mary that she is pregnant with the Son of God. Annunciation Day contains the joyful mystery of an angel's announcing the planting of the divine seed within a virgin matrix. Did the settlers imagine themselves planting the seed of a new social order in a strange wilderness, the whole enterprise blessed by God through the merits of the Virgin Mary's unique relationship to Him? Then, exactly one year later, on Annunciation Day 1634, Father White consecrated the colony of Maryland to the Virgin Mary.

The second day of July in the year 1776 was Visitation Day, commemorating the event recorded in the first chapter of Luke wherein the Virgin, pregnant with the Messiah, visits her cousin Elizabeth, who is pregnant with John the Baptist. (Nowadays Visitation Day is celebrated on May 31, but in the year 1776 it was celebrated on July second, as it had been celebrated, according to the *New Catholic Encyclopedia*'s article entitled "Visitation of Mary," every year since the Council of Basel in 1441.)

No day in the Liturgical Calendar is more suited to Bellarminian liberation theology than Visitation Day. Ste. Margaret-Marie Alacoque, whose visions inspired the Jesuit social-action cult of Sacred Heart, was a member of the Visitandines, an order of nuns devoted to the Visitation. Visitation Day's scriptural basis is the Virgin Mary's ecstatic sermon to Elizabeth at Luke 1:46-55. This famous ejaculation, known as the *Magnificat* (the opening word in the Latin Vulgate's rendering of the passage, meaning "it magnifies"), literally *defines* the social action called for by Sacred Heart in Philadelphia on the second day of July, 1776:

> My soul doth magnify the Lord, and my spirit hath rejoiced in God my Saviour. For he hath regarded the low estate of his handmaiden: for, behold, from henceforth all generations shall call me blessed. For he that is mighty hath done to me great things; and holy is his name. And his mercy is on them that fear

him from generation to generation. He hath shewed strength with his arm; he hath scattered the proud in the imagination of their hearts. He hath put down the mighty from their seats, and exalted them of low degree. He hath filled the hungry with good things; and the rich he hath sent empty away....

Scattered the proud, put down the mighty, exalted them of low degree, filled the hungry, emptied the rich.... This is the rhetoric of Christian redemption, yes, but in the context of Lorenzo Ricci's agenda it's the rhetoric of rebellion-to-tyranny, the very *point* of the Declaration of Independence, and it's spoken by the Virgin Mary, Patroness of the Society of Jesus, Patroness of Maryland, indeed, Patroness of Roman Catholic Conquest, on the day particular to her.

Even the year of Independence seems divinely validated by the perfect design of sixes and sevens contained within its expression in Roman numerals, MDCCLXXVI:

$$MDC = 1600 = (1+6) = 7$$
$$CLX = 160 = (1+6) = 7$$
$$XVI = 16 = (1+6) = 7$$

Particularly fascinating is the way the Latin equivalent of 1776 is structured upon 666 and 777. Swiss theologian E. W. Bullinger, in his scholarly guide to biblical arithmography, *Number In Scripture*, says that 6 in the Bible is always associated with humanity, 7 with divinity. The two numbers total 13, which Bullinger says is biblically associated with rebellion.

MDCCLXXVI, 1776, really does seem to be a unique convergence of time and human rebellion in the service of a divine ordination. This is eerily corroborated by John Adams' letter to Abigail on July third. He confides to his wife that independence *should have been declared in December of 1775:*

> Had a Declaration of Independency been made *seven months ago,* it would have been attended with many great and glorious effects. If I could write with freedom, I could easily convince you that it would, and explain it to you the manner how.

CHAPTER 19 THE DEATH & RESURRECTION OF LORENZO RICCI

Adams never fully explained how the earlier declaration would have produced great and glorious effects. However, the numbers suggest it would have rather fizzled. Roman numerals for 1775 fall into the following groups:

$$M D C = 1600 = (1+6) = 7$$
$$C L X = 160 = (1+6) = 7$$
$$X V = 15 = (1 + 5) = 6$$

Plain to see, December 1775 fails as cabalah. It gives no indication of divine approval to rebellious humanity. This is why, I believe, Lorenzo Ricci held out for 1776.

Of course, a sufficiently gnostic Jesuit would see in MDCCLXXVI more than good numbers. He would see an encapsulation of the very origins of the Society of Jesus. MDC would give him *milice du Christ* ("Christian militia"), the official classification of the Knights Templar and the Society of Jesus. MDC also produces Medici, the family name of Pope Leo X, whose degeneracy provoked Martin Luther to create the Protestant movement, which in turn created the need for the Society. CLX specifies the Ignatian era, which historians have ever since called the "Century of Leo X." And the last three numerals name the Century of Leo X, the sixteenth century, XVI.

WHEN it came time to sign the Declaration of Independence, how could Lorenzo Ricci not be present? How could he who had labored more than seventeen years for this superbly Bellarminian ambiance *not* participate in the excitement?

There is a story, usually told in conjunction with the Professor and the Flag Committee, involving another mysterious stranger, one who suddenly appeared in the legislative chamber of the old State House in Philadelphia on the night of July fourth.

The moment was tense. Independence had been resolved, but the document lacked signatures. Some were having second thoughts about the risks. Masonic historian Manly P. Hall writes:

> It was a grave moment and not a few of those present feared that their lives would be the forfeit for their audacity. In the

midst of the debate a fierce voice rang out. The debaters stopped and turned to look upon the stranger. Who was this man who had suddenly appeared in their midst and transfixed them with his oratory? They had never seen him before, none knew when he had entered, but his tall form and pale face filled them with awe. His voice ringing with a holy zeal, the stranger stirred them to their very souls. His closing words rang through the building: "God has given America to be free!" As the stranger sank into a chair exhausted, a wild enthusiasm burst forth. Name after name was placed upon the parchment: the Declaration of Independence was signed. But where was the man who had precipitated the accomplishment of this immortal task – who had lifted for a moment the veil from the eyes of the assemblage and revealed to them a part at least of the great purpose for which the new nation was conceived? He had disappeared, nor was he ever seen again or his identity established.[*]

Be warned. This is only a story, unsupported by primary source material. John Adams, the most talkative of the framers, said not a word about it. But we know from Adams' own pen that some kind of gag order had been imposed upon the signers – *"if I could write with freedom"* he had told Abigail in that letter dated the third of July. Could Manly Hall have received the story through Freemasory's well-insulated oral tradition? Could the stranger whose voice rang "with a holy zeal" have been the Professor, Lorenzo Ricci? Could the "wild enthusiasm" with which the legislators signed the declaration have resulted not from Ricci's inspiring pep-talk but upon his disclosure of documents taken from the oaken chest, documents easy for the Vicar of Christ in his capacity as Freemasonry's Unknown Superior to obtain, *guaranteeing that the international monetary network would indemnify the signers for their action?* My mind, informed by an ever-increasing knowledge of how the greatest clandestine warriors fight, has no problem whatsoever believing this to be the case. It is exquisitely consistent with the formation of a Febronian union of thirteen Protestant colonies, ordained to be ruled from a federal city named "Rome," a city situated within the See of Baltimore, under the protection of the Patroness of the Society of Jesus.

CHAPTER 19   THE DEATH & RESURRECTION OF LORENZO RICCI

One of the more intriguing clues that the United States of America was established under *Regimini militantis ecclesiae* is the new republic's Great Seal. As we shall see in the next chapter, the Seal is legal proof that America's true founding fathers were indeed priests of Rome.

Chapter 20

AMERICAN GRAFFITI

THERE IS A UNIVERSAL legal tradition that requires acts of a governmental authority to be marked by a seal – otherwise the acts are not authentic. Typically, a seal discloses the character of the authority it represents by means of an image which can be, and usually is, amplified by some sentence, phrase, or word.

The first seal of the United States of America, designed to authenticate all governmental actions under the Declaration of Independence, was presented to Congress in August 1776. Created by an official committee consisting of Benjamin Franklin, John Adams, and Thomas Jefferson, the seal illustrates an event based on Exodus 14:19-27. It is a cameo of Moses leading the Israelites through the parted waters while a chariot-bound Pharaoh, wielding a sword and wearing the crown of tyranny, perishes in the maelstrom. Framing the picture are the words *"REBELLION TO TYRANTS IS OBEDIENCE TO GOD."*

THE MOSAIC SEAL
of August, 1776

When I first became aware of this seal many years ago, I thought it demonstrated how intensely *biblical* was the faith of the founding fathers. But once I began discerning the hidden makers of American nationalism, my thinking changed radically. I now see this seal, despite the biblical glow of the committee that designed it, as the profession of an intensely *Roman Catholic* faith. For there is a great disparity between biblical faith and Roman Catholic faith. Indeed, this disparity was the crux of the Protestantism which Pope Paul III commissioned the Society of Jesus to extirpate.

Biblical faith regards the Bible alone, *sola scriptura,* apart from any other source, to be a sufficient and infallible rule of life. In the Bible's own words: "All scripture is God-breathed, and is profitable for teaching, for counseling, for correction, and for training in righteousness: that the man of God may be perfect, completely outfitted to perform good works" (2 Timothy 3:16).

Roman Catholic faith, on the other hand, while agreeing that the Bible is God-breathed, considers scripture neither infallible nor sufficient in itself as a rule of life, unless so interpreted by the Magisterium (the teaching authority of the Church), and then so pronounced by the infallible pope.

At Paul III's Council of Trent (1545-63), which we have learned was closely supervised over its eighteen years of existence by the Jesuits, it was decreed that the Magisterium "receives and venerates, with a feeling of piety and reverence all the books of the Old and New Testaments, *also the traditions* [italics mine], whether they relate to faith or morals, as having been dictated either orally by Christ or by the Holy Ghost, and preserved in the Catholic Church in unbroken succession.". Over the centuries, Roman Catholic faith in Scripture, as modified by tradition, as pro-

CHAPTER 20   AMERICAN GRAFFITI

nounced by the Magisterium and pope, has bound millions of consciences to a thousand doctrines not found in scripture and either unknown or rejected by the apostles and early Christian fathers.[2]

The 1776 seal agrees with Roman Catholic teaching as much as it disagrees with the Bible. Whereas the caption "Rebellion to tyrants is obedience to God" is found nowhere in Scripture, it is the cornerstone of Bellarminian liberation theology. The Bible *never* condones rebellion, not even rebellion to those tyrants under whom God's own people, the Israelites, were obliged to suffer continuously. When Scripture mentions rebellion, it is almost always referring to the disobedience of the Israelites toward their God Yahweh. The seventeenth chapter of Proverbs teaches that "the evil man seeks rebellion," and 1 Samuel 15:23 admonishes that "rebellion is as the sin of witchcraft." The God of Scripture cannot be obeyed by evil-doing and witchcraft. He will not be honored in the breach. However, sacred *tradition* authorizes *anything* in the service of Rome – *Cum finis est licitus, etiam media sunt licita,* the end justifies the means.

Depicting rebellion as a salvational act, the 1776 seal further harmonizes with the Magisterium on how the sinful soul of man is saved from eternal punishment. The Magisterium concurs with the Bible that salvation is the free gift of God's grace, but adds the nonscriptutal teaching that salvation can be *lost* if good works are not performed through the "sacred channels" of Baptism, Confession, and the Mass. Scripture (Ephesians 2:8-10) says that Jesus Christ does not share his saviorhood with *anyone or anything* ("You have been saved by grace through faith; and that not of yourselves, it is the gift of God; not as a result of works, so that no one should boast"), yet the Magisterium says that Christ is *no savior* without the sinner's cooperation with the Church and its traditions.

In fact, Scripture's account of the Exodus shows the departure from Egypt not to be a rebellion at all. When called by Yahweh to represent Israel before Pharaoh, Moses pled himself incapable (Exodus 3:11), uninformed (3:13), unauthorized (4:1), ineloquent (4:10), unadapted (4:13), unproven (5:23), and uncredentialed (6:12) – hardly the audacious mindset of a great rebel leader. What

Moses led was no rebellion but a sociological deliverance for which Yahweh alone claimed responsibility: "Come now, therefore, and I will send you to Pharaoh so that you can bring my people, the children of Israel, out of Egypt.... And I will stretch out my hand, and smite Egypt with all my wonders which I will do in the midst thereof: and after that he will let you go" (Exodus 3:10, 20). If Adams, Franklin, and Jefferson had wished the 1776 seal to express the true teaching of Scripture, they might have written *"YAHWEH REMOVES TYRANTS FOR HIS FAITHFUL."*

But even with a biblically correct motto the seal fails the biblical standard. For it is after all a *seal,* authority represented by a graven image. Although the use of seals and images is one of Roman Catholicism's proudest sacred traditions, Scripture prohibits it. The only Israelite shown to rule with a seal is king Ahab, who "did evil in the sight of the Lord above all that were before him" (1 Kings 16:30). Ahab's seal, apparently appropriated from ancient pagan tradition, was employed by his wife, the quintessentially wicked Jezebel, to commit fraud and murder (21:8-16). Scripture warns of an unlimited potential for evil inherent in graven-image seals. The apostles of Christ understood this principle well. They saw the pharisees demand Jesus show them a token of His authority, and what Jesus showed them was not an image but Scripture – the book of Jonah (Matthew 12:39). Paul the apostle had no seal except the people he'd evangelized: "for the seal of my apostleship are those of you in the Lord" (1 Corinthians 9:2). Indeed, the seal of the Body of Christ is represented in Scripture not by the miter and crossed keys of the Holy See, or the doves, flames, Bibles, bare crosses, and sunbursts of the Protestant denominations, but by *Scripture alone:* "The foundation of God stands sure, having this seal: *THE LORD KNOWS HIS OWN; AND LET CHRIST'S FAITHFUL DEPART FROM INIQUITY"* (2 Timothy 2:19).

The early Christian leaders, whose faith is historically regarded as the best-informed of any generation's, rigorously opposed the making of images or likenesses of any kind. Scripture had taught them well that Yahweh's people always suffered terrible calamity whenever they violated the commandment not to identify them-

CHAPTER 20 AMERICAN GRAFFITI

selves or their God with "any graven images or any likeness of any thing" (Exodus 20:4). Edwyn Bevan's *Holy Images: An Inquiry into Idolatry and Image Worship in Ancient Paganism and in Christianity* cites three important early churchmen who forbade images. Clement of Alexandria taught that images were "not true," and were forbidden by Yahweh "in order that we might not direct our attention to sensible objects, but might proceed to the intelligential." Origen held that images "drag the soul down instead of directing the mind to a divine invisible reality." Tertullian instructed the servants of God to avoid every form of imagery, even secular art. Indeed, as Bevan points out, Christians of the first and second centuries placed visual artists in a class with harlots, drunkards, brothel-keepers, and actors.

But for thousands of years Mediterranean cultures had been receiving their religious and political information from myths narrated by visual art. Paulinus, Bishop of Nola, said of his congregations, "They are not devoid of religion, but not able to read." This was Paulinus' excuse for beseeching the Bishop of Rome to permit him to teach with graven images. Paulinus had forgotten, or perhaps had never learned, that the basis of the Gospel of Christ was above all *literary* – else why had its Author prohibited graphic likenesses? Knowing this, the apostles devoted a large part of the evangelical process to spreading *literacy* – "blessed is he who *reads*" (Revelation 1:3). Even so, the apostle Peter foresaw the time of Paulinus, Bishop of Nola, a time when "false teachers among you shall bring in damnable heresies denying the Lord" (2 Peter 2:1). What more damnable heresy could there be than depicting a God who condemns images... *with an image?* Could such a God even be depictable by an image? Wouldn't an image purporting to be Him have to be in reality, by sheer force of logic, the image of *another God?* The apostle Paul, aware of the compelling nature of images, and their definitive incapacity to teach Jesus and the Gospel, warned the Corinthians how easily a false teacher could lead them to "another Jesus, another gospel" (2 Corinthians 11:4). The time was very close, Paul knew, when Christians "will not endure sound doctrine, but will heap to themselves teachers who will switch them from truth to myths" (2 Timothy 4:3,4). And what are graven images but the very *grammar* of myths?

The switch began noticeably happening in the third century, when teachers like Paulinus of Nola began instructing from pictures (for which Paulinus was canonized by the Roman Catholic Church). With Constantine a century later, as we've seen, a powerful new "Christian" visual language developed. Old mythic icons were renamed to fit Bible stories, and an iconic Christianity was spread through pagan images processed by missionary adaptation. What the new converts were *not* taught is that Scripture categorically rejects such attempts to iconize its contents, and that therefore (again, by sheer force of logic) the likenesses upon whom they reverently gazed were no more than the gods and goddesses originally pictured, *other gods of other gospels*. Archaeology traces these gods and their gospels back to the very earliest Babylonian cathedrals. It was in these cathedrals, erected nearly four thousand years before the Christian era, that the Roman Catholic sacred iconographic tradition was born. We shall explore this subject in some detail in a forthcoming chapter.

CONGRESS refused to adopt the 1776 seal. We may never know why. There is no record of any debate, only the notation that the seal was ordered to lay "on the table." Five years later, in the summer of 1781, a fleet of twenty-five French war vessels arrived in Chesapeake Bay with more than twenty thousand soldiers accompanied by ninety Roman Catholic chaplains and God only knows how many secularized Jesuits. A month later, the British army surrendered to General Washington at Yorktown. The legend-spinning visible war was over at last.

In June 1782, Benjamin Franklin and John Adams were meeting in Paris to perfect a treaty with envoys of the newly-elected British Prime Minister – Robert Petty. We recall Petty, Lord Shelburne, the ubiquitous "Jesuit of Berkeley Square" who teamed with Lord Bute to conclude the French and Indian Wars in terms that had made the Revolution inevitable. Franklin and Adams found themselves approaching the negotiating table without a national seal. Nothing they might do on behalf of the United States could

CHAPTER 20   AMERICAN GRAFFITI

be valid without a seal. This was the exigency that moved Congress to adopt, on June 28, the seal designed by Charles Thomson and William Barton.

The Great Seal is "written" in cabalah, that style of allegorical communication composed of seemingly unrelated symbols, numerals, and phrases. A piece in *Le Charivari* No. 18 (Paris, 1973), discussing certain symbolic motifs used by the enlightened French artist Nicolas Poussin, explains the practical advantage of cabalistic works:

> A single word suffices to illumine connections which the multitude cannot grasp. Such works are available to everyone, but their significance addresses itself to an elite. Above and beyond the masses, sender and receiver understand each other.

Cabalah goes beyond mere secret communication. Supposedly, it thrusts the sender "into direct contact with the living powers and forces of the Universe, and through them with the eternal source of all manifestation," explains Henrietta Bernstein in her *Cabalah Primer*. "In other words, you make contact with God." To a cabalist gnostic illuminatus whose special knowledge has liberated him from the clutch of matter and is speeding him toward the pure light of godliness, cabalah is "the royal art, a closed body of knowledge sacred to the elect."

Since the Great Seal is written in the language of cabalah, it appears to be a veritable Gnostic Constitution. In terms well known to initiates and God Almighty, it sets forth the origin, nature, purpose, and plan of American government. Of course, as Charles Thomson and Manly Hall have intimated, the initiates will never disclose to outsiders the meaning of the Seal's elements. But God Almighty is not so aloof. He does not resist inquiries. Nor is He a respecter of persons. Contrary to the cabalist's boast of privileged access, Scripture promises more light to any mind that seeks it from God in person. Shining that light on commonly available histories of rulers and religions, anyone can trace the Seal's elements back to their ancient origins and in the end know as much as, if not more than, the gnostics.

On the front or *obverse* side of the Seal we find an eagle clutching an olive branch and thirteen arrows, with a banner in his beak inscribed with the motto *"E PLURIBUS UNUM."* The earliest images of sacred eagles have been found in that region of present-day Iraq once known as Babylon. The eagle was identified with the Babylonian sky-god Annu. When Annu entered sacred Roman iconography as Jupiter, the eagle was still his mascot. For the more than two thousand years since the death of Rome's first emperor, Julius Caesar, Jupiter's eagle has signified Rome's imperial power – "imperial" meaning the right of the Caesars to make laws and enforce them. In many a church, Roman Catholic and Protestant alike, the Bible from which lessons are publicly read rests on a hardwood lectern carved in the shape of a magnificent eagle. Yet in the pages of this very Bible, God forbids carved images of eagles. What, then, does the eagle signify, if not a power indifferent to Scripture?

The brilliant cloud hovering over the eagle's head in the Great Seal is the *aegis*. The *aegis* is a goatskin. (We have already examined how Scripture equates the goat with worldly power and separation from God.) When Jupiter was a baby he was nursed by a she-goat named Amaltheia. (The priestly artists often portrayed the adult Jupiter as a satyr, having a man's body with the horns, hair, and legs of a goat.) When Amaltheia died, Jupiter made the *aegis* out of her hide.

The *aegis* of the Great Seal glorifies thirteen five-pointed stars, or pentagrams. Each pentagram represents an original State. In gnostic symbology, the pentagram is identified with Jupiter's wife, Venus. There is a natural reason for this. A dedicated observer, from a fixed location over an eight-year period, will discern that the planet Venus travels a unique celestial pathway that exactly describes a pentagram. Carl Ljungman, in *Dictionary of Symbols*, has written:

> As the orbit of Venus is closer to the sun than the earth's position, she is never seen more than 48 degrees from the sun. During a period of 247 days, Venus is visible as the Evening star that is, within 48 degrees or less of the sun after the sun has set. Then Venus comes too close to the sun for us to see her. She

CHAPTER 20   AMERICAN GRAFFITI

remains invisible for 14 days, then reappears as the Morning star (or Eastern star) immediately before the sun rises in the east. For 245 days we can see Venus each morning at dawn before she again disappears into the sun's light by getting too close to the sun. Venus is now invisible for 78 days. On the 79th evening, she appears again in the west immediately after the setting sun. Now she is the Evening star once more.

If one knows the ecliptic [that is, the great circle of the celestial sphere that is the apparent path of the sun among the stars] and can pinpoint the present position of the planets in relation to the constellations of fixed stars in the zodiac, one can mark the exact place in the 360 degrees of the zodiac where the Morning star first appears shortly before sunrise after a period of invisibility. If we do this, wait for the Morning star to appear again 584 days later [the synodic orbital time of Venus] and mark its position in the zodiac, and then repeat this process until we have five positions of Venus as the Morning star, we will find that exactly eight years plus one day have passed. If we then draw a line from the first point marked to the second point marked, then to the third, and so on, we end up with a pentagram.

Only Venus possesses the five-pointed star sign. Not one of the innumerable stars above us can recreate this by its own orbit.[3]

Charles Thomson, the Great Seal's co-designer, led a group of dedicated observers of Venus. The first coordinated scientific experiment of the American Philosophical Society, the club Thomson founded for politically radical young professionals, focused on Venus' celestial pathway. On the evening of June 3, 1769, with colleagues stationed at three sites in Pennsylvania and Delaware, Thomson and five others watched, from the Public Observatory on State House Square in Philadelphia, an eclipse caused by "the transit of Venus across the Sun."[4]

The goddess Venus, as we've seen, was absorbed by missionary adaptation into the Roman Catholic sacred tradition as the Virgin Mary. The adapters even ascribed to Mary the Venusian epithet "Queen of Heaven," a title never ascribed to Mary in the Bible.

"Queen of Heaven" in Scripture names only one personage, and that is Ishtar, the Babylonian Venus. Most faithful Catholics, historically insulated from Scripture by the Magisterium and the Inquisition, have not known this. Jeremiah 44 explains how the Israelites violated their covenant with Yahweh by praising the Queen of Heaven, and in turn lost their dignity, property, freedom, *everything* to the Babylonians. Scripture teaches, also, that the Babylonian interests have much to gain from inducing souls to praise the Queen of Heaven. And as we shall later see, their gain is divinely approved.

The term "Queen of Heaven" appears nowhere else in the Old and New Testaments but at Jeremiah 44, and there exactly *five times*. Did Jeremiah know that Venus' celestial trail delineated five points? And did the other thirty-five writers of the Bible's sixty-six books know as well? Did all these men, who wrote in different languages over a period of more than a thousand years, conspire *not* to mention "Queen of Heaven" in order to preserve Jeremiah's five mentions, so that the link between (a) the Queen of Heaven, (b) the five-pointed path of Venus, and (c) the curse resulting from praising her would stand as a divine lesson for the rest of eternity? Or did it just happen that way by accident? Or, as the Bible teaches, were Jeremiah and his co-authors inspired by the Author of all creation to say (and not say) things for reasons beyond their individual understanding?

THE Great Seal's eagle holds a banner in its beak inscribed "*E PLURIBUS UNUM.*" This phrase, which appears on American coinage as well, is popularly understood to signify the melting of many people into one nation, "of many, one." Or to identify the coin as one of many identical coins. The gnostic understanding of this phrase, however, borders on the psychedelic. According to Manly Hall, *e pluribus unum* refers to the ancient Bacchic Rites, which he says was "a forerunner to Freemasonry." Mysterious and fantastic, the Bacchic Rites are built upon the following story line:

In a time before the creation of mankind, the twelve Titans cause Bacchus, Jupiter's beautiful son, to become fascinated by his

CHAPTER 20   AMERICAN GRAFFITI

own image in a mirror. Enthralled by himself, Bacchus is seized by the Titans. They kill him, tear him to pieces, boil the pieces in water, and afterwards roast and eat them. This grieves all his loved ones, hence his name, from *bakhah,* "to weep" or "lament." The strewn body parts of Bacchus become the four elements of matter.

One of Bacchus' sisters, the virgin Minerva, rescues his sacred heart from the four elements and places it before Jupiter in Heaven. From Heaven, Jupiter hurls thunderbolts at his son's murderers and reduces the Titans to ashes. The rains further reduce the ashes, mingling with the four elements, to slime. From this evil slime Jupiter forms mankind, a "Titanic embodiment" from which the "Bacchic idea," or rational soul, must be released. The Bacchic idea is released by evil slime's sexual energy, especially when facilitated by alcoholic drink – hence Bacchus is associated with grapevines, wild dancing, phallic symbols, and fornication.

When death and sex have rescued the rational soul from the four slimy corners of the earth, a transfigured, eternal Bacchus is resurrected as the flaming Sun. He is *E PLURIBUS UNUM*, One from Many, a resurrection symbolized by the pentagram, the one rising out of the four to make five. This, says Manly Hall, is "the magical formula of man,"

> the human soul rising from the bondage of the animal nature. The pentagram is the true light, the Star of the Morning, marking the location of five mysterious centers of force, the awakening of which is the supreme secret of white magic.

With *"E PLURIBUS UNUM"* flowing from his beak, Jupiter's eagle preaches the Bacchic Gospel. It is a gospel of salvation that antedates that of Jesus Christ by many, many centuries. The Bacchic Gospel was preached and played out in the pagan cults. A Holy Virgin would ritually rescue the Son of God's Sacred Heart from the slime of humanity imprisoning the Son's soul. Each cult initiate – a fractional part of the Son's soul – supposedly gained increasing amounts of knowledge from mind-altering substances and sexual ecstasy administered for money, of course, by the temple priests and priestesses. The initiate looked forward to being released from his slimy humanity by ever-increasing knowledge. He yearned to be reunited ultimately with the Sacred Heart in Heaven, resurrected and transfigured for all eternity.

This salvational plan, or some variation of it, can be found at the core of all the secret or mystery religions – cults of empire. It persists from the earliest Babylonian prototype right on down through the Great Seal. It has succeeded not because it calls for repentance from sin, but because it makes sin an asset in a process of self-deification. The Bacchic Gospel serves an economy of sin management, in which sins are forgiven upon the payment of money or performance of some act of contrition valuable to society. It is about people control. Because it prospers on the addictive nature of fornication and mind-altering substances, it naturally facilitates sex and booze and drugs and all their destructive fallout in order to have a context in which to make itself useful. Unlike the Christian Gospel, which conditions forgiveness of sins upon *repentance* – "and if he repents, forgive him" (Luke 17:3) – the Bacchic Gospel forgives upon the tendering of appropriate sacrifices to the priest of the appropriate deity. The congeniality of this gospel to secular government and Roman Catholicism speaks for itself.

THE reverse side of the Great Seal contains four elements. First, the motto *"ANNUIT COEPTIS;"* second, a thirteen-coursed topless pyramid with MDCCLXXVI engraved in the foundation; third, a disembodied eye forming the pyramid's capstone, and fourth, the motto *"NOVUS ORDO SECLORUM."* These elements define exactly the "divine providence" upon whose protection the signers of the Declaration of Independence firmly relied.

The land of the Pyramid, Egypt, is where Caesarean Rome was inaugurated. By "Caesarean" I mean the empire whose head commands not only affairs of state but those of religion as well. Caesarean Rome officially began in Alexandria, Egypt, at the temple of Jupiter, on the winter solstice – December 25 – in the year 48 BC, when a fifty-two-year-old priest of Jupiter was declared to be Jupiter's incarnation, thus "Son of God." His name was Caius of the family of Marius, Caius Maria. After deification, and occasionally before, Caius Maria was referred to as "Caesar," a cabalism formed by the letter "C" (for Caius) attached to *Aesar,* the Etruscan word for "God." The God Caius. (Suetonius, the first-century biographer of the Caesars, suggests that the title was formed from prefixing Aesar with the numeral "C," meaning "hundred." God of the Hundred, or Hundreds.)

According to Scottish theologian Alexander Hislop, Caesar consented to deification in order to inherit the huge kingdom of Pergamum.[5] Consisting of most of Asia Minor (present-day Turkey), Pergamum was bequeathed to the Roman people in 133 BC by its king, Attalus III. But there was a catch: the people of Rome had to regard their leader as God.

The Pergamenian kings had begun ruling as God when the title of *Pontifex Maximus* fled the fall of Babylon in 539 BC. In that eventful year, Persian invaders assassinated the Babylonian king Belshazzar. Just moments prior, Belshazzar had seen his assassination prophesied by the famous handwriting on the wall: "Mene Mene Tekel Upharsin," ("the Numberer is *numbered*").[6] Ruling as God by divine appointment, Belshazzar had profaned the sacred vessels of the Israelite temple. This was the unpardonable sin of blasphemy, for which God sent the Persians to destroy him.

Belshazzar's priests were evidently spared. Rather than submit to the Persian conquerors, they furtively gathered together all their portable treasures, entitlements, codes, inscriptions, astrology, sacred formulae, and insignia and fled with them northwesterly to Pergamum. Since the rulers of Pergamum were already practicing Babylonian religion, they were honored to receive the fugitive Babylonian College and their great endowment.

Pergamum, the new residence of *Pontifex Maximus,* became a showplace for despotism. The neighboring Greeks reflected its sudden transformation with the myth of Midas, the king whose touch turned everything to gold. Babylonian rule graced Pergamum with the world's greatest medical complex, the Asklepion, dedicated to the god of pharmacological healing, Asklepios. Pergamum became the most important humanist learning center, its library housing more than two hundred thousand scrolls. (Marc Antony would later move these assets to Alexandria as a gift to Cleopatra. Many of them eventually found their way from Alexandria to the Medici Library in Florence.)

When Attalus III died in 133 BC, he bequeathed all his kingdom's Babylonian grandeur to the Romans. But no Roman emperor was deemed fit to receive it because the Roman constitution had never suffered a man to be deified. The bequest lay unclaimed until 48 BC, when Caius Maria Caesar was declared God Almighty in the Serapion, Alexandria's temple of Jupiter.

Deification entitled Caesar now to assume the title *Pontifex Maximus*. To indicate his infinitely holier status, he took the name "Julius."[7] The name was a claim of descent from Julius Ascanius, the legendary son of legendary Aeneas, Virgil's maritime hero who sailed westward with a band of his Trojan fellow-countrymen fleeing the sack of Troy by Greek marauders. Assisted by the whole heavenly network of mythic deities, Aeneas led his followers to sacrifice their individuality for a glorious collective existence that would one day be called "Rome."

Aeneas was considered the offspring of a union between a human being, Anchises, and Jupiter's wife Venus. (When Anchises boasted of his intercourse with the goddess, Jupiter struck him blind with a thunderbolt. The *Aeneid* opens with Aeneas carrying blind old Anchises out of Troy on his shoulders.) By taking the name of Aeneas' son Julius and claiming descent from him as well, Caesar was able to trace his lineage back to the Queen of Heaven. The divine lineage supposedly flowed through his mother, Maia, who was purported to have conceived him without losing her virginity. Maia also claimed to have remained a virgin even in childbirth by having her son delivered from the side in a surgical operation that still bears Caesar's name.

All of this "fable and endless genealogy," which Paul taught the church not to heed, is foundational to American secular government. For it is Julius Ascanius, grandson of Venus and claimed ancestor of the original Caesar, who inspired *"ANNUIT COEPTIS,"* the upper motto on the flip side of the Great Seal of the United

CHAPTER 20   AMERICAN GRAFFITI

States. The phrase, which the U.S. Department of State interprets to mean "God hath favored this undertaking," was spoken by young Julius Ascanius in the Ninth Book of Virgil's *Aeneid*.

The scene is a battleground. The Trojans are outnumbered and fearful. Young Julius Ascanius takes a position in front of his shrinking countrymen. He looks up at an evil giant named Remulus, King of the Rutulus. Remulus mocks the Trojans for sending a boy to fight him. While the giant quakes with derisive laughter, Julius slips an arrow onto his bowstring and cries toward the heavens:

> Almighty Jupiter, favor this rebellious undertaking (*AUDACIBUS ADNUE COEPTIS*)! Each year, I shall bring to thy temple gifts in my own hands, and place a white bullock at thy altar!

Jupiter then hisses an arrow from the sky that strikes Remulus in the head with such force that it passes clean through his temples. The Trojans "raise a cheer and laugh aloud; their hearts rise toward the stars." Apollo, from his throne of cloud, shouts the gnostic credo: "By striving so, men reach the stars, dear son of gods and sire of gods to come!"

A thrilling story. And one that leaves no doubt as to the identity of the god who favored the undertaking of the United States. It was a pagan deity, the god of Julius Ascanius, and not the God of the Bible. Surely, if Congress had wanted to show that the new nation was underwritten by Yahweh, God of the Bible, it could have referred to the boy-downs-giant story told in the Old Testament. Who doesn't know David and Goliath? Charles Thomson's biblical scholarship could easily have produced a motto based on I Samuel 17:47, where David says to Goliath:

"The Lord saves not with sword and spear: for the battle is the Lord's, and He will give you into our hands!"

Reduced to an original-language motto at least as comprehensible as *"ANNUIT COEPTIS,"* the passage might have appeared in the Seal as the Hebrew

והוה מלחמה

or even in translation, *"THE BATTLE IS THE LORD'S."*

But establishing a national government directly on biblical scripture was not the intent, I believe, of the founding fathers. Far more useful to them, and acceptable to the souls they knew would be populating America in good time, were the fabulous vanities of Roman religion. These souls required the sacred icons of burgeoning humanity and uninhibited sexual energy, legends that inspired hotblooded heroism and patriotism. Consent to images of this character presumed *obedience* to the omnipotent intelligence hovering inscrutably above the *ESTABLISHMENT* of ancient, stone-heavy, well-ordered pyramidic hierarchy.

LESS than four years after his deification, Julius Caesar was assassinated by an executive conspiracy. For another four years, civil war raged as two of the assassins, Brutus and Cassius, struggled for control against Caesar's immediate successor, a Triumvirate comprised of Lepidus, Marc Antony, and Caesar's adopted son (his biological grand-nephew), Caius Octavian Capias.

The Triumvirate defeated the assassins only to war against each other. Poets lamented that Rome, against whom no foreign enemy had ever prevailed, was being destroyed by the strength of her own sons. Obligations of every kind dissolved. Class fought against class. A fog of guilt and despair settled in. The poets yearned for escape beyond the world's borders, to a place of innocence and peace, perhaps to a new order of things. In his book about Rome's revolution from republic to Babylonian autocracy, Oxford historian Ronald Syme writes:

> The darker the clouds, the more certain was the dawn of redemption. On several theories of cosmic economy it was firmly believed that one world-epoch was passing, another was coming into being. The lore of the Etruscans, the calculations of

CHAPTER 20   AMERICAN GRAFFITI

astrologers and the speculations of philosophers might conspire with some plausibility and discover in the comet that appeared after Caesar's assassination the sign and herald of a new age. Vague aspirations and magical science were quickly adopted for purposes of propaganda by the rulers of the world. Already coins of the year 43 BC bear symbols of power, fertility and the Golden Age.[s]

The most influential and enduring celebration of Golden Age optimism was Virgil's prophetic-sounding *Fourth Eclogue*. This work was addressed to one of Virgil's chief benefactors, Caius Asinius Pollio, who was Consul (roughly equivalent to the office of President) when Caius Octavian, Antony, and Lepidus were reconciled in 40 BC by the Peace of Brindisi. Pollio, who represented Octavian at the Brindisi negotiations, introduced Virgil to Caius Maecenas, the media mogul of his day. He had risked his fortune supporting Julius Caesar's rise to absolute dictatorship, and he would risk no less to put Caesar's adopted son, Caius Octavian, in the same place. He scouted and subsidized the most highly talented artists, sculptors, and poets to create a totally new kind of communication. Virgil gave him the most for his money. Virgil developed a new "civic" literature whose pious rhetorical style gently guided public opinion toward accepting the rule of a deified Babylonian autocrat. In writing the *Fourth Eclogue,* Virgil borrowed heavily from the messianic verses of Isaiah, whose writings were freely accessible through the Jewish rabbis of Rome:

> Behold, a virgin shall conceive, and bear a son, and call his name 'God With Us'.... [Isaiah 7:14] For unto us a child is born, unto us a son is given: and the government shall be upon his shoulder: and his name shall be called Wonderful, Counsellor, The mighty God, The everlasting Father, The Prince of Peace. [9:6]

Six hundred years after Isaiah, Virgil solemnly announced in the *Fourth Eclogue* that the Prince of Peace would be produced by the unrolling of a New World Order *("NOVUS ORDO SECLORUM")*:

Now returns the Golden Age of Saturn, now appears the Immaculate Virgin. Now descends from heaven a divine Nativity. O! Chaste Lucina [Goddess of Maternity], speed the Mother's pains, haste the glorious Birth, and usher in the reign of thy Apollo. Thy consulship, O Pollio, shall lead this glorious Advent, and the *new world order [NOVUS ORDO SECLORUM]* shall then begin to roll. Thenceforth whatever vestige of Original Sin remains, shall be swept away from earth forever, and the Son of God shall be the Prince of Peace!

The billionaire Maecenas exploited the *Fourth Eclogue* in the media as though it were a divine summons for Caesar's adopted son Octavian to take the throne and begin sweeping the world free of Sin. A fabulous resume of Octavian was already going around – about how a thunderbolt had blasted the city wall of his birthplace, Velitre, just prior to his birth. And how the priests interpreted this to be Jupiter's way of saying the future ruler of the world would arise from the spot. And about how the Senate, upon hearing this, had decreed that all male babies should be executed. And how Octavian was saved by his mother, who pilfered the stone tablet on which the decree was engraved.

Octavian's mother was Atia of the family of Marius, Atia Maria, a vestal virgin, niece of Caius Maria, the man who would become Julius Caesar. When Octavian reached the age of twelve, great-uncle Caius became his legal father through adoption. Three years later, in Octavian's fifteenth year, his adoptive father was deified as Julius Caesar, *Pontifex Maximus*. That's when the propagandists of Maecenas got busy promoting the Son's divine origins – about how the child was born September 28, 63 BC in humble circumstances: the butler's pantry at his grandfather's mansion at Velitre. About how he had been conceived on December 25 by Apollo, who came in serpent form and impregnated the virgin Atia Maria as she lay sleeping on the floor of the Apollonian temple. About how, just prior to the child's advent, the virgin Maria had dreamed that her body was scattered to the stars and encompassed the universe. About how her husband, too, had dreamed that from within her shone the bright beams of the sun, which

CHAPTER 20   AMERICAN GRAFFITI

then "rose from between her thighs." About how the toddler Octavian's head was often seen being licked by golden solar flames.

The propaganda circulated the story of how the great astrologer Theogenes, when told Octavian's birth sign (Capricorn), rose and flung himself at the lad's feet. Theogenes knew the astrological ruler of Capricorn was Saturn, whose second Golden Age was at hand – Saturn, the celestio-mythical Father-God of Rome and father of Jupiter. Octavian, as the incarnation of Jupiter, would be ruled by Saturn, the most dictatorial house in the zodiac, terrible for his restriction, limitation, control, even to the excesses of fornication and cannibalizing of his own children. No wonder Theogenes flung himself at Octavian's feet!

In 28 BC, twelve years after the publication of the *Fourth Eclogue*, Octavian entered Rome triumphantly as the Prince of Peace. Like Julius had done, the new *Pontifex Maximus* received a new and holier name, Caesar *Augustus* ("since sanctuaries and all places consecrated by the augurs are known as 'August,'" according to Suetonius). And like Julius, he was hailed as "Son of God." Historian Alexander Del Mar describes the universal acceptance of the divine Octavian in these excerpts from his landmark exposition of Roman political deification, *The Worship of Augustus Caesar* (1899):

> In the firm establishment of the Messianic religion and ritual, Augustus ascended the sacred throne of his martyred sire and was in turn addressed as the Son of God *(Divi filius)*, whilst Julius was worshiped as the Father.... This claim and assumption appears in the literature of his age, was engraved upon his monuments and stamped upon his coins.... It was universally admitted and accepted throughout the Roman empire as valid and legitimate, according to chronology, astrology, prophecy, and tradition.... His actual worship as the Son of God was enjoined and enforced by the laws of the empire, accepted by the priesthood and practised by the people.... Both *de jure* and *de facto* it constituted the fundamental article of the Roman imperial and ecclesiastical constitution.
>
> As supreme pontiff of the Roman empire, Augustus lawfully

acquired and exercised authority over all cardinals, priests, curates, monks, nuns, flamens, augurs, vestal virgins, temples, altars, shrines, sanctuaries and monasteries, and over all religious rites, ceremonies, festivals, holidays, dedications, canonizations, marriages, divorces, adoptions, benefices, wills, burying grounds, fairs, and other ecclesiastical subjects and matters.... The common people wore little images of Augustus suspended from their necks. Great images and shrines of the same god were erected in the highways and resorted to for sanctuary. There were a thousand such shrines in Rome alone.

Augustus wore on his head a pontifical mitre surmounted by a Latin cross, an engraving of which, taken from a coin of the *Colonia Julia Gemella,* appears in Harduini, *de Numiis Antiquis* [1689], plate I.... The images of Augustus upon the coins of his own mintage, or that of his vassals, are surrounded with the halo of light which indicates divinity, and on the reverse of the coins are displayed the various emblems of religion, such as the mitre, cross, crook, fishes, labarum, and the Buddhic or Bacchic or Dionysian monogram of PX [the Greek *chi-rho,* "Cairo," site of the great pyramid].

The Augustan writers furnished materials showing that [Augustus'] Incarnation was the issue of a divine father and mortal mother, that the mother was a wife-virgin, that the birth occurred in an obscure place, that it was foretold by prophecy or sacred oracle, that it was presaged or accompanied by prodigies of Nature, that the divinity of the child was recognized by sages, that the Holy One exhibited extraordinary signs of precocity and wisdom, that his destruction was sought by the ruling powers, that his miraculous touch was sufficient to cure deformity or disease, that he exhibited a profound humility, that his deification would bring peace on earth, and that he would finally ascend to heaven, there to join the Father.

So universally were his divine origin and attributes conceded, that many people, in dying, left their entire fortunes to his sacred personal fisc, in gratitude, as they themselves expressed it, for having been permitted to live during the incarnation and earthly sojourn of this Son of God. In the course of twenty years he thus inherited no less than 35,000,000 gold aurei [nearly $1 billion at 1996 values].... Many potentates bequeathed him not

CHAPTER 20   AMERICAN GRAFFITI

only their private fortunes, but also their kingdoms and people in vassalage.... The marble and bronze monuments to Augustus still extant contain nearly one hundred sacred titles. Among them are Jupiter Optimus Maximus, Apollo, Janus, Quirinus, Dionysus, Mercurius, Volcanus, Neptunus, Liber Pater, Savus [Saviour], and Hesus.

At his death, Senator Numericus Atticus saw his spirit ascend to Heaven. The Ascension of Augustus is engraved upon the great cameo, from the spoils of Constantinople, presented by Baldwin II to Louis IX, and now in the Cabinet of France. A facsimile of it is published in Duruy's *History of Rome*....

America's Great Seal, with its obsessive fidelity to Caesarean Rome, cannot represent a nation more moral than the source of its scripture. The icons and mysterious cabalistic language of this Seal introduce a preposterous Babylonian gospel. Taken seriously (and shouldn't a government's solemn statements be taken seriously?), the Seal's gospel teaches that America's high spiritual purpose is to assist in the resurrection of the Son of God's mutilated parts from the evil slime of human flesh. It tells us that already the Holy Virgin has rescued the Son's Sacred Heart from the slime – *E PLURIBUS UNUM*, "one from many" – and has placed it high in the vault of Heaven, as her five-pointed celestial path describes for all to see. It calls for America to exert fervent sexual energy so that the Son's many parts on earth might be reunited with the *UNUM* in Heaven. It promises that America will rise toward the pure light of sinlessness and Godliness, into eternal life as part of the solar body of the Son – the Sun – of God. It signifies that this cosmic resurrective process is administered by a pyramidic hierarchy conceived in ancient Babylon, exported to Asia Minor, and bequeathed to Rome. At the top of the hierarchy sits an unseen chieftain, an unknown superior, a God of the Seal who possesses universal intelligence and authority over every soul who confederates with, or subscribes to, the Seal.

The God of the Seal wields the fasces to sweep the earth clean of the last traces of Original Sin. He is assisted by a new priestly order, a "new world order" charged with destroying all individual identity deemed inconsistent with the resurrection to godliness. Uncooperative governments and dissident citizens alike are cut down by arts of war so frugal that the liquidation increases popular faith in the fasces. Because they function in a Golden Era of Saturn, the chief and his hierarchy can be depended upon to mimic Saturn's strictness, cruelty, licentiousness, even cannabilism as the situation requires. To the charge that such is impossible in America, one comparison should be sufficient. No sooner was Augustus Caesar deified than he sacrificially murdered three hundred Senators in Perugia to atone for the assassination of his adoptive father Julius.⁹ Likewise, no sooner was an American president inaugurated than he, as Commander-in-Chief of the armed forces, authorized the sacrificial murder of nearly a hundred misguided Christians near Waco, Texas, to atone for what? A growing popular disenchantment with federal government?

What the Seal of the United States of America represents, to anyone who takes it seriously, is a *Ministry of Sin*. A speech by Jesuit political scientist Michael Novak, published in the January 28, 1989 issue of *America*, the weekly magazine of American Jesuits, sums it up eloquently enough:

> The framers wanted to build a "novus ordo" that would secure "liberty and justice for all".... The underlying principle of this new order is the fact of human sin. To build a republic designed for sinners, then, is the indispensable task.... There is no use building a social system for saints. There are too few of them. And those there are impossible to live with!... Any effective social system must therefore be designed for the only moral majority there is: sinners.

In the next chapter, we shall examine how faithfully the founding fathers reconstructed Babylonian Rome on the banks of the Potomac.

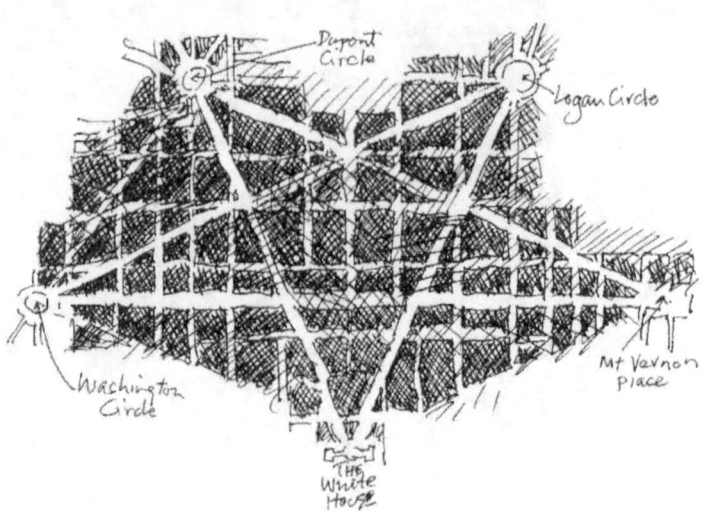

L'Enfant's celebrated plan of Washington, D.C., conforming to the cabalistic Baphomet, arranged so that the Goat's mouth (see below) is the White House.

Chapter 21

JUPITER'S EARTHLY ABODE

R OME'S GOD OF GODS, Jupiter, was served in temples called *capitolia,* from the Latin word meaning "head." As we've seen, America's temple of Jupiter was erected on land that had been known as "Rome" for more than a hundred years before it was selected by Daniel Carroll's "federal city" committee from properties owned by Carroll himself.

Subdividing the federal city, or District of Columbia, into plats was the task of an artistic Parisian engineer named Pierre-Charles L'Enfant. According to Dr. James Walsh in his book *American Jesuits,* L'Enfant got the job through the intercession of his priest, John Carroll.

L'Enfant was a Freemason. He subdivided the city into a brilliant array of cabalistic symbols and numerics. Perhaps his best-known device is the pattern that is discerned when a straight line is drawn from the White House along Connecticut Avenue to Dupont Circle, then along Massachusetts Avenue to Mount Vernon Square, then back across K Street to Washington Circle, then up Rhode Island Avenue to Logan Circle, then along Vermont Avenue back to the White House. What results is a perfect pentagram, the Queen of Heaven's eight-year-and-one-day celestial journey.

But L'Enfant's pentagram points downward, forming the shape of Baphomet, the gnostic "absorption-into-wisdom" goat's-head icon of the Knights Templar. Gnostic historian Manly Hall says the upside-down pentagram "is used extensively in black magic" and "always signifies a perverted power." The Baphomet imposed upon the federal city by Pierre-Charles L'Enfant puts the mouth of this "perverted power" exactly at the White House.

The Congressional Medal of Honor, depicting Aeneas within a Baphomet, rewards Americans who have sacrificed most for the Roman ideal.

The presence of perverted power is underscored in L'Enfant's numbering of Washington's city blocks.[1] The 600 series of blocks runs in a swath from Q Street North through the Capitol grounds down to the mouth of James Creek below V Street South. All the numbers between 600 and 699 are assigned to blocks within this swath, except for the number 666. That number is missing from the map. It must have been secretly affixed to the only unnumbered section of blocks in the 600 series. That section, we find, includes the Capitol grounds that once were called "Rome." Of course, 666 is the "number of the name of the Beast" mentioned in the thirteenth chapter of Revelation. If America's temple of Jupiter sits upon the Beast named 666, could it be that the true founding fathers soberly recognized Congress as "the great whore" of Revelation 17:1?

The Latin historians Ovid, Pliny, and Aurelius Victor all tell

CHAPTER 21   JUPITER'S EARTHLY ABODE

us that the prehistoric name for Rome was *Saturnia,* "city of Saturn." Saturnia's original settlers came from the east, from Babylon. In the Babylonian (or Chaldean) language, according to Alexander Hislop, Saturnia was pronounced "Satr" but spelled with only four characters, *Stur.* Now, Chaldean, like Hebrew, Greek, and to a limited extent Latin, had no separate numbering system. Their numbers were represented by certain characters of their alphabet. The cabalah derives its power from mathematical energies conveyed from these languages. Hislop reported a phenomenon that he said "every Chaldee scholar knows," which is that the letters of Stur, Rome's earliest name, total 666:

$$S = 60; T = 400; U = 6; R = 200 := 666$$

Hislop further reported that Roman numerals consist of only six letters, D (500), C (100), L (50), X (10), V (5), and I (1) – we ignore the letter M, signifying 1,000, because it's a latecomer, having evolved as shorthand for two D's. When we total these six letters, we discover a startling link with the Beast of Revelation embedded in the very alphanumeric communication system of the Romans:

$$D = 500; C = 100; L = 50; X = 10; V = 5; I = 1 := 666$$

Demonism, black magic, and perverted power formatted into the streets of the federal city? Well, as Michael Novak observed, the indispensable task of the founding fathers was to build a republic designed for sinners. Not all sinners can be governed with a loving call to repentance, with reason, logic, patience, understanding, and forgiveness. Sin develops cunning villains who steal, rape, destroy, torture, and kill. A republic designed for sinners must be up to the villainy of its meanest subject. This is why the great revolutionary pamphleteer Tom Paine candidly characterized human government as "a necessary *evil.*" A government must necessarily be as evil as the evildoers it's charged with regulating or it cannot protect the innocent. This just stands to reason. Scripture shows the principle as divinely ordained. Yes, God ordained the evil to rule the good. But the details of this gracious ordination, which we'll be examining presently, are so embarrassing to the flaunted piety of rulers that they must be concealed in cabalah.

Soon after completing his master plan for the federal city, Pierre-Charles L'Enfant became embroiled in a flagrant dispute with Bishop Carroll's high-ranking brother Daniel. The young engineer wanted an avenue to go where Daniel Carroll intended to build his new manor house. When Carroll refused to build elsewhere, L'Enfant ordered the work crew to tear the new house down. Before any significant damage could be done, however, President Washington dismissed L'Enfant. The whole affair diverted attention away from the demonic symbolism in L'Enfant's designs while conveniently removing him from public scrutiny. Again, blown cover as cover. The designs were executed by his successor, Andrew Ellicott, without significant alteration.

The formal creation of Jupiter's American Abode on Wednesday, September 18, 1793 was a jubilant affair. President George Washington and Capitol Commissioner Daniel Carroll departed from the White House, marching side by side. They led a magnificent parade "with music playing, drums beating, and spectators rejoicing in one of the grandest Masonic processions which perhaps ever was exhibited on the like important occasion."[2]

Arriving at the construction site on Lot 666, Commissioner Carroll presented "Worshipful Master Washington" a large silver plaque engraved with the following words:

> This South East corner stone, of the Capitol of the United States of America in the city of Washington, was laid on the 18th day of September, in the thirteenth year of American Independence, in the first year of the second term of the Presidency of George Washington, whose virtues in the civil administration of his country have been as conspicuous and beneficial, as his military valor and prudence have been useful in establishing her liberties, and in the year of Masonry, 5793, by the President of the United States, in concert with the Grand Lodge of Maryland, several lodges under its jurisdiction, and Lodge No. 22 from Alexandria, Virginia.

CHAPTER 21   JUPITER'S EARTHLY ABODE

President Washington then descended into a builder's trench prepared for the Capitol's foundations, laid the plaque on the ground, and covered it over with the cornerstone. The cornerstone was a massive rock cut from Eagle Quarry, a property in Acquia Creek, Virginia, owned by the family of Daniel Carroll's nephew, Robert Brent.

Then, just as the priests of Jupiter might have blessed their *capitolia* two millennia ago three Worshipful Masters consecrated the stone with corn, wine, and oil. Washington and the other Masters stepped out of the trench, and joined the assembled throng to listen to a patriotic speech. Afterward, said the *Gazette*,

> the congregation joined in reverential prayer, which was succeeded by Masonic chanting honors, and a 15-volley from the artillery. Then the participants retired to a barbecue, at which a five-hundred-pound ox was roasted, and those in attendance generally partook, with every abundance of other recreation....

Reading of the barbeque, I was reminded of the passage in the *Aeneid* where Julius Ascanius promised a sacrifice to Jupiter for favoring his rebellious undertaking: "I shall bring *to thy temple gifts in my own hands, and place a white bullock at thy altar...*" Could it be that the silver plaque, the corn, the wine, the oil, the chanting, the roasted ox, and the reverential prayer were the fulfillment of that promise – a burnt sacrifice to Jupiter, on the altar of his *capitolium*, upon land called Rome, land formally consecrated by *Pontifex Maximus* to the protection of the goddess Venus? Historians who believe the government of the United States was founded by Christians will certainly disagree. But the ceremony, as reported in the press, was anything but Christian. Moreover, the plaque itself reckoned time according to three systems: (1) the years of independence of the United States, (2) the years of George Washington's administration, and (3) the years of Freemasonry. It completely ignored the system that reckons time in the years of Jesus Christ.[3]

Eight years after the sacrifice, Congress met in the Capitol for the first time. Washington gave the appearance of a Roman

Catholic settlement. The most imposing houses in the city belonged to Daniel Carroll and his brother-in-law, secularized Jesuit priest Notley Young. The city's mayor was Carroll's nephew, Robert Brent, who was also purveying stone for most of the federal buildings. Over on the west side of town stood Georgetown College, established by Bishop John Carroll in 1789. Georgetown quickly became the foremost incubator of federal policy, foreign and domestic. It is still administered by the Society of Jesus.

Seal of the Black Papacy's Georgetown University, as it appears today on a campus security vehicle. The Roman eagle grasps both the world and the cross, State and Roman Catholic Church, the banner in its beak declaring "UTRAQUE UNUM," – "Both together."

When Pope Pius VII restored the Society of Jesus in August 1814, former presidents John Adams and Thomas Jefferson exchanged comments. "I do not like the resurrection of the Jesuits," wrote Adams.

> They have a general now in Russia [Tadeusz Brzozowski], in correspondence with the Jesuits in the United States, who are more numerous than everybody knows. Shall we not have swarms of them here, in the shape of printers, editors, writers, schoolmasters, etc? I have lately read Pascal's letters over again [Blaise Pascal's *Provincial Letters* helped bring about the suppression of the Society], and four volumes of the History of the Jesuits. If ever any congregation of men could merit eternal perdition on earth and in hell it is this company of Loyola. Our system, however, of religious liberty must afford them an asylum; but if they do not put the purity of our elections to a severe trial, it will be a wonder.

CHAPTER 21 JUPITER'S EARTHLY ABODE

Jefferson's reply indicates (or pretends) that he, too, was unaware that America's destiny had been shaped by the hands of Rome: "Like you, I disapprove of the restoration of the Jesuits, which seems to portend a backward step from light into darkness."

During the next seventy years, Superior Generals John Roothaan (1829-1853) and Pieter Jean Beckx (1853-1883) would pump the Society up to its original greatness, swelling the membership from a few hundred to more than thirteen thousand. In those same seventy years, the Protestants who had fought for America's independence would vastly diminish in proportion to the influx of fresh Roman Catholic refugees from European tyrannies. (There is evidence these tyrannies were Jesuit-fed, for the express purpose of populating America. Perhaps a new scholarship will investigate more thoroughly than I have time or inclination for.)

As America's public became increasingly Catholic, Generals Roothaan and Beckx were able to signify Washington's debt to the black papacy with much bolder iconographic and architectural symbols. This little-explored material is the subject of our next chapter.

Persephone, Goddess of the U.S. Capitol Dome.
Said by her priests to have been immaculately conceived, she was renamed "Freedom" for American consumption. Abducted by Hades, son of Saturn, she ruled the dead and all else that is within the earth, namely metals and precious stones.
At daybreak of May 9, 1993, helicopters lowered the Queen of the dead to ground level for her first cleaning in more than a century. The author attended this historic event and snapped the above photograph. Significantly, May 9, 1993 was…
Mother's Day.

Chapter 22

THE IMMACULATE CONCEPTION

A s IF IT WEREN'T enough that Christopher Columbus had dedicated the New World to her, and that Andrew White had dedicated Maryland to her, and that Bishop Carroll had dedicated his See of Baltimore to her, the 1846 convention of American Roman Catholic bishops declared the Virgin Mary to be "Patroness of the United States."

The first two years under her patronage enriched the national government considerably. The Oregon territory and the Southwest joined the Union. As did California, with its bursting veins of gold. The blessings had their downside, however. They precipitated a corresponding increase in intersectional tensions that erupted in a devastating interstate bloodbath some historians call the Civil War. In that war, the Patroness of the United States dealt as cruelly with the enemies of her protectorate as the vengeful goddess Ishtar did with the enemies of ancient Babylon.

In February 1849, "Pio Nono" (the popular name for Pope Pius

IX; there's a boulevard named after him in Macon, Georgia) issued an encyclical that colored America's Patroness with the fearsome aspects of Ishtar. The encyclical, entitled *Ubi primum* ("By whom at first"), celebrated Mary's divinity, saying:

> The resplendent glory of her merits, far exceeding all the choirs of angel, elevates her to the very steps of the throne of God. Her foot has crushed the head of Satan. Set up between Christ and his Church, Mary, ever lovable, and full of grace, always has delivered the Christian people from their greatest calamities and from the snares and assaults of all their enemies, ever rescuing them from ruin.

Holy as she may sound, a Satan-bashing, life-saving Virgin Mary is a fabrication of sacred pagan tradition. The Bible does prophesy that Satan's serpentine head will be violated. But not by Mary. At Genesis 3:15, we read God's vow that Satan's seed will be bruised by the seed of Eve. It may be argued that Eve's seed was Mary. But according to the inspired understanding of the apostles, it was Jesus. At Romans 16:20 Paul promises a Roman congregation that "the *God of peace* shall bruise Satan under your feet." Nor was Mary given power to deliver people from their enemies. Only the "one mediator between God and men, the man Christ Jesus" (1 Timothy 2:5), "a name which is above every other name" (Philippians 2:9), is a divinely-authorized deliverer.

No, the Mary of *Ubi Primum* will not be found anywhere in the Bible. But then Pio Nono, the first pope ever to be declared Infallible, carried about a rather famous theological ignorance. His private secretary, Monsignor Talbot, defended Pio's ineptitude in a letter cited by Jesuit author Peter de Rosa in his *Vicars of Christ:*

> As the Pope is no great theologian, I feel convinced that when he writes his encyclicals he is inspired by God. Ignorance is no bar to infallibility, since God can point out the tight road even by the mouth of a talking ass.

The truth of the matter, according to J.C.H. Aveling, is that

CHAPTER 22 THE IMMACULATE CONCEPTION

throughout Pius IX's long reign (1846-1878), most of his theology was written by Jesuits. On December 8, 1854, Superior General Beckx brought three hundred years of Marian devotion to a glorious climax with *Ineffabilis Deus* ("God indescribable"), the encyclical defining the Immaculate Conception, the extrascriptural doctrine that Mary, like Jesus, was conceived and remained free of sin:

> The doctrine which holds that the most blessed Virgin Mary, in the first instant of her conception, by a singular grace and privilege granted by Almighty God, in view of the merits of Jesus Christ, the Saviour of the human race, was preserved free from all stain of original sin, is a doctrine revealed by God and therefore to be believed firmly and constantly by all the faithful.

Ineffabilis Deus mobilized the United States Congress to pass extraordinary legislation. Congress became suddenly obsessed with expanding the Capitol's dome. According to the official publication *The Dome of the United States Capitol: An Architectural History* (1992), "Never before (or since) has an addition to the Capitol been so eagerly embraced by Congress." Within days of Pio Nono's definition of the doctrine of Immaculate Conception, legislation was rushed through Congress that effectively incorporated the new Vatican doctrine into the Capitol dome's crowning architectural platform, its cupola.

A week following *Ineffabilis Deus* Philadelphia architect Thomas Ustick Walter, a Freemason, completed his drawings for the proposed dome. It would be surmounted by a bronze Marian image which would come to be recognized as "the only authorized Symbol of American Heritage."[1] Her classical name was *Persephone,* Graeco-Roman goddess of the psyche, or soul, and leading deity in the Eleusinian Mysteries of ancient Greece. Persephone was abducted by Saturn's son, Hades, and made queen-consort of his dominion, the underworld. Persephone was distinguished for her *Immaculate Conception* – described by Proclus, head of the Platonic Academy in Athens during the fifth century of the Christian era, as "her undefiled transcendency in her generations." In fact, most of the statues of Persephone in the Christianized Roman Empire had been simply re-identified and re-consecrated as the Virgin Mary by missionary adaptation.

Congress appropriated $3,000 for a statue of Persephone. President Franklin Pierce's Secretary of War, Jefferson Davis, awarded the commission to a famous young American sculptor named Thomas Crawford. Crawford lived and worked in Rome. His reputation had been established with a statue of Orpheus which, when exhibited in Boston in 1843, was the first sculptured male nude to be seen in the United States. Since another of Persephone's ancient names was *Libera* ("Liberty"), Crawford named his Persephone "Freedom." His work has worn this title ever since.

After two years of labor in the shadow of the Gesu, Crawford completed a plaster model of Freedom. Her right hand rested on a sword pointing downward. Her left hand, against which leaned the shield of the United States, held a laurel wreath. She was crowned with an eagle's head and feathers mounted on a tiara of pentagrams, some inverted, some not. When ultimately cast in bronze, Freedom would reach the height of nineteen feet, six inches – a sum perhaps deliberately calculated to pay homage to the work's final destination, the Beast of Revelation at Lot 666, for nineteen feet, six inches works out to 6+6+6 feet, 6+6+6 inches.

Freedom would stand upon a twelve-foot iron pedestal also designed by Thomas Crawford. The upper part of the pedestal was a globe ringed with the motto of the Bacchic Gospel, *E PLURIBUS UNUM,* while the lower part was flanked with twelve wreathes (the twelve Caesars?) and as many fascia, those bundles of rods wrapped around axe-blades symbolizing Roman totalitarianism.

Crawford wanted his sculpture to be cast at the Royal Bavarian Foundry in Munich (where Randolph Rogers' great ten-ton bronze doors leading to the Capitol rotunda were cast), while architect Thomas U. Walter preferred Clark Mills' foundry, near Washington. Their transatlantic argument ended abruptly when Crawford died in London on September 10, 1857, of a tumor behind his left eye.

In that same year, 1857, the United States Supreme Court

CHAPTER 22   THE IMMACULATE CONCEPTION

handed down *Dred Scott vs. Sanford,* a decision which most historians agree ignited the Great American Civil War. The opinion was written by the Roger Brooke Taney, who succeeded John Marshall as Chief Justice. A devout Roman Catholic "under the influence of the Jesuits most of his long life" according Dr. Walsh's *American Jesuits,* Taney held that Negro slaves and their descendants could never be State citizens and thus could never have standing in court to sue or be sued. Nor could they ever hope to be United States citizens since the Constitution did not create such a thing as "United States citizenship."

Taney's opinion was widely suspected of being part of a plot to prepare the way for a second Supreme Court decision that would prohibit *any* state from abolishing slavery. American slavery would become a permanent institution. This is exactly what happened, although not quite as everyone supposed it would. First, slavery was abolished by the Thirteenth Amendment (1865). Then, the Fourteenth Amendment (1868) created a new national citizenship. Unlike State citizenship, which was denied to Negroes, national citizenship was available to *anyone* as long as they subjected themselves to the jurisdiction of the United States – that is, to the federal government, whose seat is the District of Columbia, "Rome." What is so remarkably Jesuitic about the scheme that proceeded out of Roger Taney's opinion is that slavery was *sustained* by the very amendment that supposedly *abolished it.* Amendment Thirteen provides for the abolition of "involuntary servitude, except as punishment for crime whereof the party shall have been duly convicted." In our time the federally regulated communications media, with their continually exciting celebration of violence and drug-use, have subtly but vigorously induced youthful audiences to play on a minefield of complementary criminal statutes. The fruit of this collaboration is a burgeoning national prison population of men and women enslaved constitutionally. American slavery has become a permanent institution.

Reaction to Taney's decision animated Abraham Lincoln to immerse himself in abolitionist rhetoric and challenge Stephen A. Douglas for the Senate in 1858....

MEANWHILE in Rome, Freedom's plaster matrix was packed into five huge crates and crammed, with bales of rags and cases of lemons, into the hold of a tired old ship bound for New York, the *Emily Taylor*. Early on, the *Emily* sprang a leak and had to put in to Gibraltar for repairs. Once the voyage was resumed, stormy weather caused new leaks. Despite attempts to lighten her load by jettisoning the rags and the citron, things got so bad she put in to Bermuda on July 27, 1858. The crates were placed in storage, and the *Emily* was condemned and sold.

In November, Lincoln lost his bid for Douglas' seat in the Senate, and in December, another ship, the *G.W. Norton,* arrived in New York harbor from Bermuda with some of the statuary crates. By March 30, 1859 all five crates had been delivered to the foundry of Clark Mills on Bladensburg Road, on the outskirts of the District of Columbia, where the process of casting the Immaculate Virgin into bronze and iron was begun.

Lincoln opposed Stephen Douglas again in 1860, this time for the Presidency, and this time victoriously. The northern states rejoiced. The southern states, fearing Lincoln would abolish slavery, prepared to secede. "The tea has been thrown overboard!" shouted the *Mercury,* of Charleston, South Carolina, capital of American Scottish Rite Freemasonry. "The revolution of 1860 has been initiated!"

By Lincoln's inauguration in March 1861, six states had seceded from the Union. In April, General Pierre Beauregard, a Roman Catholic who resigned his Superintendency of West Point to join the Confederacy, fired on the United States military enclave at Fort Sumter and brotherly blood began flowing. Jefferson Davis, who five years earlier had commissioned Crawford to sculpt the Immaculate Virgin, served as President of the rebellious Confederate States of America. In historian Eli N. Evans' book on Judah P. Benjamin, I happened upon a strange and interesting link between Davis and the Vatican.

While a young Protestant student at the Roman Catholic monastery of St. Thomas College in Bardstown, Davis had pled to be received into the Catholic faith, but was "not permitted to con-

CHAPTER 22 THE IMMACULATE CONCEPTION

vert." He remained "a hazy Protestant" until his confirmation into the Episcopal Church at the age of fifty. Despite outward appearances of rejection, the Confederate President maintained a vibrant communion with Rome. No one was more aware of this than Abraham Lincoln. At an interview in the White House during August 1861, Lincoln confided the following to a former law client of his, a Roman Catholic priest named Charles Chiniquy, who published the President's words in his own autobiography, *Fifty Years In The Church of Rome:*

> "I feel more and more every day," [stated the President] "that it is not against the Americans of the South, alone, I am fighting. It is more against the Pope of Rome, his Jesuits and their slaves. Very few Southern leaders are not under the influence of the Jesuits, through their wives, family relations, and their friends.
>
> "Several members of the family of Jeff Davis belong to the Church of Rome. Even the Protestant ministers are under the influence of the Jesuits without suspecting it. To keep her ascendency in the North, as she does in the South, Rome is doing here what she has done in Mexico, and in all the South American Republics; she is paralyzing, by civil war, the arms of the soldiers of liberty. She divides our nation in order to weaken, subdue and rule it....
>
> "Neither Jeff Davis nor any one of the Confederacy would have dared to attack the North had they not relied on the promises of the Jesuits that, under the mask of democracy, the money and the aims of the Roman Catholics, even the arms of France, were at their disposal if they would attack us. I pity the priests, the bishops, and monks of Rome in the United States when the people realize that they are in great part responsible for the tears and the blood shed in this war. *I conceal what I know, for if the people knew the whole truth, this war would turn into a religious war, and at once, take a tenfold more savage and bloody character....*[2]

The Great Civil War rampaged for another year. In autumn of 1862, the Confederacy's invasion of the Union was defeated at the Battle of Antietam in Sharpsburg, Maryland. As if in celebration, the Immaculate Virgin was moved from the foundry and brought to the grounds of the Capitol construction site. The lower floors of the building were teeming with the traffic of a Union barracks and makeshift hospital. Above all this loomed Thomas U. Walter's majestic cast-iron dome, patterned after that of St. Isaac's Cathedral in St. Petersburg, Russia.

In March 1863, Freedom was mounted on a temporary pedestal, "in order that the public may have an opportunity to examine it before it is raised to its destined position," as stated in Walter's Annual Report dated November 1, 1862. One would expect photographers to be climbing all over themselves to make portraits of "the only authorized Symbol of American Heritage" while she was available for ground-level examination. America's pioneer photographer, Matthew Brady, had shot a comprehensive record of the Capitol under construction, including portraits of both Capitol architect Thomas U. Walter and Commissioner of Public Buildings Benjamin B. French. But neither Brady nor anyone else photographed Freedom while she was available for closeups.[3] Why? Was there a fear that perhaps some Protestant theologian might raise a hue and cry about the pagan icon about to dominate the Capitol building?

Apparently, not too many Protestants ever examined Freedom at ground-level. The District of Columbia was still virtually a Roman Catholic enclave. Moreover, the nation in 1863 had been drastically reduced in size. The secession of the southern states had left only twenty-two northern states, and these twenty-two were heavily populated by Catholic immigrants from Europe and Ireland. "So incredibly large," we recall from Sydney E. Ahlstrom's *Religious History of the American People*, "was the flow of immigrants that by 1850 Roman Catholics, once a tiny and ignored minority, had become the country's largest religious communion." Thus, Crawford's towering goddess was being examined mostly by Roman Catholic eyes, eyes that could not help but see in her the dreadnaught Mary described by Pius IX in *Ubi Primum:* "ever lovable, and full of grace, set up between Christ and his Church, always delivering the Christian people from their greatest calami-

CHAPTER 22   THE IMMACULATE CONCEPTION

ties and assaults of all their enemies, ever rescuing them from ruin."

The war rapidly advanced to conclusion while Freedom held forth on the east grounds of the Capitol. The Union forces under Burnside lost to Lee at Fredericksburg, but Rosecrans defeated the Confederates at Murfreesboro, and Grant took Vicksburg. In summer, Lee's second attempt to invade the North failed at Chancellorsville and Gettysburg. By fall, Grant won the Battles of Chattanooga and Missionary Ridge with Sherman and Thomas. By the end of November 1863, the Union had taken Knoxville, and the Confederacy found its resources exhausted and its cause hopelessly lost.

On November 24, a steam-operated hoisting apparatus lifted the Immaculate Virgin Mother of God's first section to the top of the Capitol dome and secured it. The second section followed the next day. Three days later, in a driving thunderstorm, the third section was secured. The fourth section was installed on November 31.

At quarter past noon December 2, 1863, before an enormous crowd, the Immaculate Virgin's fifth and final section was put into place. The ritual procedure for her installation is preserved in Special Order No. 248 of the War Department. Her head and shoulders rose from the ground. The three-hundred-foot trip took twenty minutes. At the moment the fifth section was affixed, a flag unfurled above it. The unfurling was accompanied by a national salute of forty-seven gunshots fired into the Washington atmosphere. Thirty-five shots issued from a field battery on Capitol Hill. Twelve were discharged from the forts surrounding the city. Reporting the event in the December 10 issue of the *New York Tribune,* an anonymous journalist echoed the qualities that Pius IX had given Mary:

> During more than two years of our struggle, while the national cause seemed weak, she has patiently waited and watched below: now that victory crowns our advances and the conspirators are being hedged in, and vanquished everywhere, and the bonds are being freed, she comes forward, the cynosure of thousands of eyes, her face turned rebukingly toward Virginia

and her hand outstretched as if in guaranty of National Unity and Personal Freedom.

If *Tribune* readers felt more nationally united and personally free because Freedom was glaring at rebellious Virginia and outstretching her hand to her beloved America, they were deceived. For the goddess faced in *precisely the opposite direction!* She faced *east,* as she does to this day, faced east across Maryland, the "land of Mary," across the Atlantic, toward her beloved Rome. In fact, neither hand outstretches in any direction. Both are at rest, one on her sword, the other holding the laurel wreath.

And her forty-seven Jupiterean thunderbolt-gunshots? They were a tribute to the Jesuit bishop who had placed the District of Columbia under her protection. For December 2, 1863 tolled the *forty-seventh year from John Carroll's last full day alive, December 2, 1815!*

ONCE the pressures of the installation were over, an exhausted but relieved Capitol Architect Thomas U. Walter wrote his wife, Amanda, at their Philadelphia home, to say that "her ladyship looks placid and beautiful – much better than I expected, and I have had thousands of congratulations on this great event, and a general regret was expressed that you were prevented from witnessing this triumph." Someone else had missed the triumph, too, someone who by all the rules of protocol should have been there no matter what: the Commander-in-Chief of the United States Armed Forces, whose War Department had engineered the whole Capitol project from top to bottom – *President Abraham Lincoln.* At noon on the day the temple of federal legislation was placed under the patronage of Persephone, Freedom, Wife of Hades, Queen of the Dead, Immaculate Virgin of Rome, Protectress of the Jesuits, Protectress of Maryland, and Patroness of the United States, the record shows that Lincoln sequestered himself inside the White House, touched with "a fever." A telling detail.

But the sacred iconography was still not complete. The engineers began now preparing the interior of the dome, its canopy, for a massive painting Congress had approved back in the spring of

CHAPTER 22   THE IMMACULATE CONCEPTION

1863. This painting would depict George Washington undergoing the secular version of the canonization of Ignatius Loyola. It contains even more data useful to our understanding of the character and provenance of American government. We examine this masterpiece in our next chapter.

APOTHEOSIS OF WASHINGTON.
(Photograph: Architect of the Capitol)

Chapter 23

THE DOME OF THE GREAT SKY

""It's like St. Peter's!"
— Tourists describing the rotunda fresco,
as quoted in the official Capitol guidebook
WE, THE PEOPLE

ARCHBISHOP JOHN HUGHES of New York sailed for Rome in the autumn of 1851, just after Congress had approved funds to enlarge the Capitol. Hughes had laid the cornerstone for St. Patrick's Cathedral in Manhattan, and had helped the Jesuits establish Fordham University in Westchester. Now he was helping them decorate the Capitol's interior.

In Rome, Superior General John Roothaan introduced the Archbishop to Constantino Brumidi, an artist boasting an impressive list of credits. Brumidi had painted an acclaimed portrait of Pio Nono (which the Vatican still exhibits), an Immaculate Conception in the little Sanctuary of the Madonna dell'Archetto in Via San Marcello, and the restoration of three sixteenth-century frescoes in the Vatican Palace. Brumidi was good. General Roothaan had determined to make him America's Michaelangelo. Archbishop Hughes let it be known that Brumidi would be welcome to paint some frescoes in churches of the New York bish-

Constantino Brumidi

opric. General Roothaan then went about making the Vatican's artist acceptable to American egalitarianism.

Soon after the Archbishop left Rome for New York, the Vatican accused Constantino Brumidi of criminal acts. Supposedly, Brumidi had committed crimes during his membership in the Republican Civil Guard under Giuseppe Mazzini, the Italian Freemason who had recently led ill-fated nationalist revolutions against the papacy. These crimes were said to have included (a) refusing to fire on his Republican friends, (b) looting several convents, and (c) participating in a plot to destroy the Catholic Church — acts reasonably sure to merit a hero's welcome in Protestant America. The Architect of the Capitol's unpublished dossier on Brumidi, which I was permitted to examine during 1993, notes that "several widely divergent accounts suggest that Constantino Brumidi himself was probably the source of at least some of the legends."

Vatican justice found the artist guilty in December 1851 and sentenced him to eighteen years in prison. Several weeks later the sentence was reduced to six years. And within two months, on March 20, Pio Nono himself quietly granted Brumidi an unconditional pardon. General Roothaan then placed his newly-created republican freedom fighter on a ship bound for America.

Brumidi arrived in New York harbor on September 18. On November 29 he filed for state citizenship with the New York Court of Common Pleas. Although the invite had come to paint New York churches, there was no such work to be done there. Instead, the Archbishop sent him to Mexico City — by way of Washington, D.C. In Washington, Brumidi was received by his Masonic brother Thomas Ustick Walter. For two years Walter had been serving President Millard Fillmore as Architect of the Capitol. When the cornerstone for Walter's Capitol expansion plan was

CHAPTER 23 THE DOME OF THE GREAT SKY

laid on the Fourth of July of 1851, President Fillmore and Commissioner of Public Buildings Benjamin B. French, who also happened to be "Grand Master of the Masonic fraternity," led a colorful ceremony. Washington's popular *National Intelligencer* reported the occasion was "welcomed by a display of National flags and the ringing of bells from the various churches and engine houses."[1]

Thomas Walter needed Constantino Brumidi. An edifice as important as the United States Capitol – like the palaces of Augustus and Nero, the Baths of Titus and Livia, the Loggia of Raphael at the Vatican – required the most noble and permanent interior decoration possible. Only fresco painting, in which pigments are mixed with wet mortar immediately before application to the surface, would suffice. And only Constantino Brumidi, of all the artists living in America, knew how to paint fresco. But the dome was not yet ready to be frescoed. So the artist was routed to the sunny, Italianate climate of Mexico City to enjoy life, to ponder his subject matter at a casual pace, to wait for the call.

Two years later, on December 28, 1854, less than three weeks following Pio Nono's decree of the doctrine of Immaculate Conception, Constantino Brumidi appeared in the office of Montgomery C. Meigs, Supervising Engineer of the Capitol extension project. The Capitol's unpublished dossier on Brumidi relates that as the two men conversed in broken French, Brumidi struck Meigs as "a lively old man with a very red nose, either from Mexican suns or French brandies." The immediate upshot of their conversation was a commission to paint a fresco covering an elliptical arch at one end of Meigs' office in the Capitol. It was the first fresco ever painted in the United States, as well as Brumidi's first in five years. The fresco celebrated the coming Civil War in terms of Roman history. According to the commission's report it depicted "a senator, who points to Rome and appeals to Cincinnatus to come to the help of his country." Cincinnatus, the fifth-century BC Roman dictator, was called to defend Rome twice, first from foreign invaders, then from his own common people. Likewise, American heroes first defended their Rome against foreign British invaders, and were now about to be called to defend the same Rome against her own seceding states.

Brumidi completed the Cincinnatus in March 1855. Meigs invited various Congressmen to behold it. They were impressed. Thomas U. Walter was "much delighted." On March 20, Jefferson Davis approved of the Cincinnatus and authorized Meigs to negotiate a salaried contract with Brumidi. Constantino Brumidi's lifetime career spent decorating the Capitol began on a salary of $8.00 a day. His contract allowed him to accept other artistic projects but not to leave Washington. In November 1855 he began a canvas painting of the Blessed Virgin for St. Ignatius' Jesuit church in Baltimore, but was not present for its December 4th installation, on the occasion of the Feast of the Immaculate Conception.

IN the summer of 1862, even as Thomas Crawford's statue was being cast at the Mills foundry, Thomas U. Walter wrote to Brumidi asking him to paint something monumental "in real fresco" to cover the 4,664-square-foot inner surface of the Capitol's dome. Three weeks later, Brumidi submitted sketches of something he entitled "Apotheosis of Washington." The word *"apotheosis"* was then commonly understood by its definition in Webster's 1829 Dictionary:

> Apotheosis – the act of placing a prince or other distinguished person among the heathen deities. This honor was often bestowed on illustrious men of Rome, and followed by the erection of temples, and the institution of sacrifices to the new deity.

Walter responded ecstatically to the "Apotheosis," writing the artist that "no picture in the world will at all compare with this in magnitude." He praised the design before Worshipful Master and Commissioner of Buildings Benjamin French as "probably the grandest, and the most imposing that has ever been executed in the world." French enthusiastically agreed, adding that the Secretary of Interior was also greatly impressed. Final approval of "Apotheosis" at a price of $40,000 came on March 11, 1863, just

CHAPTER 23   THE DOME OF THE GREAT SKY

as the Immaculate Virgin was being placed on her temporary pedestal on the Capitol's east grounds. "Frustrating delays in manpower," according to official histories, would hold the fresco in abeyance until December 1864.

On April 9, 1865, Richmond fell and the Confederacy surrendered to Ulysses S. Grant. Less than a week later, on the evening of April 14 at Ford's Theatre, during an instant of hilarious laughter, one of the country's leading actors, John Wilkes Booth, cried out an oath summarizing the liberation theology of Cardinal Robert Bellarmine: *"Sic Semper Tyrannis"* ("Always this [i.e., death] to tyranny"), and fired a shot into the head of President Abraham Lincoln. *Sic Semper Tyrannis* is also the motto of Virginia, then considered a State in rebellion. Might Booth's cry have been intended to give the assassination the look of an official act of the Confederacy, much in the way Lee Harvey Oswald's much-touted sympathy for Cuba initially gave the Kennedy assassination the look of communist revenge? An illusion of official Confederate responsibility for a beloved president's assassination justified the elaborately cruel revenge which the federal government inflicted upon the southern states in order to bring all the states under the jurisdiction of Washington D.C. (The inferiority of states to the federal "Rome" is expressed in the law of flag. Wherever state and national flags are flown together, the national is always higher.)

Booth had associated with seven people who were brought to trial less than a month following the assassination. It was not a civilian trial but a special eleven-man military tribunal appointed by President Andrew Johnson called "The Hunter Commission."

Counsel for the defendants objected to the Commission, arguing that the military had no jurisdiction over civilians, and therefore the proceeding was unconstitutional. The objection was overruled and the trial moved forward. Within seven weeks, the Commission (a two-thirds majority, not the unanimity required of a civilian jury) found four of the conspirators guilty. On July 7, 1865 they were hanged.

"The great fatal mistake of the American government in the prosecution of the assassins of Abraham Lincoln," wrote Rev.

Charles Chiniquy, the excommunicated priest whom Lincoln had successfully defended in his early law career (see note 2, Chapter 22), was to cover up the religious element of that terrible drama. But this was carefully avoided throughout the trial.[2]

The religious element — the fact that all seven of the conspirators were devoted Roman Catholics — was carefully avoided because of who controlled the trial. As Commander-in-Chief of the armed forces, it was Johnson himself who quite constitutionally reigned supreme over the Hunter Commission. But Johnson was also a Freemason, which meant that he followed the wise directives of the Unknown Superior. Thus, the real power behind the Hunter Commission was Superior General Pieter Jean Beckx, a relatively young Belgian who was a great favorite of Pio Nono, Pope Pius IX, the only head of state in the world to recognize the Southern Confederacy as a sovereign nation. Obedient to the will of General Beckx, President Johnson issued an executive order closing the courtroom to the working press. At the end of each day, officials would ration to selected reporters from the Associated Press news carefully evaluated to keep "the religious element" out of the public consciousness.

Charles Chiniquy

Charles Chiniquy tirelessly investigated the assassination. After the conspirators were executed, he went incognito to Washington and found that;

> not a single one of the government men would discuss it with me except after I had given my word of honor that I would never mention their names. I saw, with a profound distress, that the influence of Rome was almost supreme in Washington. I could not find a single statesman who would dare to face that nefarious influence and fight it down.[3]

CHAPTER 23   THE DOME OF THE GREAT SKY

One official told him: "This was not through cowardice, as you might think, but through a wisdom you ought to approve, if you cannot admire it." Had there not been censorship, had the witnesses been pressed a little further, "many priests would have been compromised, for Mary Surratt's [one of the four executed conspirators] house was their common rendezvous; it is more than probable that several of them might have been hanged."

Thirty years after the assassination, a member of the Hunter Commission, Brigadier General Thomas M. Harris, published a small book revealing that Lincoln's assassination had actually been a Jesuit murder plot to extirpate a Protestant ruler. Harris stated:

> It is fact well established that the headquarters of the conspiracy was the house of a Roman Catholic family, of which Mrs. Mary E. Surratt was the head; and that all of its inmates, including a number of boarders, were devoted members of the Roman Catholic Church. This house was the meeting place, the council chamber, of Booth and his co-conspirators, including Mrs. Mary E. Surratt, and her son, John H. Surratt, who, next to Booth, were the most active members of the conspiracy.[4]

Commissioner Harris went on to relate that Mary Surratt's son John had been a Confederate spy for three years, "passing back and forth between Washington and Richmond, and from Richmond to Canada and back, as a bearer of dispatches." John's mentor during this period was a Jesuit, Father B.F. Wiget, president of Gonzaga College and a priest noted for his sympathies for the Confederacy. John introduced Father Wiget to his mother and the priest became Mary Surratt's confessor and spiritual director. As well, Father Wiget gave spiritual direction to the famous John Wilkes Booth who, though "a drunkard, a libertine, and utterly indifferent to matters of religion," was spiritually attracted to him. "The wily Jesuit, sympathizing with Booth in his political views, and in the hope of destroying our government, and establishing the Confederacy ... was able to convert him to Catholicism." Hard evidence of that conversion was found on the assassin's corpse: "On examination of Booth's person after his death, it was found that he was wearing a Catholic medal under his vest, and over his heart."

At the conspiracy trial, Father Wiget testified to Mary Elizabeth Surratt's "good Christian character." Even assuming her complicity in the assassination, Wiget as a Jesuit could truthfully say Surratt was a good Christian simply by reserving mentally (a) that by "Christian" he meant "Roman Catholic;" (b) that under the terms of the *Directorium Inquisitorum* (see Chapter 8), "Every individual may kill a heretic;" and (c) that President Lincoln was twice a heretic: for his Protestantism and for his having successfully defended an excommunicated priest.

But Mary after all "kept the nest that hatched the egg," as President Johnson put it, and was hanged. Conditional to her death sentence was a provision that a petition for mercy would be attached and sent to Johnson. By execution day, July 7, 1865, Surratt's daughter Anna had heard nothing from the President. Distraught, she appeared at the White House to beg him for clemency. Two government men stood in her way. Preston King and Senator James Henry Lane denied her access to the President, who later declared he had never received any petition for mercy. The following November, Preston King drowned, his body laden with weights. In March, Senator Lane shot himself. (In the judgment of one modern investigator, "Some person or persons were apparently determined that Mary Surratt should not live."[5]) Shortly thereafter, the Supreme Court rendered a landmark decision that would have won all the conspirators a jury trial. *Ex parte Milligan* held that military courts have no jurisdiction over civilians. *Milligan* lent Mary Surratt's death at the hands of Protestants an aura of tragedy and Catholic martyrdom.

Charles Chiniquy obtained important testimony supporting the widely held suspicion of Jesuit responsibility for the assassination. He received from Rev. Francis A. Conwell, Chaplain of the first Minnesota Regiment, a sworn affidavit saying that on April 14, 1865, he was visiting St. Joseph, Minnesota, location of a Roman Catholic seminary. Rev. Conwell swore that at about six o'clock that evening the man in charge of the seminary, a storekeeper by the name of J.H. Linneman, told him and another visitor, Mr. H.P. Bennett, that President Lincoln had "just been killed."

CHAPTER 23   THE DOME OF THE GREAT SKY

The next day, Rev. Conwell journeyed ten miles to the town of St. Cloud. As soon as he arrived, he asked the hotelier, Mr. Haworth, if he had heard any news of a presidential assassination. Mr. Haworth had heard nothing, as St. Cloud had neither railroad nor telegraph. On the following morning, April 16th, on his way to preach a sermon in church, Rev. Conwell was handed a copy of a telegram brought up by stagecoach from Anoka, Minnesota. The telegram announced that President Lincoln had been assassinated on Friday evening at about nine o'clock.

On the morning of Monday the 17th, Rev. Conwell hurried to St. Paul and reported to the newspaper that in St. Joseph he had been informed of President Lincoln's assassination three hours before the event took place. The paper published his report.

"We have now before us," wrote Commissioner Harris, positive evidence that these Jesuit Fathers, priests of Rome, engaged in preparing young men for the priesthood away out in the village of St. Joseph, in far off Minnesota, were in correspondence with their brethren in Washington City, and had been informed that the plan to assassinate the President had been matured, the agents for its accomplishment had been found, the time for its execution had been set, and so sure were they of its accomplishment, that they could announce it as already done, three or four hours before it had been consummated. The anticipation of its accomplishment so elated them that they could not refrain from passing it around ... as a piece of glorious news.

MEANWHILE, through the Lincoln assassination and its aftermath, the Vatican's artist, Constantino Brumidi, along with some seventy French and Italian assistants, applied pigmented mortar to the interior canopy of the Capitol dome. They were still working when the first session of the Thirty-ninth Congress met on December 4, 1865. Not until the following January did the scaffolding come down. When it did, viewers were awestruck by what they beheld. Brumidi had crowned the ceiling of America's legislative center with a glorious, panoramic visualization from Book VI of Virgil's *Aeneid,* where Aeneas' blind father, Anchises, explains *NOVUS   ORDO   SECLORUM*:

"Here is Caesar, and all the line of Julius, all who shall one day pass under the dome of the great sky. This is the man, this one, of whom so often you have heard the promise, Caesar Augustus, son of the deified, who shall bring once again an Age of Gold to Latium, the land where Saturn reigned in early times. He will extend his power beyond the Garamants [Africans] and Indians, over far territories north and south of the zodiacal stars, the solar way...."

The epicenter of "Apotheosis of Washington" is a solar orb, the Sun-God into which Augustus Caesar was said to have been absorbed when his body died. From the Capitol's highest interior point Augustus radiates his golden light outward and downward to the next in the "line of Julius," the deified George Washington. The god Washington occupies the judgment seat of heaven, sword of Justice firmly clasped in his left hand. Basking in the light of Augustus – *Pontifex Maximus* – he rules "over far territories north and south of the zodiacal stars, the solar way." Like his Caesarean forebears, Washington is God, Caesar, Father of his Country.

On the right hand of the Father sits Minerva, holding the emblem of Roman totalitarianism, the fasces. Minerva, we recall, was the virgin goddess of the Sacred Heart – it was she who rescued the heart of the Son of God, and placed it with Jupiter in heaven. She was called "Minerva" when praised for her justice and wisdom. When praised for her beauty and love, Minerva was known as Venus, the Queen of Heaven. She and Venus were often identified with each other, just as statues of both were reconsecrated "Mary" through Roman Catholic missionary adaptation. Minerva's most persistent role in ancient paganism was *Dea Benigna,* "The Mediatrix." She heard the prayers of sinful mortals and passed them on to Jupiter, in the same way the Roman Mary is believed to pass Catholic prayers on to Christ.

Completing the circular composition around the solarized Augustus are thirteen nubile goddesses. These are the original States. They dance weightlessly in space, supporting a white banner inscribed with the soul of the Bacchic Gospel, *"E PLURIBUS UNUM."* Above the head of each State-goddess floats a magical white pentagram.

CHAPTER 23   THE DOME OF THE GREAT SKY

Beneath all this celestial revelry, Brumidi painted more Roman gods mingling with American mortals. Here is Vulcan, the god of fire and craftsmanship, planting his foot on a cannon, while his workers prepare munitions and weapons of death and destruction. And over here Neptune rises with his trident from the sea in a horse-drawn scallop-shell chariot. And here the wise Mediatrix communicates with American scientists Benjamin Franklin, Samuel F. B. Morse, inventor of the Code, and Robert Fulton, inventor of the steamship.

The States

And here, the Goddess Immaculately Conceived, the Dreadnaught Mary. Wearing the pentagrams and eagle headdress of Thomas Crawford's statue atop the dome's exterior, she mobilizes her sword and shield against a pack of fleeing sinners labeled "Tyranny" and "Kingly Power." Jupiter's mascot, the Roman eagle, glides just behind her clutching a bunch of thunderbolts in his talons. Innocent in her flowing scarlet cape, the Goddess is situated *exactly* beneath the deified George Washington, coming between him and the embattled viewing public gazing up from ground level. It is the graphic realization of Pio Nono's *Ubi primum,* which decreed the Virgin Mary was "set up between Christ and his Church, always delivering the Christian people from their greatest calamities and from the snares and assaults of all their enemies."

The Virgin pursues evildoers

The eagle gliding behind Mary explains the otherwise inscrutable seal of the United States Justice Department, which contains a wingspread eagle surrounded by the motto *"QUI PRO DOMINA JUSTITIA SEQUITUR"* ("He who follows the Goddess Justice"). Persephone, or Minerva the Mediatrix, when judging the sinfully dead in

Hades was called *Justitia,* or Justice. The *"HE"* of the Justice Department's motto identifies the eagle, symbol of Rome. Rome follows the Goddess Justice – that is, the Immaculately Conceived Mother of God in her judicial capacity.

A rainbow sweeps across the lower quadrant of the Dome of the Sky from Benjamin Franklin to a young boy wearing a Smurf-cap and a toga. The boy attends a goddess who reclines on a large horse-drawn reaper. She is Persephone's mother Ceres, who was reconsecrated by early missionary adaptation as Anna, mother of the Virgin Mary. The golden boy is officially designated "Young America." Although Brumidi has hidden the boy's face from us, he deserves our careful scrutiny for one very important reason. Bearing the name "America," he is the only element in the sacred national iconography that defines the character of the *American person as perceived by government.*

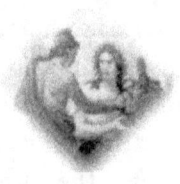

YOUNG AMERICA

Young America's Smurf-cap is a style of headgear known as the "Phrygian cap." Phrygia was a district in the Kingdom of Pergamum. We remember Pergamum. It was the middle point in the transfer of Babylonian religion westward to Rome. *Phrygia* is a Greek word meaning "freemen" (our English word "free" comes from the first syllable, "phry-"). Phrygian caps were given to freed Roman slaves to indicate their new liberated status. Roman law regards liberty as a conditional status. Once *granted* by a patron, it could be *revoked* at any time for cause. Phrygian-cap freedom, then, means liberty (freed Roman slaves, by the way, were called *"liberti"*) to please Caesar. We remember from Chapter 8 how Ignatius described such freedom in Section 353.1 of his Exercises: "We must put aside all judgment of our own, and keep the mind ever ready and prompt to obey in all things the hierarchical Church." Of course, those *liberti* bold enough to protest what their superiors commanded lost their freedom, no matter how lucid and

CHAPTER 23   THE DOME OF THE GREAT SKY

reasonable their own judgment might have been. They were reverted to slavery. Since the advent of the Febronian State Church, the reversion of protestant *liberti,* or Protestants, to slavery has been so methodically insidious that it's hardly noticeable. The shackles are psychological, humanely fitted by increasing varieties of spiritual exercise. Like Aeneas, Anchises, Julius Ascanius and their Trojan followers, most Americans are indeed Phrygian-cap freemen, free to sacrifice their individuality to the greater glory of Rome.

The Black Obelisk of Calah, which stands in the Babylonian-Assyrian Wing of the British Museum, records the great accomplishments of the ninth-century BC god-king Shalmaneser II. In a scene depicting various monarchs paying obeisance to Babylon, we

THE FREEDOM CAP
Jehu submitting to Shalmaneser

see one monarch kneeling before Shalmaneser, worshiping him. Shalmaneser in turn offers a sacrifice to an eight-pointed star set within a bird's wings and tail-feathers. Inscriptions identify this kneeling monarch as King Jehu of Israel. Remarkably, according to the New Catholic Encyclopedia, Jehu's likeness here is the only known contemporaneously-rendered portrait of a biblical personage. More remarkably, Jehu is wearing the Phrygian cap. Like Brumidi's Young America, Jehu's liberty is subject to the mood of his god-king.

The Bible confirms the testimony of the Black Obelisk. At II Kings 10:31 we read: "Jehu took no heed to walk in the law of the Lord God of Israel with all his heart." Scripture further tells us that

Jehu worshiped the golden calf, a sacred Babylonian icon made fashionable in tenth-century-BC Israel by Jehu's predecessor, Jeroboam. Jeroboam renounced "the law of the Lord God of Israel" and instituted... *democracy.* Democracy opened the Israelite priesthood, originally appointed by Yahweh exclusively to the family of Levi, to all applicants. Consequently, Yahweh's priesthood was infiltrated by non-believers and foreign sympathizers. They prepared the way for Jehu to make of himself a Phrygian freeman, obligated to concur with obedience of the understanding in all things which his superior, Shalmaneser II, commanded – exactly as the Black Obelisk explains in lucid visual terms. As a direct result of Jehu's departure from the God of Israel, the Israelite nation began falling apart. It was ultimately destroyed by Caesarean Rome, the legitimate heir to Shalmaneser's Babylonian authority as it passed down through Pergamum.

Running throughout this cosmic Battle of the Faiths is a highly refined cabalah involving the concept of "golden calf." The word "calf" in Hebrew, the language of Jehu and Jeroboam, is עגל, pronounced *"eagle."* Whereas Jehu gave his people Shalmaneser's golden עגל to worship, the Church Militant has trained the American public to worship Rome's golden *eagle,* which surmounts every flagpole. Could it be that if we show respect, affection, or loyalty toward the national eagle we create the presumption of worshiping the golden calf, and so alienate ourselves from the God of the Bible and in the vacuum find ourselves under the rule of the Church Militant?

ACCORDING to J.C. Judson, in his *Biography of the Signers of the Declaration of Independence,* as General Washington was planning his famous expedition against Cornwallis at Yorktown, "the army was destitute, the government treasury was empty, her credit shivering in the wind." Suddenly, a miracle in the annals of philanthropy occurred. Robert Morris, Superintendent of Finance, the highest officer in the United States under the Articles of Confederation (1781), personally raised eighty cannon and a hundred pieces of field artillery. In addition, he raised "all other necessary

CHAPTER 23 THE DOME OF THE GREAT SKY

supplies not furnished from other sources" and became personally responsible to the amount of $1,400,000 upon his own notes, which were promptly paid at maturity. This enabled the American army to give the finishing stroke to the revolution, and triumph, in victory complete, over a proud and merciless foe.

So goes a historian's version of how Robert Morris saved America. The *official* version is revealed in Constantino Brumidi's "Apotheosis of Washington." Here we see Superintendent Morris gazing up from his accounts ledger at yet another Roman deity. We recognize the deity from the familiar *caduceus* in his right hand, from the winged sandal he's thrust to within kissing distance of Morris' lips, and from the shadowy bag of gold he tantalizingly dangles in Morris' face. The deity is Mercury, the Psychopomp, the Trickster, the patron deity of commerce, deceivers, and thieves. Mercury, the brilliant, lovable Pied-Piper deity who deceives the souls of sinful humanity into following him exuberantly down into the oblivion of Hades. Just as Sebastiano Ricci's painting subtly established Mercury as the guiding spirit of modern Roman Catholicism, Brumidi's painting acknowledges the same deity's ascendancy over the fulfillment of the American Revolution.

Mercury & Robert Morris

Amazing stuff, these pictures. And like so many of the testimonies presented in this book – the supremacy of the Church Militant, the publication of Sun-Tzuan strategies in a western language, the names, the numbers, the dates, the locus and layout of the federal city, the architecture, the statuary, the monuments, the emblems, the frescoes, the ceremonies – they come not from the Trickster's victims, *but from the Trickster himself.* It's as if the point of the trick is to warn the victim beforehand, in words and pictures, that he or she is about to be tricked. A con is much sweeter when the mark actually *consents* to the con. That way, the Trickster's conscience is clear.

CONSTANTINO Brumidi continued decorating the Dome of the Great Sky well into his seventies. In 1879, at the age of 74, while painting "Penn's Treaty with the Indians" on the Rotunda frieze, he slipped from a scaffold. Dangling fifty-eight feet from the marble floor, he held on until help came. He escaped a deadly fall. But the shock of the experience killed him a few months later.

Chapter 24

THE MARK OF CAIN

> "The mark of Cain is stamped upon our foreheads.
> Across the centuries, our brother Abel has lain in blood which we drew, and shed tears we caused by forgetting Thy love."
> —Pope John XXIII, A Prayer (1960),
> cited in *VICARS OF CHRIST*

WE LIVE IN THE New World Order, just as people under Augustus Caesar did. Not a future thing to be feared or avoided, the New World Order is a present reality to be identified, understood, and dealt with in a way most pleasing to God. It was God, after all, who established the New World Order. We can read about it in the Bible. In fact, the Bible is the only record we have that publicly and truthfully sets forth the essentials of the Order's origins and development through time.

The Bible records the great decisive events in the progress of human life up to the close of the first century AD. Creation of earth and the fullness thereof, creation of man and woman, their turning away from God, the first conception, the first birth, the first sacrifice, the first murder, the first insignia, the first city, the first and only great flood, the surviving family and its peculiar relationship through time with God – all of this momentous data is given in the Bible with a stark truthfulness that is invariably supported, often to the surprise of many, by the results of scientific inquiry. The writers of the Bible, Israelite prophets inspired by their God Yahweh, held no monopoly on reporting these events. Priests of other nations reported them, too. But in doing so, they cunningly adapted them to fit prevailing administrative needs. The result of their adaptations is what we call mythology.

One very persistent myth, based on a crucial event accounted for in the Bible, explained to people under Babylonian rulership the divine origin of their government. This was the myth of Marduk.[1]

The Naram-Sin [Enoch] Stele, with Annu's name over the mountain-top.

The myth of Marduk begins with Annu, "the head deity of Babylonian mythology,"[2] looking down upon earth in dismay. The land is in chaos, overrun by flood-waters and monstrous serpents. Annu senses that bringing order to such chaos is a job for Marduk, the first-born son of the moon goddess Ea. So Annu summons Marduk and asks him to organize the earth. Marduk agrees to the task, but "only on the condition that he be made first among the gods and that his word shall have the force of the decree of Annu."[3] Annu accepts Marduk's terms and vests him with "the powers and insignia of kingship – and Marduk's word was declared to have the authority of Annu." Armed with divine power, Marduk goes to earth and separates dry land from sea. He polices the monsters, and any evildoer foolish enough to oppose him receives the wrath of God.

The result of Marduk's ordination was depicted in the Stele of Naram-Sin, now in the Louvre. In this very ancient Babylonian monument, Annu is shown imbuing Naram-Sin (Enoch to the

CHAPTER 24   THE MARK OF CAIN

Marduk policing the evildoer Tiamat with thunderbolts. From a bas-relief on the walls of the palace of the Assyrian king Assur-nasir-pal (9th century bc at Calah, now in the British Museum). Note the repeated Annu signature in the sacred hem of Marduk's garment. And the scythe under his left arm: is the artist subtly revealing that Marduk was once a farmer?

Hebrews) with power over a mass of other beings. Annu's name, seen in the tip of the stele, is the cuneiform symbol for "heaven," the double-cross, or ✳.

Marduk wears the Annu signature like a cop with his badge. It makes him a god. In fact, the ordination-of-power iconography of ancient Babylonian nations was never without it. Even today (see Appendix: "Fifty Centuries of the Annu Signature"), we find it in the flag of Great Britain, said to be the union of St. Andrew's Scottish cross and St. George's English cross. We find it prominently displayed in the decor of government buildings, especially courtrooms. It forms the motif for much of the decorative architecture of the U.S. Supreme Court Building, interior and exterior. The pavement surrounding the Obelisk of Caligula in St. Peter's Piazza, where the multitudes stand to receive papal edicts and blessings, is inlaid with a gigantic Annu signature. No doubt about it: a very ancient symbol has remained consistently identified with the presence of rulership. Could it be that a symbol of so much power is based on a myth? Or is it based on the fact from which the myth sprang?

THE sensitive Bible-reader immediately sees in the myth of Marduk a missionary adaptation of the biblical account of Cain. The two protagonists are remarkably similar. Both Cain and Marduk were firstborn sons of mothers bearing almost the same name: Marduk, son of Ea; Cain, son of Eve. Both firstborns were appointed to rule over evil, albeit for different reasons: Marduk because of his heroism, Cain because of his own wickedness.[4] So that they might move effectively among evildoers, both were given protective seals of immunity by the God of Heaven. God said to Cain,

> Therefore whosoever slayeth Cain, vengeance shall be taken on him sevenfold. And the Lord set a mark upon Cain, lest any finding him should kill him.[5]

In Marduk's case, the evildoers were chaotic beings ruining Annu's earth. Cain's evildoers were persons who might slay him because he had become a homeless trespasser. The Bible details exactly why Cain became homeless. His farm refused to yield harvests because he had defiled the soil with the blood of his brother. Cain "rose up against Abel his brother and slew him." We're not told why. It may have been jealous rage, and it may not. Nothing in Scripture indicates that Cain hated Abel. The most we know of their relationship is that "Cain talked with his brother," and afterward, in a field, murdered him.[6] Nor are we given details of the murder, except that it was bloody.[7] The blood is an important clue as to motive.

We know that Cain was first crestfallen then angry at God for preferring Abel's sacrifice to his own.[8] Abel, the shepherd, sacrificed lambs from his flock.[9] Cain, the farmer, apparently thinking sacrifice was about returning the best of his productivity to God, sacrificed the best of his harvest. God found Cain's sacrifice offensive and Abel's pleasing.[10] Elsewhere in Scripture we learn why. It involves a principle that is very difficult for many of us to comprehend. The principle is this: *without shedding of blood there is no*

CHAPTER 24   THE MARK OF CAIN

remission of sin.[11] Abel pleased God because he shed blood, the blood of sacrificial animals.

The great teaching of the Bible is that the death sentence mankind has inherited from the original breaking of God's Law by Cain's parents ("Thou shalt not eat of the fruit...") is pardonable only by death, by the extreme act of *shedding blood fatally.* This teaching is the bedrock of the Old Testament and the whole point of the New. In the Old Testament, the people of God were pardoned the sinfulness inherited from Adam by shedding the blood of animals, as Abel had dutifully done. In the New, the people of God were pardoned this same sinfulness by doing exactly as Cain had done, *shedding the blood of a man.* To this day, according to the Scriptures, all who believe that Jesus Christ's blood has power to remit sins are imputed sinless by God.[12] Imputed sinless, their sentence of eternal separation from God is commuted, and they are given eternal life in Heaven.[13]

Now, Scripture does not tell us that God ever explained the purpose of blood sacrifice to Cain.[14] But we know that God is the greatest of all teachers. And we know he wants the best for mankind. It's unthinkable, then, that He would want Cain ignorant of the life-saving effect of blood sacrifice. He must have taught Cain as thoroughly as he taught Abel. And Cain must have listened attentively, for we know he was anxious to please God – otherwise, why would he have been angry and crestfallen at learning of God's dissatisfaction with his sacrifice? But Cain was more creative than obedient. It's entirely consistent with his character for him to have decided;

> Okay, if it's blood sacrifice He wants, I'll give Him the sacrifice He deserves, a better sacrifice than lambs: I'll give Him the blood *of an innocent man!*

Cain's intent was evil only in that he sought to *improve* on what God had commanded, in the way Saul improved on God's commandment to annihilate the Amalekites by sparing their king and certain valuable livestock.[15] Cain knew the logic of God – he was, after all, the first human being born with the knowledge of good and evil. And we know from what happened to Jesus that God's logic calls for the sacrifice of the only One whose perfect innocence overcame death. In his obsession to *please* God, wouldn't Cain have regarded spilling Abel's blood as the *ultimate* godliness?

What I am suggesting is that, in Cain's mind, Abel was not so much murdered as *sacrificed,* nailed to Annu's very name —

— *hanged upon a cross!* Wouldn't this explain why Scripture shows no evidence that Cain sensed any guilt? Wouldn't it also explain the hundreds of ancient, pre-Christian myths of young shepherds (such as Tammuz, Bacchus, Attis, Mithras) who were slain in cold blood by various villains only to rise from the dead, their shed blood having supposedly propitiated original sin and resurrected them to eternal life? The myths, obviously based on the fact of Abel's crucifixion, all pointed to a *universally anticipated event* foretold by the Israelite prophets: Messiah's death and resurrection, which would pardon the sins of mankind and restore eternal life.

Thus emerges the possibility that the "lamb slain from the foundation of the world" mentioned at Revelation 13:8 might have indeed been Abel, God's first obedient servant. For it is a fact that "the World" – by which the New Testament writers meant the ordering of human institutional systems which God admitted into existence – did actually begin, as we are about to see, in the immediate aftermath of Abel's death. If this is the case, then mankind owes a strange debt to Cain. No Cain, no death of Abel. No death of Abel, no World. No World, no incarnation of God as only begotten Son. No Son of God, no true death and resurrection. No true death and resurrection, no hope of mankind for eternal intimacy with God.

IT was the complaint of an earth outraged by Abel's spilt blood that moved God to banish Cain from his accustomed habitat

CHAPTER 24   THE MARK OF CAIN

forever. Just as Marduk demanded protection from the monsters he had been asked to control, Cain demanded protection from possible assailants in his exile. God graciously accommodated Cain by "set[ting] a mark" upon him which made Cain seven times more powerful than any mortal competitor. The mark served as the very "powers and insignia of kingship" Annu had granted Marduk. It empowered Cain to rule all human beings likely to challenge his protective mark, beings unafraid of Yahweh's name,[16] beings who shared Cain's environs "out from the presence of the Lord."[17]

Armed with his mark, Cain began the rulership of evil. The Bible accounts for Cain's movements after his ordination. He took a wife and sired a son. Then, he built a city and named it after his son, "Enoch."[18] Centuries later, Enoch disappeared under the silt of Noah's flood. It passed from memory to mystery to oblivion, until the 1840s, when archaeologists following the Bible's descriptions of Babylonia began excavating in present-day Iraq. Along the Euphrates River, near Al Khidr, they discovered numerous strata of ancient settlements. The deepest stratum, beneath which there was nothing but bedrock, had called itself Unuk. "Unuk was founded on the oldest bricks," declared one of the leading archaeologists, a renowned classical linguist from Queens College, Oxford, named Archibald Sayce.

Having deciphered and evaluated large numbers of clay tablets from the site, Professor Sayce issued the opinion in 1887 that Unuk was indeed biblical Enoch, the city built by Cain and his son.[19] Lecturing at Oxford, Sayce also pointed out that one of Cain's mythological names was Marduk[20] – an important contribution to the Marduk-equals-Cain hypothesis. Unuk's dominant temple bore the title "house of Annu," further enhancing the probability that Marduk's myth was spun from Cain's murder of Abel. As ruler of Unuk, Cain was known as Sargon – or, as other translators have rendered the spelling, Shargani, Sarrukinu, Sargoni, etc.[21] These variations of Sargon are composites of the Babylonian *shar*, meaning "king" and *gani*, *kinu*, or *goni*, meaning "Cain."[22] It would be hard to say Sargon means anything other than "King Cain."

271

Unuk had been no primitive village. *Encyclopedia Britannica* noted that "transparent glass seems to have been first introduced in the reign of Sargon."[23] Sargon built a metropolis of enormous complexity. But what astonished the archaeologists most was the city's miraculous historical *suddenness*. Unuk seemed to have materialized from out of nowhere:

> We have found, in short, abundant remains of a bronze culture, but no traces of preceding ages of development such as meet us on early Egyptian sites.[24]

The suddenness factor severely challenged those scholars who viewed history through Darwinian anti-biblicalism, which had become the fashion in Jesuit-influenced academic circles. To fit evolutionary theory, Unuk should have evidenced development from a much older civilization. As a contributor to the London Times' prestigious *Historians' History of the World* grumbled,

> Surely such a people as this could not have sprung into existence as a *Deus ex Machina* [a person or thing introduced or appearing unexpectedly so as to provide an artificial or contrived solution to an otherwise insoluble problem]. It must have had its history – a history which presupposes development of several centuries more.[25]

But Unuk as a social organization had no previous history. This maddening circumstance drove the British Museum's H. R. Hall to rationalize that its "ready-made" culture must have been "brought into Mesopotamia from abroad."[26] Modern anti-biblicists find it easier to accept that Unuk's sudden complexity came from other galaxies than from something as simple as... acquiring divine intelligence from biting into a piece of forbidden fruit. Of course, eating the fruit of disobedience is how the Bible explains the suddenness factor. Cain had extraordinary powers because he inherited from his parents the knowledge of good and evil which the Trickster had encouraged them to obtain at the price of eternal life.[27] In Mrs. Bristowe's words: "Cain was born and bred in the

CHAPTER 24   THE MARK OF CAIN

atmosphere of the miraculous; his parents were possessed of supernatural knowledge, some of which must have been imparted to their children."[28]

King Cain was no primitive chieftain. On one of his many autobiographical inscriptions, he boasted that "in multitudes of bronze chariots I rode over rugged lands ... I governed the upper countries," and "three times to the sea I have advanced."[29] A brilliant, well-organized military emperor – the prototypical Caesar – Cain controlled a "vast empire." The Cambridge History tells us he divided his imperium;

> from the [Persian Gulf] to the [Mediterranean], from the rising to the setting of the sun into districts of five double hours march each, over which he placed the 'sons of his palace.' By these delegates of his authority he ruled the hosts of the lands together.[30]

Cain's empire was founded on slavery[31] – the inevitable result of one man's retributive power exceeding all others sevenfold. For the most part, however, it appears that Cain exercised his advantage in the public interest. Professor Sayce tells us that his empire was "full of schools and libraries, of teachers and pupils, and poets and prose writers, and of the literary works which they had composed." Furthermore,

> the empire was bound together by roads, along which there was a regular postal service, and clay seals which took the place of stamps are now in the Louvre bearing the name of Sargon and his son.... It is probable that the first collection of astronomical observations and terrestrial omens was made for a library established by Sargon.[32]

The insignia of power and kingship did not vanish with Cain's death. That Cain built the original city with his son implies that the mark was intended to be an hereditary entitlement. The son's name implies that he received the power of the mark from his father. "Enoch" in Hebrew means "the initiated" – to be inducted by special rites, to be instructed in the rudiments or principles of something." Scripture implies that Enoch and perhaps Cain in turn initiated other deputies and successors. Four generations after Cain's birth, we find Enoch's great-great grandson Lamech still exercising, in fact *augmenting,* the prerogative of divine vengeance:

> Lamech said to his wives, "Adah and Zillah, listen to me; wives of Lamech, hear my words. I have killed a man for wounding me, a young man for injuring me. If Cain is avenged seven times, then Lamech seventy-seven times."[34]

Receiving authority to govern requires taking an oath which binds the initiate to a code of rights and responsibilities. Interestingly, our word "oath" is cognate with the Hebrew אות (pronounced "oath"), which is the word translated "mark" at Genesis 4:15, "the Lord set a *mark* upon Cain." Knowing this, we may accurately say "the Lord put Cain under oath," an oath visibly represented by the various insignia governments display. The mark, then, stands for a covenant between God and Cain. It is not the all-encompassing sort of covenant which God struck with the humbly obedient Abraham – "And I will establish my covenant between me and thee and thy seed after thee in their generations for an everlasting covenant, to be a God unto thee, and to thy seed after thee."[35] Cain's unwillingness to obey the letter of Yahweh's commandments made him unfit for intimacy with the divine. In Cain's own words, "from thy face shall I be hid."[36] The exile covenant was strictly limited to assuring God's vengeance against anyone who would threaten Cain's life. In matters of wisdom, correction, instruction in righteousness, Cain was on his own. He was on his own, also, if he should try to attack the peaceful. *The mark was a covenant of retribution only.*

Early on, Cain saw there was great profit in provoking assailants. The more enemies, the more spectacular the displays of vengeance. The more vengeance, the more justice; the more justice, the more power to Cain; a more powerful Cain could do more excellent public works. Thus, it became essential to the self-interest of the bearer of the mark – which remains to this day a first

CHAPTER 24   THE MARK OF CAIN

principle of ordered government – to provoke and encourage evildoing, particularly the form that manifests itself in rebellion.

Cain terrorized evil with awesome dependability. His faith that God would avenge his enemies made him a highly reliable public protector. Down through the ages, righteous people could live secure in the knowledge that the mark-bearer would stop at nothing to persecute evildoers. This fact is marvelously declared in Scripture. In the seventh century BC, the mark-bearing Babylonians were appointed by God to capture the wayward Israelites and show them some harsh discipline. Israel couldn't understand why God would put a vain, evil Babylonian king over His own chosen people. God explained saying: "See, he is puffed up, and his desires are not upright, but the *righteous shall live by his faith*."[37]

How has the mark managed to remain vibrant for nearly six thousand years? Grand Commander Albert Pike, in his influential *Morals and Dogma*, threw valuable light on the subject. He declared that "from the earliest time," Freemasonry has been the "custodian and depository" of the "symbols, emblems, and allegories ... erected by Enoch."[38] The Commander was careful to say he meant not Cain's son Enoch, but the Bible's other Enoch, Enoch-2, the good Enoch, the Enoch "who walked with God."[39] However, his attempt to dissociate his institution from Cain puts the Commander at variance with Masonic and biblical chronology. For if a biblical Enoch erected the earliest imagery of Freemasonry, it could not possibly have been Enoch-2. It had to have been Enoch-1. Let's examine the chronology.

Enoch-2 was descended from Seth, whom Eve conceived after the death of Abel – "for God, said she, hath appointed me another seed instead of Abel, whom Cain slew."[40] When Eve conceived Seth, Adam was 130 years old.[41] According to the scripturally faithful computations of the Archbishop of Armagh, James Ussher (1581–1656), Adam was created in 4004 BC. Thus, Seth was born in 3874 BC. Genesis 5:6–20 gives us an exact toll of the years between Seth and his great-great-great-great grandson Enoch-2:

Father	Son	Age of father at son's birth
Seth	Enos	105
Enos	Cainan	90
Cainan	Mahaleel	70
Mahaleel	Jared	65
Tared	Enoch-2	162
	Total years	492

According to the Bible, Enoch-2 was born 492 years after the birth of Seth, or in 3382 BC. NOW, Commander Pike's book, *Morals and Dogma,* reckons its date of publication in both Christian (1871 AD) and Masonic (5680 AM) chronology. To find out the beginning of Masonic history – that "earliest time" in which Enoch erected his "symbols, emblems, and allegories" – in terms of Christian chronology, we subtract the given Christian year from its Masonic equivalent (1871 from 5680). This gives us a first Masonic year of 3809 BC.[42] But the figures show that Enoch-2 was not born until 3382, some 427 years *after* Freemasonry's "earliest time"! Enoch-2 could not possibly have erected the prototypical symbolic devices of which Freemasonry has ever been custodian and depository. However, Cain's son, Enoch-1, very well could have!

Cain began his wandering after Abel's death, which the Bible marks with Seth's conception and Adam's age, 130 years, in about 3876 BC. If we give Cain ten years to find a wife, settle down, and sire a child, Enoch-1 would have been born in 3866 BC. This would make him a 55-year-old man in the first Masonic year, 3809. At that age, Enoch-1 would have been fully equipped to erect symbols and allegories memorializing his father's divine appointment to rule populations "out from the presence of the Lord."[43]

Incidentally, Professor Sayce placed Cain in Masonry's early years *against his previous determinations.* Sayce admitted to being compelled by the scholarly diligence of a latter-day Babylonian king to accept the evidence that Sargon lived as early as four thousand years before Christ:

The last king of Babylonia, Nabonidas, had antiquarian

CHAPTER 24 THE MARK OF CAIN

tastes, and busied himself not only with the restoration of the old temples of his country, but also with the disinterment of the memorial cylinders which their builders and restorers had buried beneath their foundation. It was known that the great temple of the Sun-god at Sippara ... had originally been erected by Naram-Sin [Enoch], the son of Sargon, and attempts had been already made to find the records which, it was assumed, he had entombed under its angles. With true antiquarian zeal, Nabonidas continued the search until he had lighted upon 'the foundation stone' of Naram-Sin himself. This 'foundation-stone' he tells us had been seen by none of his predecessors for 3200 years. In the opinion, accordingly, of Nabonidas, a king who was curious about the past history of his country, and whose royal position gave him the best possible opportunities for learning all that could be known about it, Naram-Sin and his father Sargon lived 3200 years before his own time, or 3750 BC.

What we see in the Bible's account of how Unuk came about is nothing less than *the foundation of the world's legal system.* That God would ordain an evil man to administer the law makes sublime sense to me.

In our final chapter, I shall ask your indulgence in a few personal reflections of my own as to how a system designed to process evil can do as much good as it does.

Chapter 25

THE TWO MINISTRIES

> "The years pass so quickly – where do they go? – so quickly, and then we get old. We never knew what any of it was about."
> —WOODY ALLEN, *RADIO DAYS*

WHAT, TO ME, makes the Bible such an inviting resource is the vigor with which the rulers of evil have suppressed its unlicensed reading. It's been my experience that as predictably as such rulers play with truth, the Bible forthrightly tells it.

The previous chapters have been written in the presumption that ruling institutions *are* what they say they are (under the Cain covenant they must truthfully identify their origins, which they do with cabalah). It's only fair, then, that I write this chapter in the presumption that the Bible really is what it says it is. It claims to be the unique, revealed Word of God,[1] and the veritable literary embodiment of Jesus Christ.[2] If we disbelieve that claim, we must disbelieve all the mottoes, insignia, bulls, encyclicals, laws, acts, ordinations, constitutions, oaths, and decrees of the rulers of evil.

According to God (as given in Scripture), the purpose of law is to regulate evildoers. Hear the apostle Paul:

> We also know that law is made not for the righteous but for lawbreakers and rebels, the ungodly and sinful, the unholy and irreligious; for those who kill their fathers or mothers, for murderers, for adulterers and perverts, for slave traders and liars and perjurers – and for whatever else is contrary to the sound doctrine that conforms to the glorious gospel of the blessed God.[3]

In other words, any behavior not conforming to "the glorious gospel" of God belongs to the law, which, obviously from its subject matter, is a jurisdiction foreign to Jesus Christ.

Scripture teaches us that the glorious gospel commands (1) repenting of sinful lifestyles,[4] (2) loving neighbor as oneself,[5] (3) loving and blessing one's enemies,[6] (4) giving freely without thought of reward,[7] (5) forgiving debts and injuries,[8] and (6) preaching that whoever believes the evidence of Christ's life, death, and resurrection enters the royal family of God for all eternity.[9] Not every personality is drawn to the glorious gospel,[10] although Scripture tells us that everyone is asked (in some way) to know it.[11] For the protection of those drawn to the glorious gospel, and for the management of those foreign to it, there exists the "rule of law." Rule of law is the system by which authorities bearing Cain's "powers and insignia of kingship" rule the World. Very briefly, it compares with the glorious gospel in the following ways:

Glorious gospel	Rule of law
Repent of sinful lifestyle	Manage sinful lifestyle
Love neighbor as oneself	Achieve advantage over neighbor
Love and bless one's enemies	Conquer one's enemies by legal means
Give freely without thought of reward	Give requiring reward
Forgive debts and injuries	Enforce payment of debts and injuries with interest
Preach that whoever believes the evidence of Christ's life, death, and resurrection enters the royal family of God for all eternity	Preach the absentee, impersonal God of Cain, Deism, and other faiths

CHAPTER 25 THE TWO MINISTRIES

The following table shows how readily the Roman Catholic Church-State organism conforms to the rule of law:

Rule of law	Secular Government	Roman Catholicism
Manage sinful lifestyle	Legislation, police, criminal justice, philanthropy, media	Pontification, Inquisitioin of the Holy Sacraments, media
Competition: Achieve advantage over neighbor	Self-interested political action, competition, partisanism, nationalism	Self-interested political action in the guise of ecumenism (e.g., Trent)
Conquer one's enemies by legal means	War and emergency powers, Darwinian survivalism, patriotism	"End justifies the means" rationale of the Church Militant *(Regimini militantis ecclesiae)*
Give, requiring reward	Profit-based trade and commerce	Salvation earned by good works; the selling of indulgences
Enforce payment of debts and injuries with interest	Judiciary, police	Forgiveness of sins in exchange for payments and penances
Preach the absentee, impersonal God of Cain, Deism, and other faiths	Preaching "In God We Trust" while prohibiting Bibles in schools	Praying to saints for intercession with an absentee, impersonal Saviour

The rule of law is what Scripture calls a "ministration of condemnation."[12] The "strength" of the rule of law is sin.[13] This is observable in how law is at its most vibrant when ferreting out, prosecuting, and punishing crime. Officials of the rule of law are called "ministers of righteousness, whose end shall be according to their works."[14] (I take this to mean "Good works, good end; bad works, bad end.") As might be expected of a ministry appointed to Cain, who Scripture tells us was "of that wicked one,"[15] the ministration of condemnation – the rule of law – belongs to Satan. It is a shocking thing to realize that, according to Scripture, world law is Satan's province. But surprisingly, Scripture also teaches that a certain degree of cordiality exists between God and Satan.

We learn from the book of Job that Satan is welcome in God's heavenly throne room,[16] even though he has led a rebellion in Heaven for which one third of the angelic population were cast out.[17] His business consists of "going to and fro in the earth, walking up and down in it."[18] Since he is an angel, and therefore incapable of a bodily existence, Satan can only affect human affairs by (1) providing spiritual direction to human beings who consent to him as "the god of this world,"[19] and (2) manipulating the forces of nature as "prince of the power of the air."[20] To secure popular consent to his spiritual direction, he employs his supernatural abilities to make himself irresistibly attractive. He's an angel of light,[21] the author of the humanist extravaganza – pomp and circumstance, breathtaking visual experience, disorienting emotionalism, architecture that overwhelms. He means to convince us (1) that he wields the power of God Almighty on earth, and (2) that we are therefore bound to follow his moral guidance.[22] Jesus Christ agreed with the first proposition (and in so doing affirmed, in my opinion, the covenant between God and Cain), but admonished Satan that *only the written word of God* is fit to guide mankind and Trickster alike.[23] Quite apart from its infallible moral guidance, the written word of God appears to be *the only truthful disclosure of Satan's origin, scope, and purpose.* Its potential for damaging his appeal is why the highest rulers of law have traditionally prohibited, or at least not diligently encouraged, Bible reading.

THE earliest Christians well understood Rome's indispensable satanic role in human affairs. In the legal process which Christ established for members of his Church, the harshest sentence an offender could receive was abandonment to Caesarean authority:

> If your brother sins against you, go and show him his fault, just between the two of you. If he listens to you, you have won your brother over. But if he will not listen, take one or two others along, so that 'every matter may be established by the testimony of two or three witnesses.' If he refuses to listen to them, tell it to the church; and if he refuses to listen even to the church, treat him as you would a pagan or a tax collector.[24]

CHAPTER 25   THE TWO MINISTRIES

Writing about "Hymenaeus and Alexander, whom I have *handed over to Satan* to be taught not to blaspheme,"[25] the apostle Paul was not talking about committing unruly churchmen to some satanic cult. Nor did he mean by the following counsel that the church at Corinth should engage in demonic incantations:

> When you are assembled in the name of our Lord Jesus and I am with you in spirit, and the power of our Lord Jesus is present, *hand this man over to Satan,* so that the sinful nature may be destroyed and his spirit saved on the day of the Lord.[26]

In both cases, Paul was heeding Christ's commandment concerning brethren who rejected both the glorious gospel and the rule of law: turn them over to the Caesarean criminal justice system *for their own good and for the good of the church.* Thus, the earliest Christians were keenly aware that Rome's purpose, as the spiritual heir of Cain and the incarnation of the satanic spirit, was (1) to teach the people of God not to blaspheme, (2) to destroy the sinful nature, thereby (3) to save man's spirit from eternal damnation on judgment day. This violent good-working spirit is characterized at Psalm 2:9 and again at Revelation 2:27 as a "rod of iron" with which Christ rules nations and dashes them to pieces. The Judaean political leaders, anticipating a Messiah who would overthrow Caesar, didn't understand that *Rome* was Christ's rod of iron. Because He would not dash Rome to pieces, they declared Him an impostor, demanded His crucifixion, and gloated when He failed to come off the cross. They could not fathom His consenting to suffer under the violent justice of His own rod. Nor could they foresee that He would use this same rod on September 8, 70 in the person of the Roman general Vespasianus Titus, who captured their rebellious city, Jerusalem, and dashed it to pieces.

Paul, whom his non-believing Israelite brethren continually mugged, persecuted, jailed, tortured, and hounded throughout his Mediterranean and Aegean ministry, understood the rod of iron. It was in his letter to the Romans that we find perhaps the most eloquent statement on the New World Order ever written (I cite from the New International Version):

> Everyone must submit himself to the governing authorities, for there is no authority except that which God has established. The authorities that exist ["powers that be" in the King James Version] have been established by God.
>
> Consequently, he who rebels against the authority is rebelling against what God has instituted, and those who do so will bring judgment on themselves.
>
> For rulers hold no terror for those who do right, but for those who do wrong. Do you want to be free from fear of the one in authority? Then do what is right and he will commend you.
>
> For he is God's servant to do you good. But if you do wrong, be afraid, for he does not bear the sword for nothing. He is God's servant, an agent of wrath to bring punishment on the wrongdoer.
>
> Therefore, it is necessary to submit to the authorities, not only because of possible punishment but also because of conscience.
>
> This is also why you pay taxes, for the authorities are God's servants, who give their full time to governing.
>
> Give everyone what you owe him: If you owe taxes, pay taxes; if revenue, then revenue; if respect, then respect; if honor, then honor.
>
> Let no debt remain outstanding, except the continuing debt to love one another, for he who loves his fellowman has fulfilled the law.[27]

Since the epoch of Emperor Constantine, the Roman papacy has fostered the concept that the ruler who terrorizes wrongdoers is necessarily a Christian. Pope Sylvester, the Bishop of Rome who supposedly converted Constantine to Christianity, saw nothing strange in a warrior coming to faith in a crucified Christ by slaughtering his enemies."[28] This thinking pervaded Sylvester's successors, as well as the Crusades, the Holy Roman Empire, European nationalism, the American Revolution, the War of Southern Secession, and the wars of the twentieth century. Indeed, perhaps the black papacy's most admirable psychological conquest is that Protestants generally agree that armed rulership is an authority instituted by God for Christians to exercise. Since there is no scrip-

CHAPTER 25   THE TWO MINISTRIES

tural authority for a member of the Body of Christ to bear any kind of armament whatsoever other than the figurative weaponry of God's Word, agreeing to such a principle signifies *prima facie* adherence to the moral guidance of him who bears the power of Almighty God on earth, the person who legitimately bears the mark of Cain in a long succession begun with Peter. Yes, the popes can truthfully declare that "Peter" is their foundation by holding in mental reservation that the Hebrew פטר, pronounced "payter," means... *firstling,*[29] which of course is Cain's primary attribute as firstborn of Eve.

Supporters of the argument favoring lethal-force Christian rulership usually stand on a single scriptural passage. It's that verse in Luke 22 wherein, as the betrayal nears, Christ admonishes his disciples, "If you don't have a sword, sell your cloak and buy one."[30] I have often heard Christian militiamen (some of whom I am not ashamed to call my friends) use this to justify arming themselves against the minions of unjust rulers. But Jesus explained otherwise in the very next verse: "It is written: 'And he was numbered with the transgressors' [see Isaiah 53:12]; and I tell you that this must be fulfilled in me." In order to fulfill prophecy, Christ had to be numbered among lawbreakers, which bearing swords would certainly make them disciples of any true Prince of Peace. As soon as the disciples produced two swords – the minimum number constituting the plural "transgressors" – prophecy was fulfilled. Christ then told them "It is enough." From then on, no more cloaks were sold, no more swords bought.

ROMAN Christianity's success at avenging evil has resulted in a world that severely mistrusts the Christian gospel. It's to Rome's advantage that the Christian gospel be mistrusted, for any soul that mistrusts Christ is Rome's lawful prey. It's to Rome's advantage that governing bodies be rebelled against as tyrannical, for rebellion against tyrants is disobedience to the glorious gospel. Much as I despaired over the vicious taking of innocent life in the Waco massacre, I had no choice but to see it as a rather standard Church-Militant inquisitorial procedure against perceived rebelliousness. ATF Special Agent Davy Aguilera's affidavit,[31] which resulted in the warrant under which governing bodies invaded the Davidian compound, *dutifully listed the scriptural errors of David Koresh*. According to the affidavit, Vernon Howell adopted the name David Koresh because he "believed that the name helped designate him as the messiah or the anointed one of God" (p2). Yet one group member stated that Koresh's teaching "did not always coincide with the Bible" (p11). This allegation is supported by Aguilera's finding that the "anointed one of God" and his followers had spent at least $44,000 on guns and explosives during 1992 alone, including hand grenades and rifle grenades, gunpowder and potassium nitrate (p6). Where in Scripture are the anointed ones of Christ told to stock up on destructive weaponry? According to Aguilera's inquisition, "David Koresh stated that the Bible gave him the right to bear arms" (p15). Where in the glorious gospel is an anointed one of God given the right to bear arms? Koresh prophesied the immanent end of the world, "that it would be a 'military type operation' and that all the 'non-believers' would have to suffer" (p9). Where in Scripture are Christians commanded to make war against non-believers?

From the Inquisition's standpoint, the Davidians paid lip-service to Jesus Christ but demonstrated a substantive infidelity to Him by infringing upon the ancient Cain franchise – the mark – which flows through the United States government from the black papacy. Against Christ's commandment, even while professing scriptural knowledge, the Davidians chose to brandish deadly weapons – weapons that Cain could envision pointed at himself someday. How could any mark-bearing ruler resist mobilizing sevenfold vengeance in self-defense? How could Cain resist holding these professed Christians responsible under Christ's warning at Revelation 13:10: "He that killeth by the sword must be killed by the sword"? Is it any wonder that government regards memories of Waco as little more than annoyances to be stonewalled?

YET one can live intelligently, freely, and safely in a World legitimately governed by the Trickster. The secret is revealed in the

CHAPTER 25   THE TWO MINISTRIES

resource which the Trickster has labored so tirelessly to marginalize: the Holy Bible. I cite again that remarkable verse in Habakkuk (2:4), in which God tells us that although governing bodies have the wrong desires, we can live safely in *their faith* that God will not punish them for annihilating their mortal enemies.

Scripture reduces all human interaction to two great ministries: the ministry of Condemnation"[32] and the ministry of Reconciliation.[33] Condemnation is the rulership of evil by law; it judges and does justice. Since its subject is the criminal mind ("the strength of the law is sin"), Condemnation requires the brilliance of the firstling, Cain, along with the deviousness of Jesuitry and Sun-Tzu. Condemnation enforces its authority with deadly force – it "does not bear the sword for nothing."

The ministry of Reconciliation teaches and administers the glorious gospel of Christ. Reconciliation does not judge executably or do justice. Rather, it judges spiritually, it loves, nurtures, suffers patiently, forgives, and rejoices in the truth. Reconciliation never fails because its strength is not sin but the power of God.

The ministry of Condemnation operates "out from the presence of the Lord." Its only proof of divine association is an inert substance, a seal, a pallium, a miter, a collar, a badge, the mark of Cain, the insignia of its authority to terrorize evildoers. The ministry of Reconciliation is directly animated by the Lord operating within. It proves divine association by everything it does: its mere *existence* is its seal.

There are exceptions, of course: Condemnors who Reconcile and Reconcilers who Condemn. Many loving Roman Catholic priests dedicate their lives to a form of reconciliation, Confession and Absolution. But aren't these sacraments really a process of Condemnation in which the confessant pleads guilty and is sentenced on the spot by the priestly judge to certain penitential acts which pardon the guilt? Reconciliation according to Scripture forgives the sin *free of charge* and directs the confessant's energies not to punishments but toward a repentant, constructive *life* within the mind of Christ. I suspect there are lots of Catholic priests who do true Reconciliation, even though it's technically heretical. My elderly British Jesuit friend stationed at the Gesu was a Reconciler of sorts: he took confession every weekday afternoon by the clock in Italian, a language he didn't understand.

My father was a good lawyer who denied himself many a handsome legal fee by trying to reconcile marriages out of divorce court. He was a minister of Condemnation by trade, yet the word of God written on his heart made a Reconciler out of him almost in spite of himself. This, I believe, is what Scripture calls "every knee bow[ing] at the name of Jesus Christ, in heaven and on earth, and under the earth."[34] It's proof of the great power of Reconciliation that the World highly esteems Condemnors who Reconcile, Condemnors for whom the name of Jesus Christ may not be important or even credible. (My private opinion is that many who find Christ uninteresting have been sold an inferior gospel by hypocritical preaching. I tend to agree with G.K. Chesterton's remark, "It's not that Christianity has been tried and found wanting, but that it's hardly been tried at all.")

Despite crossovers, Condemnation and Reconciliation work together as opposites, like male and female, sea and land, night and day, yin and yang. Condemnation punishes us for alienating God; Reconciliation lovingly brings us together with God. Condemnation cannot bring us to God, but it can drive us to Him. Reconciliation cannot punish us for alienating God, but it can release us to Condemnation, which walks to and fro in search of corrupt Reconcilers to persecute along with the usual suspects. Release is a conciliatory operation. The spiritual judgments of Reconciliation are executed in release, while the natural judgments of Condemnation are executed by the opposite of release: restriction – restriction of body, comfort, freedom, property, options, life.

Restriction is the flexure of Condemnation's muscle, and this is good for Reconciliation. It provides God a captive audience. I saw it in a dozen jail cells in Tennessee, Oklahoma, Georgia, Mississippi, and California. Condemnation can so restrict that its subject cries out for Reconciliation. In jail, God is not a philosophical proposition to be deliberated at leisure. He's a vivid benefit grasped

CHAPTER 25   THE TWO MINISTRIES

as though He were a key to the jailhouse lock. I have seen it so often, under so many circumstances, that I have to regard it as a principle: The More Restriction, the Closer to God.[35] So even though the ministry of Condemnation is directed by Satan to do justice among evildoers (and what could be more just than for Satan to rule evil?), the ultimate beneficiary is He who ordained the whole system in the first place.

For, just as Paul says, Satan is an angel of light and his ministers are ministers of righteousness whose end shall be according to their works. Scripture is a catalog of satanic ministers who were absolutely necessary for Christ to perform His finished work: the Serpent, Cain and Enoch, Ham, Nimrod, Esau, Pharaoh, the Amalekites, Nebuchadnezzar, Belshazzar, Cyrus, Ahasueras, Haman, Judas, and many, many others. Some were deplorably wicked, other surprisingly moral – it was Judas' sense of guilt that drove him to suicide. The Jesuit priest who inaugurated my prosecution on the Feast Day of St. Ignatius was a satanic minister, and he was absolutely necessary for my maturity as a Christian. He sent me on a fifteen-year journey that has brought me to this page.

ONCE I understood the two ministries, hard questions answered themselves. What can a responsible citizen do to restore moral, fair, constitutional government? First, realize that no judgment that government is immoral, unfair, or unconstitutional can be executed unless by an authorized person. Only Condemnation has authority to alter government's patterns of conduct. To change government by conventional means, I must become a Condemnor. (Can anyone name a true Reconciler who is great in the World?) To gain influence among Condemnors, I must master the arts of Sun-Tzu and the Trickster. Little good this will do, for as my investigation has tended to show, always the preponderance of Condemnation's resources go into keeping the system evil. If I build forces capable of meaningfully altering the system, the masters will terminate me because they are authorized by God to avenge sevenfold those who would slay Cain. In short, the potential for improvement *within* the system of Condemnation appears to be limited to cyclical periods of pretty good times, pretty bad times. Isn't this obvious from history and the news?

Of course, God could change government by a simple miracle, and Revelation says He will, on the "last day," the fearful day of cosmic shakedown when unrepentant evildoers will burn with their beast and only the perfect will remain. Scripture is silent as to when that day will come. In the meantime, Reconcilers are told that improving human rulership is *their* responsibility. Not by taking control of the system, and not by sealing themselves off in well-fortified communes, either. Reconcilers improve the system by making themselves... *available*. Reconcilers are attractive to Condemnation because they don't judge or attempt to do justice. They don't put down, attach blame, or pin guilt. Consequently, Reconcilers are not perceived as a threat. They are wise as serpents and harmless as doves.[36]

This is not to say that Reconcilers condone evil. Their posture toward sin is this: People know right from wrong. People don't need to be told they're sinful. People know. God's law written on their hearts continually reminds them. What the World needs is the *friendship* of someone who is God-minded (if not well-versed in the Word of God), someone confident in the *Love* of God who can patiently and non-judgmentally hold the most evil of souls in friendship while helping it work through repentance to healthier values at its own pace.

Many years in Condemnation have driven me into the ministry of Reconciliation, and the heart of Reconciliation is love. I now appreciate the simple wisdom in Felix Mendelssohn's question, "Why should any man offend the people in power?" Offending people in power – offending anyone – is no longer attractive to me. I do good, or at least try to with our Lord's help. The most reliable instruction I've yet found for this purpose is the Bible with its glorious gospel, and the Bible tells me that if I do good (not good as I see it, but good as the gospel defines it: *Love God with all your heart, soul, and mind; love your neighbor as yourself*), the rulers of evil will commend me.

And so I freely subject myself to Condemnation for examina-

CHAPTER 25   THE TWO MINISTRIES

tion of my conscience. Who knows? I might just interest the examiner in the joys of Reconciliation. Taxes? I continue to pay every tax for which I am liable, and none for which I'm not.

Finally, I anticipate that some may disagree with certain of the conclusions in this and other chapters. I welcome disagreement. Disagreement is the mother of this book. Nobody is paying me to market any particular doctrine. I'm not the kind of person who has to be right. I let the evidence lead me. The evidence shaped my conclusions. The evidence wrote this book. To anyone who knows of countervailing evidence, evidence that might point me in a different direction, this is my request to see it. I'm not above repenting again, nor would I shrink from printing retractions. I want Reconciliation, and I want Truth.

If St. Francis Xavier can say "I would not even believe in the *Gospels* were the Holy Church to forbid it," with no less commitment I can say that I would not believe even the *Bible* were Truth to forbid it.

Appendix A

FIFTY CENTURIES OF THE ANNU SIGNATURE

Above. The hem of Marduk's garment (see page 267) consists of the Annu signature, authorizing Marduk to rule evildoers.

Right. Ancient Babylonian cylinder in the British Museum depicts the Queen of Heaven, Ishtar, empowered by four Annu signatures.

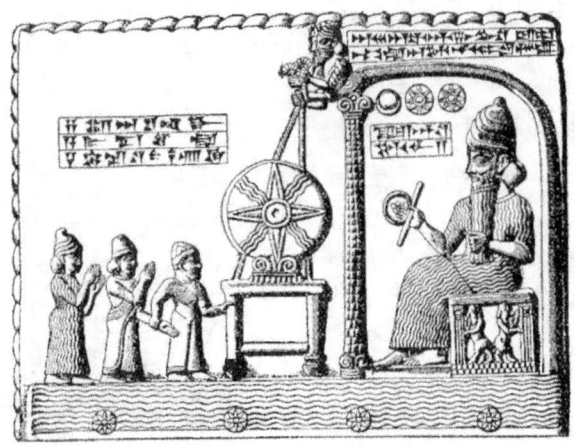

Left. Stone tablet in the British Museum depicts Nabonidas, the scholarly Babylonian *Pontifex Maximus,* supervising the placement of the ancient Annu signature during the restoration of Annu's temple at Sippara eight or nine centuries before Christ.

Left. St. Peter's Piazza at Rome, where throngs gather to give audience to the popes, is inlaid with the Annu signature

Below. Front and back-side of an ancient Assyrio-Babylonian bronze tablet "representing the world in the clutches of an evil demon" (1959 *Britannica* Vol. 7, p 190). The "demon" is just a dog, who shepherds unruliness for Annu, as does Satan for Yahweh "by going to and fro in the earth, and walking up and down in it." Note the Annu signature just below and to the left of the dog's gaping mouth. Canines are a favorite metaphor for Cain. There's no brighter star in the heavens than the "dog star," named Canis Major after Cain. The Egyptians called Canis the "second sun" because it ruled the mysterious world of night, a ruler of what Paul calls "the darkness of this world" (Ephesians 6:12). Homer called Canis "the evil star" because its rising brought on the hot summer season and its attendant pestilence. Human sacrifices were offered to appease the dog star, believed by many scholars to be the "Lucifer" of Isaiah 14:12.

Right. The Annu signature declares the entrance to Harvard Law School.

APPENDIX A   FIFTY CENTURIES OF THE ANNU SIGNATURE

Left. As the Commander Albert Pike attested, the Annu signature and other emblems representing Cain's authority to rule have been protected by Freemasonry since their creation by Enoch. Every Masonic temple proclaims its devotion to Annu.

Below. The U.S. Supreme Court Building reveals the Annu signature in its exterior stone and bronze work, as well as its interior throughout. American justice avenges its offenders at least sevenfold not because it is corrupt but because it has inherited Cain's divine empowerment to do so.

Appendix B
Superior Generals of the Society of Jesus

according to *The Historical Catechism, chiefly relating to the English Province of the Society*, Ed. by George Oliver, St Nicholas Priory, Exeter, 1838; amplified by current research)

1. Ignatius Loyola, 1 April 1541 – 31 July 1556 (65 yrs at death)
2. Diego Laynez, 2 July 1558 – 10 Jan 1565 (53)
3. Francis Borgia, 2 July 1565 – 1 October 1572 (62)
4. Everard Mercurian, 23 April 1573 – 1 August 1580 (?)
5. Claudius Aquaviva, 19 Feb 1581 – 31 Jan 1615 (72)
6. Mutius Vitelleschi, 15 Nov 1615 – 9 Feb 1645 (82)
7. Vincent Caraffa, 7 Jan 1646 – 8 June 1649 (65)
8. Francis Piccolimini, 21 Dec 1649 – 17 June 1651 (69)
9. Alexander Gottifred, 21 January 1652 – 13 March 1652 (58)
10. Goswin Nickel, 17 March 1652 – 31 July 1664 (82)
11. John Paul Oliva, who had been elected *Vicarius Generalis perpetuus cum jure succedendi 7 Junii 1661* was immediately invested with the government of the Society at Nickel's death. He died 96 November 1681 (81)
12. Charles de Noyelle, 5 July 1682 – 12 Dec 1686
13. Thyrsus Gonzales, 6 July 1687 – 19 Nov 1705 (78)
14. Michaelangelo Tamburini, 31 Jan 1706 – 28 February 1730
15. Francis Retz, 30 Nov 1730 – 19 Nov 1750 (78)
16. Ignatius Viconti, 4 July 1751 – 4 May 1755
17. Luigi Aloysius Centurioni, 30 November 1755 – 2 October 1757
18. Lorenzo Ricci, 21 May, 1758 – 24 Nov 1775 (72)

The brief of Clement XIV for suppressing the Society, dated 21 July 1773 was put in execution 16 August.

APPENDIX B SUPERIOR GENERALS OF THE SOCIETY OF JESUS

Superior Generals of the Society of Jesus

according to *The Historical Catechism, chiefly relating to the English Province of the Society,* Ed. by George Oliver, St Nicholas Priory, Exeter, 1838; amplified by current research)

IN RUSSIA

19. Stanislaus Czerniewicz, permitted by Catherine the Great to feign for life as "Superior General for Russia" 17 Oct 1782 – 21 Oct, 1785 (57)
20. Gabriel Lenkiewisz, 8 October, 1785 – 21 October 1798 (77)
21. Francis Karew, 12 Feb 1799 – 4 Aug 1802 (71)
22. Gabriel Gruber, 22 Oct 1802 – 6 April 1805 (67)
23. Thaddeus Brzozowski, elected in 1805, would serve as head of the whole Society when it was restored 7 August 1814 by the Bull of Pope Pius VII *Solicitudo omnium Ecclesiarum,* but would never remove to Rome because the Russian Government refused him permission to leave, died 5 Feb 1820

24. Aloysius Fortis, 18 Oct 1820 – 29 Jan 1829 (81)
25. John Roothaan 1829 – 1853
26. Pieter Jean Beckx, 1853 – 1887
27. Ludovico Martin, 1892 – 1901
28. Franz Xavier Wernz, 1907 – 1914
29. Vladimir Ledochowski, 1915 – 1942
30. Jean-Baptiste Janssens, 1946 – 1964
31. Pedro Arrupe, 1965 – 1981 (removed by Pope John Paul II)
32. Paolo Dezza, Giuseppe Pittau, 1981 – 1983 (appointed by John Paul II)
33. Peter Hans Kolvenbach, 1983 –

Appendix C

GLOSSARY

absolution: a remission of sins pronounced by a priest

acronym: a word formed from the initial letter or letters of each of the successive parts or major parts of a compound term

anathema: a ban or curse solemnly pronounced by ecclesiastical authority and accompanied by excommunication

Assyria: an ancient west Asian empire extending along the middle Tigris River and over foothills to the east, identified with Babylonia

autocracy: government in which one person possesses unlimited power

Babylon: the ancient civilization spawned on foundations built by the historical Cain and his son Enoch; a metaphor for Rome

black pope: informal name for the Superior General of the Society of Jesus

bull: a solemn papal letter sealed with a bulla or with a red-ink imprint of the device on the bulla

cabalah: (cabala, qabbala, etc): a system of signs, letters, numbers, and images believed to put one in private communication with God and like-minded persons; a gnostic system marked by mysticism, magic, and a belief in creation through emanation; esoteric doctrine or mysterious art

Caesar: a powerful, autocratic ruler, dictator, head of religious and civil governments but limited in Matthew 22:21 to the civil power. First to hold the title was Gaius Julius Maria (100-44 B.C.)

Calvinism: the theological system of John Calvin (c. 1570) and his followers marked by strong emphasis on the sovereignty of God, the depravity of mankind, and the doctrine of redestination

casuistry: a resolving of specific cases of conscience, duty, or conduct through generally false interpretation of ethical principles or religious doctrine; specious argument, rationalization

Christendom: the part of the world in which Christianity prevails

Christian: one who professes belief in the teachings of Jesus Christ

Christianity: the religion derived from Jesus Christ, based on the Bible as sacred scripture, and professed by Eastern, Roman Catholic, Protestant, and non-denominational bodies

condemnation: authoritatively judging a matter and rendering an enforceable opinion

Deism: a movement or system of thought advocating natural religion independent of scriptural revelation, emphasizing morality, and denying the personal involvement of the Creator in human affairs or with the laws of the universe

Diet: (from Middle English *diete*, day's journey, day set for a meeting, from Medieval Latin *dieta*, daily regimen): a formal deliberative assembly of princes or estates; any of various national or provincial legislatures

ecumenical: of, relating to, or representing the whole of a body of churches; promoting or tending toward worldwide Christian unity or cooperation

empire: from Latin *imperium*, absolute authority; a major political unit having a territory of great extent or a number of territories or peoples under a single sovereign authority

encyclical: a papal letter to the bishops

Encyclopedists: the writers of the French *Encyclopedia of Sciences, Arts and Trades* (1743–51) who were identified with the Enlightenment and advocated deism and scientific rationalism

Enlightenment: a philosophic movement of the 18th century marked by a rejection of traditional social, religious, and political ideas and an emphasis on rationalism

equivocation: to use tricky language especially with intent to deceive; to avoid committing oneself in what one says; lying

extirpate: to destroy completely, to wipe out, to pull up by the roots, to cut out by surgery, to exterminate

fascism: a political philosophy, movement, or regime that exalts nation above the individual and that stands for a centralized autocratic government headed by a dictatorial leader, severe economic and social regimentation, and forcible suppression of opposition

Gesu, the: the international headquarters of the Society of Jesus, at

No. 5 Borgo Sancto Spiritu, Rome

gnosticism: the thought and practice especially of various cults of late pre-Christian and early Christian centuries distinguished by the conviction that matter is evil and that emancipation comes through *gnosis* ("knowing")

gospel: sacred writing, the message or teachings of a religious teacher, something accepted as infallible truth or as a guiding principle; the message concerning Christ, the kingdom of God, and salvation

hierarchy: a ruling body of clergy organized into orders or ranks each subordinate to the one above it: a body of persons in authority; the classification of a group of people according to ability or to economic, social, or professional standing

Holy Roman Empire: the commonwealth of Europe ruled by papacy and Holy Roman Emperor as co-ordinate sovereigns. At various times, the Emperor claimed authority over the German states and Hungary, Poland, France, Spain, the Scandinavian peninsula, and the British Isles. However, the "effective empire" embraced only Germany, Burgundy, and the old Lombard kingdom in Italy's Po Valley

Ignatian: noun: a person under special oath to perform services, usually clandestine, for the Superior General of the Society of Jesus

Illuminati: any of various groups claiming special religious enlightenment; persons who are or who claim to be unusually enlightened

illuminism: belief in or claim to a personal enlightenment not accessible to mankind in general

Inquisition: an investigation conducted with little regard for individual rights; a severe questioning; a Roman Catholic tribunal for the discovery and punishment of heresy, presently functioning under the title Congregation for the Doctrine of the Faith

Israel: a complex identifier, being (1) the name given by Yahweh to Jacob, signifying Jacob's acquiring his twin brother Esau's birthright to lead God's chosen people; (2) the ancient Hebrew nation which, after the death of Solomon, divided into two kingdoms, Israel to the north, Judah to the south; (3) the biological nation of which the man Jesus Christ was a descendant through his mother; (4) a modern state occupying the rough geographical perimeters of Caesarean Judaea and Samaria, having an official policy of denying the New Testament Gospel; (5) the amorphous body of those who, through studious belief in and love for Jesus Christ, have been grafted by divine surgery to the ancient Hebrew nation

APPENDIX B GLOSSARY

Judaea: Greek term for Judah, the southern Hebrew kingdom whose inhabitants were called Jews

learning against learning: concept advanced by Cardinal Thomas Wolsey that pitted humanist doctrine against scriptural Christian teaching

liberation theology: a religious movement especially among Roman Catholic clergy in Latin America that combines political philosophy usually of a Marxist orientation with a theology of salvation as liberation from injustice

Majesterium: the teaching authority of the Roman Catholic Church

mental reservation or reserve: intentional withholding of truth when it is regarded as inconvenient to disclose it (as from people who are regarded as unable to understand it or receive it with benefit)

missionary adaptation: process by which populations are brought under subjection to the Roman papacy by harmonious cultural integration

notariqon: cabalistic technique in which the initials of an acronym create a word that enhances the acronym's meaning

pagan: a follower of a polytheistic religion (as in ancient Rome); one who delights in sensual pleasures and material goods

pallium: a white woolen band with pendants in front and back worn over the chasuble by a pope or archbishop as a symbol of full episcopal authority

papacy: the office of pope; a succession or line of popes; the term of a pope's reign; the system of government of the Roman Catholic Church of which the pope is the supreme head

Papal States: lands ruled directly by the popes in central Italy between 755-1870

penance: an act of self-abasement, mortification, or devotion performed to show sorrow or repentance for sin

philosophes: the deistic or materialistic writers and thinkers of the 18th century French Enlightenment

Pontifex Maximus: ancient title first applied to head of Babylonian civil and religious government, meaning "supreme (or sovereign) bridgebuilder;" first assumed by Roman autocrats at the deification of Gaius Maria as Julius Caesar in 48 BC; title owned by the Roman popes

Protestant: one who makes or enters a protest; any of a group of German princes and cities presenting a defense of freedom of conscience against an edict in 1529 intended to suppress the Lutheran movement; a member of any of several church denominations denying the universal authority of the Pope and affirming the

Reformation principles of justification by faith alone, the priesthood of all believers, and the primacy of the Bible as the only source of revealed truth; a Christian not of a Catholic or Eastern church

Psychopomp: from Greek *psychopompas,* "soul director;" a name often applied to Mercury, Roman god of commerce, communication, and thievery

ratio studiorum: Latin "method of study;" the educational process by which the Jesuit schools and colleges obscure the moral supremacy of the Holy Bible and secure tacit obedience to the will of the black papacy

reconciliation: restoration of harmony and friendship; in Roman Catholicism: penance, the result of the sacrament of absolution

salvation: deliverance from the power and effects of sin; the agent or means that effects salvation

sacrament: a Christian rite (in Roman Catholicism: baptism, Holy Eucharist or Mass, penance, matrimony, anointing of the sick, confirmation by the Church, and holy orders) that is believed to have been ordained by Christ and that the Magisterium holds to be a means of divine grace

sodality: from Latin *sodalitas,* "comradeship": an association of Roman Catholic laity

Sibylline prophecies: utterances of any of several prophetesses usually accepted as ten in number and credited to widely separate parts of the ancient world (as Babylonia, Egypt, Greece, and Italy)

Spiritual Exercises: Loyola's 30-day intensive program of psychological indoctrination designed to align individual thought with papal authority

Vulgate: a Latin version of the Bible authorized and used by the Roman Catholic Church

Appendix D

NOTES

PP 1-16

Chapter 1: Subliminal Rome

1. "Holy Alliance: How Reagan and the Pope conspired to assist Poland's Solidarity movement and hasten the demise of Communism." Time, February 24, 1992.
2. An updating of this list will not reflect a significant change in the presence of Roman Catholic lay-persons in the higher legislative reaches. According to the Association of Jesuit Colleges and Universities, in the 106th Congress there are 40 Jesuit alumni who graduated from 17 Jesuit institutions. There are 5 alumni in the US Senate and 35 alumni in the House of Representatives. Out of these 40 alumni, 23 received graduate or professional degrees from Jesuit Universities. Georgetown University has the most graduates, boasting 15 alumni in the U.S. Congress. President William J. Clinton is a graduate of Georgetown University and Secretary of Commerce, William M. Daley, is a graduate of Loyola University of Chicago.
3. Scharf, *History of Western Maryland*, Baltimore (1882), pp 27-30
4. *We, the People: The Story of the United States Capitol: Its Past and Its Promise*, U.S. Capitol Historical Society, p 56.

Chapter 2: Missionary Adaptation

1. 1989 Catholic Almanac, p 175.
2. U.S. Court of Appeals for the Third Circuit, Case No. 85–1309.
3. Just as the Roman priests traditionally took as their own the name of the god or goddess they served, judges on the United States Supreme Court ceremonially adopt the appelation of the goddess Justitia, as in "Mr. Justice Antonin Scalia."
4. Alexander del Mar, Middle Ages Revisited, California 90250: Hawthorne, Omni Book Club (orig. pub. 1899), pp 101–102.
5. *Ibid.*, p 86
6. *Ibid.*, pp 144–146
7. Chadwick, *The Early Church*, Eerdmans (1967), p 243
8. The New Catholic Encyclopedia, "Missionary Adaptation."

Chapter 3: Marginalizing the Bible

1. J. Edwin Hendricks, *Charles Thomson and the Making of A New Nation 1729-1824*, Fairleigh Dickinson University Press (1979), pp 136-137

2. Council of Toulouse, 1229.
3. Peter de Rosa, SJ, *Vicars of Christ: The Dark Side of the Papacy,* New York: Crown Publishers (1988), p 162 ff.
4. *Pontifex Maximus* has laundered the Inquisition's name twice. In 1908, Pope Pius X renamed it "the Holy Office," which Paul VI transformed into "Congregation for the Doctrine of the Faith" in 1965,

Chapter 4: Medici Learning

1. Peter de Rosa, *Vicars of Christ,* p 116–118
2. *Ibid.*
3. De Rosa, *Vicars of Christ,* p 120
4. "Since printing cannot be put down, it is best to set up *learning against learning,* and by introducing all persons to dispute, to suspend the laity between fear and controversy. This at most will make them attentive to their superiors and teachers." Quoted in Lord Herbert's *Life of Henry VIII.*

Chapter 5: Appointment At Cyprus

1. In constructing this brief biography of Loyola, I draw from the following sources: Barthel's *Jesuits,* Martin's *Jesuits,* Aveling's *Jesuits,* Meissner's *Ignatius,* Caraman's *Ignatius,* Letson & Wiggins' *The Jesuit Mystique,* Paris' *Secret History of the Jesuits,* Catholic Encyclopedia, New Catholic Encyclopedia, and Encyclopedia Britannica. In certain needful instances, an individual source will be endnoted.
2. W.W. Meissner, SJ, MD, *Ignatius of Loyola: The Psychology of A Saint,* New Haven, London: Yale University Press (1992), P55.
3. Louis J. Puhl, *The Spiritual Exercises of St. Ignatius,* Westminster, MD: The Newman Press (1959)
4. *Ibid.*
5. Manfred Barthel, transl. by Mark Howson, *The Jesuits: History and Legend of the Society of Jesus,* New York: Quill, William Morrow (1982-84), p 29.
6. Michelet, *Life of Luther,* p 70, 71
7. Philip Caraman, SJ, *Ignatius Loyola: A Biography of the Founder of the Jesuits,* San Francisco: Harper & Row (1990), p 48

Chapter 6: The Epitome of Christian Values

1. While the unanimously-acclaimed Celestine II was being installed, "the Frangipani family, with the connivance of Chancellor Aimeric, broke into the assembly and at sword-point had Cardinal Lamberto acclaimed Honorius II." *The Oxford Dictionary of Popes,* p 165 ff.
2. Encyclopedia Britannica, "China."
3. Piquet, *Des Banqiers au Moyen Age: les Templiers,* Paris, (1931), as cited in *Holy Blood, Holy Grail,* p 451
4. Daraul, *History of Secret Societies,* pp 46ff.
5. J. M. Ragon, *Cours Philosophique et Interpretatif des Initiations anciennes et modernes,* edition sacree a l'usage des Loges et des Macons SEULEMENT (Masonic year 5,842) p 37.

6. J. B. Fabre Palaprat, *Recherches historiques sur les Templiers*, (1835) p 31
7. Michelet, *Procès des Templiers*, II, 404. This work largely consists of the publication in Latin of the Papal bulls and trials of the Templars before the Papal Commission in Paris.
8. Jules Loiseleur, *La doctrine secrète des Templiers*, p 141
9. Leviticus 16:6–10
10. I Kings 11:4
11. The Zohar, Section Ahre Moth, folio 70a.
12. I Kings 3:12.
13. *Ibid*, 11:4.

Chapter 7: The Fingerstroke of God

1. The Statute of Uses (27 Henry VIII, c. 10) Parliament concurred in Henry's assumption of Rome's clerical power with its Act of Supremacy, which stated: "Albeit the king's Majesty justly and rightfully is and ought to be the supreme head of the Church of England, and so is recognized by the clergy of this realm in their convocations, yet nevertheless, for corroboration and confirmation thereof, and for increase of virtue in Christ's religion within this realm of England, and to repress and extirpate all errors, heresies, and other enormities and abuses heretofore used in the same, be it enacted, by authority of this present Parliament, that the king, our sovereign lord, his heirs and successors, kings of this realm, shall be taken, accepted, and reputed the only supreme head in earth of the Church of England, called Anglicans Ecclesia; and shall have and enjoy, annexed and united to the imperial crown of this realm, as well the title and style thereof, as all honors, dignities, pre-eminences, jurisdictions, privileges, authorities, immunities, profits, and commodities to the said dignity of the supreme head of the same Church belonging and appertaining; and that our said sovereign lord, his heirs and successors, kings of this realm, shall have full power and authority from time to time to visit, repress, redress, record, order, correct, restrain, and amend all such errors, heresies, abuses, offenses contempts and enormities, whatsoever they be, which by any manner of spiritual authority or jurisdiction ought or may lawfully be reformed, repressed, ordered, redressed, corrected, restrained, or amended, most to the pleasure of Almighty God, the increase of virtue in Christ's religion, and for the conservation of the peace, unity, and tranquillity of this realm; any usage, foreign land, foreign authority, prescription, or any other thing or things to the contrary hereof notwithstanding." [From: Milton Viorst, ed., *The Great Documents of Western Civilization* (New York; Barnes and Noble, 1965) pp. 97-98]
2. Peter de Rosa, *Vicars of Christ*, page 28
3. Part IX, Sections 764 and 765

4. J. Huber, *Les Jesuites*, Paris: Sandoz et Fischbacher (1875), pp 71ff

Chapter 8: Moving In

1. Fourth session, April 8, 1546, *The Canons and Decrees of the Council of Trent*, translated by H.J Shroeder, Rockford IL: TAN Books (1978)

2. Barthel, *The Jesuits*, p 101
3. II Timothy 3:16.
4. Encyclopedia Brittanica, Livy ii, 21, 7; 27,5.
5. Barthel, *The Jesuits*, p 49

Chapter 9: Securing Confidence

1. La Chaize probably directed the King through the Fifth Exercise, the famous "meditation on hell," which became the centerpiece of Protestant "hellfire and brimstone" preaching. The Fifth Exercise, in its entirety, is as follows: "First point. This will be to see in imagination the vast fires, and the souls enclosed, as it were, in bodies of fire. Second point. To hear the wailing, the howling, cries, and blasphemies against Christ our Lord and against His saints. Third point. With the sense of smell to perceive the smoke, the sulphur, the filth, and corruption. Fourth point. To taste the bitterness of tears, sadness, and remorse of conscience. Fifth Point. With the sense of touch to feel the flames which envelop and burn the souls. Colloquy. Enter into conversation with Christ our Lord. Recall to memory that of those who are in hell, some came there because they did not believe in the coming of Christ; others, though they believed, because they did not keep the Commandments. Divide them all into three classes: 1. Those who were lost before the coming of Christ; 2. Those who were lost during His lifetime; 3. Those who were lost after His life here on earth. Thereupon, I will give thanks to God our Lord that He has not put an end to my life and permitted me to fall into any of these three classes. I shall also thank Him for this, that up to this very moment He has shown Himself so loving and merciful to me. Close with an *Our Father*."
2. Samuel Smiles, *The Huguenots*, New York: Harper & Brothers (1869), p 153
3. James J. Walsh, MD, *American Jesuits*, New York: The Macmillan Company (1934), p 174
4. Manfred Barthel, *The Jesuits*, p 125
5. Henry Foley, SJ, *Records of the English Province SJ*, VII, Part 2, London (1877-1883), pp 1162ff.
6. Garry Wills, *Witches & Jesuits: Shakespeare's Macbeth*, New York: Oxford University Press (1995), p 20.
7. Barthel, *The Jesuits*, page 42
8. *Ibid.*
9. Edmond Paris, *The Secret History of the Jesuits* (translated 1975, original publisher and publication date unknown), distributed by Chino CA: Chick Publications, pp 127-8
10. Peter de Rosa, *Vicars of Christ*, p 5
11. *Ibid.*, p 138
12. Barthel, *The Jesuits*, p 260
13. *Education Reporter*, May 1996, published monthly by Eagle Forum Education & Legal Defense Fund, St. Louis, MO 63105

Chapter 11: The Thirteen Articles Concerning Military Art

1. Estimation in 1784 of then Father Superior of the American Mission, John Carroll,

NOTES   pp. 87-144

a Jesuit priest and brother of Daniel Carroll, upon whose land, "Rome," the U.S. Capitol building was erected.

2. M. Martin, SJ, *The Jesuits: The Society of Jesus and the Betrayal of the Roman Catholic Church,* New York: Simon & Schuster (1987), p 490. Prof. Martin concludes that since the currently-reigning Supetior General, Peter Hans Kolvenbach, "sanctions" a book by Jesuit Juan Luis Segundo, *Theology and the Church* (1985), the book constitutes Kolvenbach's "ultimate answer to the continued dissatisfaction of Popes with the new Society."

Chapter 12: Lorenzo Ricci's War

1. J.C.H. Aveling, *The Jesuits,* p 225
2. Hyneman and Lutz, editors, *American Political Writing During the Founding Era 1760-1805,* Indianapolis: Liberty Press (1983), Vol. I, p 383.
3. *Ibid.* The anonymous author of this 1776 material on the Penn Charter and the city of Philadelphia was, in the editors' opinion "probably a lawyer – or at least had considerable knowledge of legal matters."
4. Aveling, *The Jesuits,* p 225
5. Martin, *The Jesuits,* p 215
6. Aveling, p 278
7. Barthel, *The Jesuits,* p 208
8. Martin, p 212

9. *Catholic Encyclopedia,* "Lorenzo Ricci"

Chapter 13: The Secret Bridge

1. Martin, *The Jesuits,* p 23
2. *Oxford Book of Popes*
5. Sidney Hayden, *Washington and His Masonic Compeers,* New York: Masonic Publishing and Manufacturing Company (1868)
3. Hendricks, *Charles Thomson and the Making of A New Nation,* p. 189
4. Rush, *Autobiography,* p. 155

Chapter 15: The Madness of King George III

1. Koch and Peden, *The Selected Writings of John & John Quincy Adams,* New York: Alfred A. Knopf (1946), letter of July 3, 1776
2. In 1779, they would divide Bute County into two new counties, named Warren and Franklin, after patriots Joseph and Benjamin. Bute County no longer exists.
3. John G. Miller, *Origins of the American Revolution,* New York: Little, Brown (1943), p 190
4. S. Bullock, *Revolutionary Brotherhood: Freemasonry and the Transformation of the American Social Order,* 1730-1840, Chapel Hill: University of North Carolina Press, (1996), p 106
5. David S. Muzzey, *Our Country's History,* Boston: Ginn & Company (1961), p 92

Chapter 16: Tweaking the Religious Right

1. Denis Gwynn, *Bishop Challoner,* London:Douglas Organ (1946), p 192
2. Gwynn, *Challoner,* p 191
3. Finke & Stark, *The Churching of America,* New Jersey: Rutgers University Press (1993), p 25
4. Theodore Sedgwick, Jr., *A Memoir of the Life of William Livingston,* New York (1844), p 136
5. *The Literary Diary of Ezra Stiles,* New York (1901), Vol I, p 490
6. Jonathan Boucher, in Miller, *Origins,* p 195
7. Thomas O'Gorman, *History of the Roman Catholic Church in the United States,* New York (1895), p 208
8. Sidney Hayden, *Washington and his Masonic Compeers,* New York: Masonic Publishing and Manufacturing Co., (1868), p 371. Before the Provincial Grand Lodge of New York, Rev. Seabury delivered an address December 27, 1782, as seen by the following record of that body: "Resolved unanimously, that the thanks of this Lodge be given to our Rev. Bro. Dr. Seabury, for his sermon delivered this day, before this and other Lodges, convened for the celebration of St. John the Evangelist."
9. Ahlstrom, *Religious History of the American People,* pp 368-70

Chapter 17: A Timely Grand Tour

1. The Barony of Stourton, according to *Burke's Peerage,* is "the oldest surviving barony created by Letters Patent." A "letter patent" is a royal grant.
2. The John Catroll Papers, Georgetown University,
3. J.C. Papers, Letter to Thomas Ellerker, October 26, 1772
4. Matthew 24:24
5. Garcia's manuscript translation from the French of Amiot's *Thirteen Articles Concerning Military Art,* used by permission of La Belle Eglise.

Chapter 18: The Stimulating Effects of Tea

1. As such, East India seems likely to have been the source of funding for Amiot's translation of Sun-Tzu. Perhaps someday this connection can be investigated.
2. *Country Life,* October 10, 1968
3. *Ibid.*
4. Geoffrey Holt, S.J, *St. Omers and Bruges Colleges, 1593-1773: A Biographical Dictionary,* London (1979)
5. Black's Law Dictionary, 5th edition, page 709
6. Pat Shannan, who investigates clandestine government involvement in great public catastrophes such as the bombing of the Murrah Building in Oklahoma City, suggests that the mysterious shot might have been fired by Sam Adams himself. When I spoke with Shannan in July 1999, he had just returned from several weeks of sleuthing around Lexington Green. He told me the following: "Sam Adams and John Hancock had big prices on their heads and were hiding out during the early morning hours of 19 April in the home of Rev. Jonas Clarke. Clarke's house is less

than a quarter mile from Lexington Green. Adams delivered many of his rabble-rousing speeches at the meeting-house near the Green. It was from behind this meeting-house shortly after daybreak that the initial shot was fired on the redcoats. As to who was responsible for firing that shot, really the first of the Revolution, my number one suspect since my first visit to Lexington years ago has always been Sam Adams. He had motive, he had access, and he, more than anyone else, had been in the King's face for a long time with his firebrand speeches. He was always urging the people to value liberty more than life itself – which is really what that shot was about."

Chapter 19: The Death & Resurrection of Lorenzo Ricci

1. Hall, *The Secret Teachings*,etc., p CLXVIII
2. *Ibid.*, CC

Chapter 20: American Griffiti

1. Council of Trent, *Decree Concerning the Canonical Scriptures,* Fourth Session.
2. The best-documented, most reasoned, and certainly most energetic analysis of the conflict between Roman Catholicism and Scripture is regularly published by Dave Hunt, of Bend, Oregon. His monthly newsletter, "The Berean Call," is studiously researched, wonderfully written, and free for the asking. Other finely reasoned works on the subject are James R. White's *The Roman Catholic Controversy,* and *Roman Catholics and Evangelicals: Agreements and Differences* by Norman Geisler and Ralph MacKenzie.
3. *Dictionary of Symbols,* Malmo, Sweden: Merkur International KB
4. *Pennsylvania Gazette,* June 8, 1769
5. Hislop, *The Two Babylons,* pp 240,241. Hislop cites the *Phocica* of Pausanius (Book x, chap xv, p 833)
6. Daniel 5:25, 26
7. Del Mar, *The Worship of Augustus Caesar,* p 306. "In all the earlier works referring to [Julius] he is called Caius Caesar, and sometimes simply Caius."
8. Syme, *The Roman Revolution,* p 218 ff
9. Del Mar, *Worship of Augustus Caesar,* p 318

Chapter 21: Jupiter's Earthly Abode

1. As published in Senate Document 332, 71st Congress, 3d Session, and available through the Library of Congress as "Johnson's Map of Georgetown and Washington." This phenomenon was first pointed out to me by Daniel Salmons, who has explored the cabalism of the federal city's layout with incredible fervor and imagination.
2. *Maryland Gazette* for September 26, 1793
3. According to the office of the Architect of the Capitol, the silver plaque has been lost, along with the cornerstone, despite two scientific excavations in recent years.

Chapter 22: The Immaculate Conception

1. *National Republic,* March 1960
2. Chiniquy, *Fifty Years in the Church of Rome: The Conversion of a Priest,* orig. pub. London, 1886, by Protestant Literature Depository. Abridged version published 1985 by Chick Publications, Chino CA. For refusing to obey his bishop's order to send a rich parishioner to a nunnery (thereby expropriating her wealth for the Church), Rev. Chiniquy was first excommunicated, then criminally prosecuted in Urbana, Illinois, on trumped-up sexual impropriety charges. Young Abraham Lincoln won his acquittal in 1856 by exposing perjury in the testimony of several priests. Chiniquy and Lincoln remained good friends.
3. I was personally informed by the Architect of the Capitol in 1992 that "no ground-level photographs of Freedom are known to exist."

Chapter 23: The Dome of the Great Sky

1. See *The Dome of the United States Capitol: An Architectural History* (U.S. Government Printing Office, 1992), and *We, the People: The Story of the United States Capitol* (U.S. Capitol Historical Society, in association with the National Geographic Society, 1985). Most of the material relative to Brumidi's association with the Capitol project is derived from these two handy resources.
2. Chiniquy, *Fifty Years in the Church of Rome,* p 312
3. *Ibid.*
4. Brig. Gen. Thomas Harris, *Rome's Responsibility for the Assassination of Abraham Lincoln,* orig. pub. 1897, repub. by Petersburg OH 44454: Pilgrim Brethren Press (1989), p 19.
5. John Cottrell, *Anatomy of an Assassination,* New York: Funk & Wagnalls (1966)

Chapter 24: The Mark of Cain

1. S.H. Hooke, *Babylonian and Assyrian Religion,* Norman OK: University of OklahomaPress (1963), p 15
2. George Smith, *The Chaldean Account of Genesis,* New York: Scribner, Armstrong & Co. (1876), pp 54-55
3. Hooke, *Babylonian Religion,* p 61
4. Genesis 4:7. God cautioned Cain that if he failed to do well, the Evildoer would lie at his door. "And unto thee shall be his desire, and thou shalt *rule over him.*"
5. Genesis 4:15
6. Genesis 4:8
7. Genesis 4:10
8. Genesis 4:5
9. Genesis 4:2
10. Genesis 4:4
11. Hebrews 9:22
12. Matthew 26:28, Acts 20:28, Romans 3:25, 5:9, Ephesians 1:7, 2:13, Colossians 1:14, Hebrew 9:12, 9:20, 10:19, 13:12, I Peter 1:2, 19, I John 1:7, Revelation 1:5, 7:14, 12:11.

13. Ephesians 2:6
14. Genesis 4:6, 7
15. I Samuel 15:9
16. Genesis 4:26. Only upon the birth of Seth's son Enosh did "men [begin] to call on the name of the Lord." Up to that time, most of humanity apparently ignored or denied the Holy Name. These were Cain's lawful subjects.
17. Genesis 4:16
18. Genesis 4:17
19. Sayce, *The Hibbert Lectures on Babylonian Religion* (1887), p 185
20. Mrs. Sidney Bristowe, *Sargon the Magnificent,* Canada: Burnaby, B.C., Association of the Covenant People (undated, but estimated c. 1925), p 83. Sayce used the term Merodach, which is the Hebrew variant of Marduk.
21. H. S. Williams, Editor, *The Historians' History of the World, A Comprehensive Narrative of the Rise and Development of Nations As Recorded by the Great*, London: The Times (1980), Vol I, p 373. See also George Smith, *The Chaldean Account of Genesis: Containing the description of the creation, the fall of man, the deluge*, London: Sampson Low (1976), p 295.
22. *Ibid.* See also Bristowe, *Sargon,* for a well-documented presentation favoring the identification of Cain with Sargon and numerous mythological personages.
23. Edition 2, Vol. 3, "Babylonia"
24. Leonard King, *Egypt, Babylon and Palestine*, p 28 (noted in Bristowe)
25. Williams, *Times History,* Vol. I p 356.
26. H.R. Hall, *The Ancient History of the Near East,* London: Mithuen & Co. (11th Edition, 1950), p 172
27. Genesis 3
28. Bristowe, *Sargon,* pp 39-40
29. Ragozin, Zenaide A., *Chaldea from the Earliest Times to the Rise of Assyria*, London: T. Fisher Unwin (1886), pp 205-207
30. *Cambridge History*, Vol I, p 406 (noted in Bristowe)
31. "Slavery was part of the foundation upon which Babylonian society rested." Sayce, *Babylonia and Assyria*, p. 67
32. *[London] Times History,* Vol. I, p 362
33. Webster's definition.
34. Genesis 4:23-24
35. Genesis 17:7-8
36. Genesis 4:14
37. Habakkuk 2:4
38. Pike, *Morals and Dogma,* p 210
39. Genesis 5:17
40. Genesis 4:25
41. Genesis 5:4
42. There is a discrepancy of 191 years between Pike's reckoning and that inscribed into the plaque of the Capitol Cornerstone (1793 AD from 5793 AM) I am inclined to believe Pike's is more scientifically determined.
43. Genesis 4:16

Chapter 25: The Two Ministries

1. Hebrews 1:1
2. John 1:1-14
3. 1 Timothy 1:9-10 (NIV)
4. Matthew 3:8
5. Matthew 19:19
6. Matthew 5:44
7. Matthew 10:8
8. Matthew 6:12; 18:22
9. Mark 16:15
10. John 6:44
11. I Timothy 2:4
12. II Corinthians 3:9
13. I Corinthians 15:56
14. II Corinthians 11:15
15. I John 3:12
16. Job 1:6,7
17. Isaiah 14:12, Revelation 12:12
18. Job 1:7
19. II Corinthians 4:4
20. Ephesians 2:2
21. II Corinthians 11:13
22. Matthew 4:1-10
23. *Ibid.*
24. Matthew 18:14-17. In other words, "Respect his wish to avoid you, as the pagans do." The tax collectors known to the Israelites were disloyal brethren hired by Romans to tax other Israelites for personal profit. Today's equivalent might be undercover agents working to create tax liability for a church.
25. 1 Timothy 1:20
26. 1 Corinthians 5:4-5
27. Romans 13:1-8
28. De Rosa, *Vicars of Christ,* p 36
29. Strong's Hebrew Lexicon, no. 6363
30. Luke 22:36
31. U.S. District Court, Western District of Texas, filed February 26, 1993, No. W-93-15M.
32. II Corinthians 3:9
33. II Corinthians 5:18
54. Philippians 2:10
35. The principle is proved by its reverse: The Less Restriction, the Farther from God, which is borne out by high recidivism statistics. The free world tends to dilute the intimacy with God which restriction has established.
36. Matthew 10:16

Appendix E

BIBLIOGRAPHY

Ahlstrom, Sydney E., A *Religious History of the American People*, New Haven & London: Yale University Press (1972)

Aveling, J.C.Hugh, *The Jesuits*, New York: Stein 6k Day (1981)

Barthel, Dr. Manfred, transl. by Mark Howson, *The Jesuits: History and Legend of the Society of Jesus*, New York: Quill, William Morrow (1982-84)

Baigent, Michael, Richard Leigh and Henry Lincoln, *Holy Blood, Holy Grail*, New York: Delacorte Press (1982)

Black's Law Dictionary, 5th edition

Bristowe, Mrs. Sidney, *Sargon the Magnificent*, Canada: Burnaby, B.C., Association of the Covenant People (undated, but estimated c. 1925)

Bullock, Steven C., *Revolutionary Brotherhood: Freemasonry and the Transformation of the American Social Order*, 1730-1840, Chapel Hill: University of North Carolina Press (1996)

Caraman, Philip, SJ, *Ignatius Loyola: A Biography of the Founder of the Jesuits*, San Francisco: Harper & Row (1990)

Carroll, John (edited by Thomas O'Brien Hanley), *The John Carroll Papers, 1755-1791*, in 3 volumes, University of Notre Dame Press (1976)

Catholic Almanac

Chadwick, *The Early Church,* Eerdmans (1967)

Chiniquy, Rev. Charles, *My Fifty Years in the Church of Rome: The Conversion of a Priest,* orig. pub. London, 1886, by Protestant Literature Depository. Abridged version published 1985 by Chick Publications, Chino CA

Cottrell, John, *Anatomy of an Assassination,* New York: Funk & Wagnalls (1966)

Daraul, Arkon, A *History of Secret Societies,* Citadel Press (1995)

Del Mar, Alexander, *Middle Ages Revisited,* California 90250: Hawthorne, Omni Book Club (orig. pub. 1899); *The Worship of Augustus Caesar,* Hawthorne, CA: Christian Book Club of America (1976)

De Rosa, Peter, *Vicars of Christ: The Dark Side of the Papacy,* New York: Crown Publishers (1988)

Dictionary of Symbols, Malmo, Sweden: Merkur International KB

Dillenberger, John, ed., *Martin Luther: Selection from his writings,* New York: Doubleday Anchor Press (1961)

Dome of the United States Capitol, The: An Architectural History, U.S. Government Printing Office (1992)

"Education Reporter," published monthly by Eagle Forum Education & Legal Defense Fund, St. Louis, MO 63105

Fabre Palaprat, J.B, *Recherches historiques sur les Templiers,* (1835)

Finke & Stark, *The Churching of America,* New Jersey: Rutgers University Press (1993)

Foley, Henry, SJ, *Records of the English Province SJ,* London (1877-1883)

Geisler & MacKenzie, *Roman Catholics and Evangelicals: Agreements and Differences,* Grand Rapids: Baker Book House, (1995)

Gwynn, Denis, *Bishop Challoner,* London:Douglas Organ (1946)

Hall, H.R., *The Ancient History of the Near East,* London: Mithuen & Co. (11th Edition, 1950)

Hall, Manly P., *The Secret Teachings of All Ages: an Encyclopedic Outline of*

APPENDIX D   BIBLIOGRAPHY

Masonic, Hermetic, Qabbalistic & Rosicrucian Symbolical Philosophy, Philosophical Research Society, (1988)

Harris, Brig. Gen. Thomas, *Rome's Responsibility for the Assassination of Abraham Lincoln,* orig. pub. 1897, repub. by Petersburg OH 44454: Pilgrim Brethren Press (1989)

Hayden, Sidney, *Washington and His Masonic Compeers,* New York: Masonic Publishing and Manufacturing Company (1868)

Hendricks, J. Edwin, *Charles Thomson and the Making of A New Nation 1729-1824,* Fairleigh Dickinson University Press (1979)

Herbert of Cherbury, Edward, Lord, *The Life and Raigne of King Henry the Eighth,* London: Printed by E. G. for Thomas Whitaker (1649)

Hislop, Alexander, *Two Babylons,* Neptune, New Jersey: Loiseaux Brothers (1916)

Holt, SJ, Geoffrey, *St. Omer's and Bruges Colleges, 1593-1773: A Biographical Dictionary,* London (1979)

Hooke, Samuel H., *Babylonian and Assyrian Religion,* Norman OK: University of Oklahoma Press (1963)

Huber, J., *Les Jesuites,* Paris: Sandoz et Fischbacher (1875)

Hunt, Dave, Editor, "The Berean Call," P.O. Box 7019, Bend, Oregon 97708

Hyneman and Lutz, editors, *American Political Writing During the Founding Era 1760-1805,* Indianapolis: Liberty Press (1983), two volumes

Kaster, Joseph, *Putnam's Concise Mythological Dictionary,* The Putnam Publishing Group (1963)

Kelly, J.N.D.,The Oxford Dictionary of Popes, Oxford & New York:Oxford University Press (1986, 1989)

King, Leonard W., *A History of Babylon,* London: Chatto and Windus (1919)

Koch and Peden, *The Selected Writings of John & John Quincy Adams,* New York: Alfred A. Knopf (1946)

Letson & Wiggins, *The Jesuit Mystique,* Chicago: The Loyola Press (1995)

Martin, Malachi, SJ, The Jesuits: *The Society of Jesus and the Betrayal of the*

Roman Catholic Church, New York: Simon & Schuster (1987)

Meissner, W.W., SJ, MD, *Ignatius of Loyola: The Psychology of A Saint,* New Haven, London: Yale University Press (1992)

Michelet, M., *Life of Luther, written by himself,* London: David Bogue (1846). Luther's texts collected, arranged, and translated by Michelet

Miller, John G., *Origins of the American Revolution,* New York: Little, Brown (1943)

Muzzey, David S., *Our Country's History,* Boston: Ginn & Company (1961)

Needham, Guil. (Imprimatur), A *Brief Historical Account of the Behaviour of the jésuites and their Faction, for the First twenty five Years of Q. Elizabeth's Reign, with an Epistle of W. Watson, a Secular Priest, shewing, How they were thought of by the other Romanists of that Time,* London: James Adamson (1689)

New Catholic Encycyclopedia (1967)

O'Gorman, Thomas, *History of the Roman Catholic Church in the United States,* New York (1895)

Paris, Edmond, *The Secret History of the Jesuits* (translated 1975, original publisher and publication date unknown), distributed by Chino CA: Chick Publications

Piquet, *Des Banqiers au Moyen Age: les Templiers,* Paris, (1931)

Pike, Albert Commander, *Morals and Dogma of the Ancient and Accepted Scottish Rite of Freemasonry,* Richmond, Virginia: Jenkins, Inc. (1871, 1923)

Puhl, Louis J., *The Spiritual Exercises of St. Ignatius,* Westminster, MD: The Newman Press (1959)

Ragon, J.M., *Cours Philosophique et Interpretatif des Initiations anciennes et modernes,* edition sacree a l'usage des Loges et des Macons Seulement (Masonic year 5,842)

Ragozin, Zenaide A., *Chaldea from the Earliest Times to the Rise of Assyria,* London: T. Fisher Unwin (1886)

Rush, Benjamin (Ed. by George W. Comer), *The Autobiography of Benjamin Rush,* Princeton University Press, (1948)

Sayce, Archibald, *The Hibbert Lectures on the Origin and Growth of Religion, as*

APPENDIX D   BIBLIOGRAPHY

Illustrated by the Religion of the Ancient Babylonians, London: Williams & Norgate, (1909)

Scharf, *History of Western Maryland,* Baltimore (1882)

Sedgwick, Jr., Theodore, *A Memoir of the Life of William Livingston,* New York (1844)

Shroeder, H.J., trans., *The Canons and Decrees of the Council of Trent,* Rockford IL: TAN Books (1978)

Smiles, Samuel, *The Huguenots,* New York: Harper & Brothers (1869)

Smith, George, *The Chaldean Account of Genesis,* New York: Scribner, Armstrong & Co. (1876)

Stiles, Ezra, *The Literary Diary of Ezra Stiles,* New York (1901)

Strong's *Exhaustive Concordance with Hebrew & Greek Lexicons*

Syme, Ronald, *The Roman Revolution,* Oxford University Press (1966)

U.S. Court of Appeals for the Third Circuit, Case No. 85-1309

We, the People: The Story of the United States Capitol: Its Past and Its Promise, U.S. Capitol Historical Society

Viorst, Milton, ed., *The Great Documents of Western Civilization,* New York; Barnes and Noble, 1965

Walsh, James J., MD, *American Jesuits,* New York: The Macmillan Company (1934)

White, James R., *The Roman Catholic Controversy,* Minneapolis: Bethany House Publications (1996)

Williams, H. S., Editor, *The Historians' History of the World, A Comprehensive Narrative of the Rise and Development of Nations As Recorded by the Great,* London: The Times (1908)

Wills, Garry, *Witches & Jesuits: Shakespeare's Macbeth,* New York: Oxford University Press (1995)

Appendix E

INDEX

A

Abel 268, 269,270,271,275,276
Abigail 198, 200
 Adams 196
abolition 239
Abraham 77
Abraham Lincoln 240, 241, 244, 251
Acadia 150
Acquaviva, Superior General Claudio 69
actors 72, 207, 251
Adams, John 104, 139, 140, 179, 184, 194, 196, 198, 200, 203, 208, 232
Adams, Samuel 140, 143
Addison, Judge 151
Admiralty 139, 141, 184
adultery 80
Aeneas 15, 121,216, 228, 256, 259
Aeneid, The 15, 16, 216, 231
Aguilera, ATF Special Agent Davy 286
Ahlstrom Sydney E. 242
Aimeric of Santa Maria Nuova, Cardinal 36
Alacoque, Ste. Margaret-Marie 108, 197
Albany congress 122
Alissiardi, Fathers 70
American colonists 85, 89, 126, 133, 139, 141, 142, 143, 148, 149, 161, 184, 195
American Inquisition xvi
American Jewish Congress 9
American Revolution 66, 85-86, 109, 115, 125, 129-131, 140, 156, 159, 173, 176, 261, 284
Americans United for Separation of Church and State 9
Amiot, Josef-Marie 86, 87, 88
Anacostics 176
Anathema 57
Anathematized 57
Andrea Gritti 32
Anglican 148, 151, 152, 184
annals 260
Annapolis 178

Annu 210, 266, 267, 268, 270, 271
Annuit Coeptis 5, 15, 214, 217, 218
Annunciation Day 197
Annunzio, Frank 3
Antietam 242
Antioch, Ignatius of 44
Apollo 11, 60, 217, 220, 223
Apostolic Nunciature of the Holy See 9
apotheosis 35, 69, 250, 256, 261
Appeal to the Ruling Classes 24, 65
Aquinas, St. Thomas 130
Aragon 110
Aranda, Count de 118
Aranzazu, Virgin of 30
Archbishop John Hughes 247
Archibald Sayce 271
Aristotle 14, 130
Ark 175
Articles of Confederation 260
artillery 111, 150, 231,261
Arundell, Earl of (Thomas Howard) 123
Arundell, Lord (Henry Howard) 172
Asher 77
assassination 115, 215, 219, 224, 251, 252, 253, 254, 255
Athens 23, 237
Atonement, Day of 39
Augsburg
 Confession 55
 Peace of 56
Augusta of Saxony 135
Avignon 38

B

Bacchus 11, 12,213
Baltimore 146, 151, 152, 174, 201, 235, 250
banking 37, 57, 161, 169, 188
Baptist Joint Committee on Public Affairs 9
Barcelona 30, 32, 43, 44
Barton, William 124, 209
Basel, Council of 197
Basque country 24

APPENDIX E   INDEX

Batso Furnace 179
Bavaria 64, 70, 170
Beauregard, Gen. Pierre 240
Beckx, Superior General Pieter Jean 233
Beijing 167
Belgium 44, 67, 123
belli legum dormit 82
Benjamin, Judah P. 241
Berkeley Square 139, 168, 208
Berkeley, Dr. Edmund xiii, xiv
Bernard, Abbot of Clairvaux 35
Bernstein, Carl 1, 2
Berthier, the Jesuit 107
Beza, Theodore 130
Biden, Sen.Joseph 2, 3
Bidermann, Jacob 66
Bishop of Rome (pope) 85, 104, 207
Black Madonna of Montserrat 30, 70
Black Papacy 57, 82, 95, 97, 103, 120, 123,
    133, 137, 139, 152, 159, 161, 177, 187,
    194, 196, 232, 233
Black Pope 6, 47, 59, 71, 87, 103, 184
blood 20, 29, 39, 50, 51, 94, 121, 162, 182,
    240, 241, 265, 268, 269, 270
Bohemia 31, 176
Boleyn, Anne 46
Boling, Kenneth 124
Booth, John Wilkes 251, 253
Bordeaux 38, 170
Boscawen, Admiral Edward 100
Boston 140, 141, 142, 143, 150, 162, 171,
    173, 174, 177, 178, 181, 184, 185, 190,
    193,238
Boston Massacre 143
Boston Tea Party 171, 173, 178, 185
Bourbon(s) 109, 111, 112, 118
Braddock, General Edward 100
Brady, Matthew 242
Branch Davidians 286
Braschi, Cardinal Giovanni 180
Brent, mayor Robert 4, 232
Briand, Bishop 194
Bristowe, Mrs. Sidney 272
Britannus Americanus 142
British colonies 82, 85, 147
British Empire 88, 89, 138, 140
broadcasting 70, 71, 72
Brown 1
Bruges 155, 157, 164, 171, 172, 177, 184
Brumidi, Constantino 5, 247, 248, 249, 250,
    255, 257, 258, 259, 261, 262
Buddha 59
Bullinger, E. W. 198

Busenbaum, Hermann 79, 81
Bute, third Earl of (Lord Bute) 134, 136
    137, 138, 139, 140, 155, 168, 184
Butterbriefe (indulgence) 21

C

cabalah 23, 31, 33, 36, 38, 39, 175, 196, 199
    209, 230, 260
Caesar
    Augustus 5, 221, 224, 256
    Julius 6, 152, 210, 218, 219, 220
Cain 265, 267, 268, 269, 270, 271, 272, 273,
    274, 275, 276, 277, 279, 280, 281, 282,
    283, 285, 286, 287, 289
Caius Maecenas 5, 219
Calvert 174, 175, 176, 177
Calvert, Cecilius 175, 176
Calvert, George (Lord Bute) 174
Calvert, Leonard 175
Calvin, John 44, 130
Cambridge 130, 177, 182, 189, 190, 191, 195
Campbell, Robert Allen 189,190
Canada 98, 100, 185, 194, 195, 253
canonization 10, 69, 245
Capitol *(capitolium)*, U.S. 70, 234
Cardinal Thomas Wolsey 23, 102, 117
Carroll
    Charles 104, 156, 177, 178, 179, 181, 194
    Daniel 227, 230, 231, 232
    John xvii, 65, 123, 146-164, 169, 172, 88,
        193,227,232,244
Casey, William 2
Cassio 150, 188
Castel Sant'Angelo 114, 171, 180, 185, 187,
    188, 190
Castille 110
Castle William 143
Casuist 78, 81
casuistry 78, 79, 80, 81, 82, 120, 150, 157
Catholic Action 70, 71, 72
Catholic Almanac 12
Catholic Church of the United States 152
Catholic Encyclopedia
    1902 edition 4
    New (1967) 4
Celebrano, Father 70
Cenodoxus 66
Centurioni, Superior General Luigi 103
Ceres 5, 258
Chaize, Francois de la 64
Challoner, Bishop Richard 147
Champagne 36
Charles Habsburg 18, 27, 30, 32, 55

Charles Stuart 137, 174
Charleston 141, 171, 240
Chase, Samuel 194
Chattanooga, Tennessee xiv, xv, 243
children 24, 27, 46, 64, 93, 102, 103, 135, 206,221
Chinese 37, 86, 87, 88
Chiniquy, Rev. Charles 241, 252, 254
Christ, Jesus 15, 49, 50, 62,68, 150, 151, 205, 213, 231, 237
Christian Corurot'ers)' (Bellarmine) 130
Christianity xvi, 11, 12, 71, 208
Christopher Columbus 27, 235
Christopher Dodd 2, 3
Church Militant 51, 74, 103, 260, 261
Church of England 101, 102, 103, 129, 136, 148, 149, 152, 158, 174
Cincinnatus 249, 250
cinema 70, 71, 72
Civil War, American 239
Civitavecchia 111
Clark Mills 239, 240,250
Clark, Judge William 2
Clinton, William J. 3
coadjutors (lay agents) 52, 191
coin xvii, 59, 212, 222
College of Cardinals 112
Collegio Anti-Bellarminianum 130
Colombière, Claude de la 108
Columbine murders 73
commerce 2, 37, 57, 58, 59, 65, 167, 188, 196, 261
Company of Jesus 42, 45
condemnation 68, 121, 281, 287, 288, 289, 290, 291
Confederacy 240, 241, 242, 243, 251, 252, 253
Confederate States of America 240
confession 10, 28, 57, 63, 64, 107, 205
confessor, Jesuit 64, 98, ill
Confucius 118
Congregation for the Propaganda 97
Congregationalist 148
Connecticut 152, 173, 178, 227
Constantine, Emperor 11, 16, 206, 284
Constitution of the United States 66
Constitution of the United States Article VI, section 3 86
Constitution of the United States First Amendment 86
Conte, Silvio Rep. 3
contemplativus in actione 47
Continental Congress 124, 178, 179, 181, 185, 194
cowboys 70
Coxe, Jr., Daniel xix, 121-122
Coxe, Sr., Dr. Saniel 122
Crawford, Thomas 5, 238, 250, 257
Creighton, Bishop Mandell 1
critics 72
Crown 52, 94, 99, 101, 102, 106, 122, 142, 149, 156, 160, 169, 172, 173, 182,203
Cuellar, Juan de 44, 45
Cybele 11
Cyprus 12, 27, 29,31,32,33

D

Dark Ages 16
Darnall, Eleanor 104, 174, 176
David 12, 217, 286
Davidians 286
Davis, Jefferson 238, 240, 250
Declaration and Resolves of October 14, 1774 179
Declaration of Independence 40, 66, 78, 132, 133, 185, 193, 195, 198, 199, 200, 203,214, 260
Declaration of the Causes 182
Declaratory Act 142
Deism 118
Delaware 85, 124, 211
Diatriba theologica 112
Diet of Nuremberg 22
Dionysus 10, 12, 223
Directorium inquisitorum 57, 254
Discourses concerning Government (Locke) 131
Disestablishment 94, 114, 118, 169, 170, 180, 187, 188
divine right 120, 129, 130, 133
Dominus ac Redemptor noster 113, 169
Dorset coast 151
Douglas, Stephen A. 240
Dove 128, 130, 131, 132, 133, 150, 175, 251
Dover, Treaty of 122
Dr. Benjamin Rush 125
Dred Scott vs. Sanford 239
Due de Choiseul 118
Duties 141, 143, 172, 179, 184

E

Ea 266, 268
eagle 5, 210, 213, 231, 232, 257, 258, 260
East India Company 164, 167, 168, 169, 171, 173, 185, 186, 192, 193, 194
Edinburgh 40

APPENDIX E   INDEX

Edison, Thomas Alva 70
education 4, 10, 41, 44, 66, 73, 102, 138
Egham races 136
emotional 73, 74, 82, 137, 183
emotions 74
Encyclopedia of Sciences, Arts, and Trades 117
Encyclopedists 117
England ii, 4, 23, 31, 36, 44, 45, 46, 49, 64, 67, 68, 69, 89, 94, 98, 101, 102, 103, 104, 108, 111, 113, 114, 121, 122, 123, 131, 132, 133, 137, 138, 139, 140, 142, 143, 148, 149, 151, 155, 157, 160, 161, 164, 168, 171, 172, 173, 174, 176, 180, 182, 184, 185, 195, 196, 197
English College 114, 170, 171, 177, 185
Enlightenment, the 102, 117, 119, 120, 126
Enoch (Unuk) 59, 266, 272-276, 294
entertainment 66, 73
Episcopal Church 153, 241
equivocation 78, 79, 80, 82, 101, 120, 157
Erasmus, Desiderius 20
Escobar, Antonio 81
esoteric experience 43
Eton 136
Etruscans 6, 219
euse 138, 141, 142, 143, 164, 168, 169, 182
Evangeline 150
Eve 31, 236, 268, 275
evil 21, 22, 31, 39, 70, 72, 73, 123, 150, 170, 205, 206, 213, 217, 223, 229
Exercises 29
Exercises, Spiritual 28, 30, 31, 43, 45, 47, 66, 73, 108, 157

F

Family Compact 109
Farnese, Alessandro (Paul III) 46
Farnese, Giulia 46, 167
Farnese, Ranuccio 59
fasces 6, 153, 224, 256
Fascism 6
Faust, Dr. Johannes 19
Fazio, Rep. Vic 3
Feast Day of St. Ignatius Loyola xiv, 289
Febronianism 158, 159
Febronius, Justinius (see Hontheim) 113, 154, 157
Fillmore, Millard 248
Filmer, Sir Robert 130, 131, 133
Fiorentini 188
Firth of Clyde 136
Fitch, Ralph 168
Flag Committee 189, 193, 199

Flanders 4, 36, 164, 175
Floquet, Father Pierre 194
Florence 23, 157, 164, 216
Florida vii, 98, 122
Florio, Rep. James 3
flying money *(fei-chi'en)* 37
Foley, Rep. Thomas 2
Fort Sumter 240
founding fathers 5, 66, 201, 204, 218, 224, 228, 229
Fourteenth Amendment 239
Fox, George 101
France 11, 12, 28, 31, 36, 37, 38, 45, 46, 64, 71, 85, 98, 102, 106, 108, 109, 122, 137, 138, 139, 170, 174, 177, 184, 223, 241
Franciscan 112, 152
Franklin, Benjamin 100, 103, 107, 122, 139, 142, 172, 179, 180, 189, 190, 194, 195, 203, 208, 257, 258
Frederick II of Hesse-Hanover 160
Frederick William, Prince of Wales 135
"Freedom" 234
"Freedom" (see Libera, Justitia) 5
Freemason 36, 118, 123, 124, 152, 160, 169, 191, 195, 227, 237, 248, 252
Freemasonry 40, 58, 98, 100, 115, 117, 118, 119, 120, 121, 135, 140, 155, 160, 170, 173, 194, 200, 212, 231, 240
Freemasons 119, 120, 168, 170, 173, 185
French and Indian War 100
French, Benjamin B. 242, 249
fresco 5, 247, 249, 250, 251
Fromm vs. Carroll 152
Fullam, Judge John 10

G

Gadsden, Christopher 139
Ganganelli, Lorenzo 112
Garcia, Hermine F. 87
Garza, Rep. Kika De la 3
George William (George III) 137
Georgetown College 232
Georgetown University 81, 146, 170, 232
Germanicum, the 56
Germany xiv, 31, 36, 40, 45, 49, 56, 63
Gesu 114, 120, 175, 188, 238, 288
glorious gospel 280, 283, 285, 286, 287, 290
Gnosticism 23, 101
Goa 168
goat 39, 210, 226, 228
god 5, 12, 15, 19, 20, 21, 24, 28, 29, 30, 31, 38, 39, 40, 42, 43, 44, 46, 51, 57, 59, 69, 72, 82, 93, 101, 105, 110, 113, 115, 125,

321

129, 130, 132, 159, 161, 169, 193, 194, 196, 197, 198, 200, 203, 204, 205, 206, 207, 208, 209, 210, 213, 215, 216, 217, 219, 220, 221, 223, 224, 227, 229, 236, 237, 238, 243, 244, 256, 257, 258, 259, 260
Gonzalez, Henry 3
Got, Bertrand de 38
Governor Richard Penn 178
Governor Thomas Hutchinson 143
Grand Union Flag of Great Britain 192
Grant, Ulysses S. 251
Great Britain vii, 68, 71, 82, 86, 95, 98, 99, 104, 122, 126, 139, 140, 142, 149, 178, 184, 191, 192, 195
Guillotin, Dr. Josef 112
guillotine 112
Gulf of Mexico 98, 122
Gunpowder Plot 68, 69
Gury, Father 80, 81
Gutenberg, Johannes 17,19

H

Hades 60, 234, 237, 258, 261
Haifa 32
Haig, Alexander 2
Hall, Manly P. 123, 199
Hamilton, Alexander 157
Harkin, Sen. Thomas 3
Harnett, Cornelius 139
Harris, Brigadier General M. Thomas 253
Harrison, Benjamin 189
Harriton 124
Harvard 149, 150
Hayden, Sidney 122
heaven 5, 30, 39, 45, 48, 62, 69, 212, 213, 216, 220, 222, 223, 228, 256
Hebrew 77, 118, 218, 229, 260
hell 24, 29, 50, 64, 73, 232
Hendricks, J. Edwin 124
Henry, Patrick 139, 142, 143, 181, 184
Hermes 59
Hesse-Hanover 160, 161, 180
Hierarchy 57, 70, 106, 121, 148, 218, 223, 224
High Church Party 174
Historians 22, 40, 44, 74, 106, 111, 115, 131, 176, 194, 199, 229, 231, 235, 239
history ix, x, xii, xvii, xix, 22, 46, 71, 73, 74, 109, 123, 124, 125, 136, 169, 171, 174, 190, 196, 223, 232, 237, 242, 249
Hitler, Adolf 40, 71
Holland 49, 143

Holy Land 30, 35, 36, 37, 45
Holy Roman Emperor Charles V 32, 40, 44
Holy Roman Emperor Maximilian 27
Hontheim, Nikolaus von xix, 154, 157, 158, 159, 160
Howard, Edward 155
Howard, Rev. Simeon 150
Howard, Thomas 123, 135
Huguenots xiii, xiv, xvi, 49, 85
humanism 65, 159
humanist 46, 69, 121, 159, 216
Hunter Commission 251, 252, 253

I

Iago 150
idolatry 80, 149, 207
Illuminati 31, 40, 68, 170
illuminism 44
Immaculate Conception 237, 239, 241, 243, 245, 247, 249, 250
In eminenti 119
Indian 99, 100, 107, 139, 168, 176, 184, 208
indulgences 21, 22, 57
infallibility 236
Ingolstadt College 70
Inquisition
   American xvi
   Roman xvi, 52, 57
   Spanish 44, 52
Inter mirifica 72, 73
Intolerable Acts 174, 185
IRS, income tax system xv, xvi
Isaiah 15, 219
Islam 32

J

Jacobite 137, 152
Jacobite Rebellion 137
Jerusalem 30, 32, 40, 43, 45
Jesui 77
Jesuit drama 67
Jesuit schools and colleges 65, 68
Jesuit theatre 66, 67, 69, 70, 71, 73
Jesuit warfare 83, 104
Jesuited 78, 106, 120, 159, 184
Jesuitess 78
Jesuitic 78, 89, 121, 195, 239
Jesuitry 78, 107
Jesuits xviii-xvi, xix, 45, 51, 52, 56, 57, 58, 63, 64, 65, 68, 69, 70, 72, 77, 78, 82, 83, 101, 102, 104, 105, 106, 108, 109, 110, 111, 112, 113, 114, 115, 117, 118, 120, 123, 126, 131, 133, 137, 147, 150, 157,

APPENDIX E INDEX

160, 161, 167, 169, 171, 174, 175, 176, 177, 180, 181, 184, 185, 187, 191, 192, 195, 204, 208, 224, 227, 232, 233, 237, 239, 241, 244, 247, 286, 289
Johannites 38
John MacCoon xiv, xv, xvi, xix
John Mattingly 170, 185
John the Baptist 38, 197
Johnson, Andrew 251
journalists 72
Jupiter 5, 11, 67, 210, 213, 215, 216, 217, 220, 221, 223, 227, 228, 229, 230, 231, 238, 256, 257
Justinian, Emperor 23
Justitia 10, 258

K

Kao-tsung, Emperor 37
Kaunitz, Prince von 118
Kennedy, Sen. Edward 3
Kerry, Sen. John 2, 3
Keystone Cops 107
King
  Charles I (England) 4, 133, 174, 175
  Charles I (Spain) 27
  Charles II (England) 101, 131
  Charles III (Spain) 184
  Ferdinand V (Spain) 40
  Francis I (France) 46
  Frederick the Great (Prussia) 118
  George II (England) 100
  George III (England) 113, 166
  Henry III (England) 37
  Henry III (France) 63
  Henry VIII (England) 46, 129
  James I (England) 68, 99, 174
  James II (England) 152
  Louis XIV (France) 64, 85, 122, 131
  Louis XV (France) 63, 98, 108, 112, 113, 118, 184
  Philip IV (France) 37, 109
  William of Orange 152
Kino, Eusebio 70
Kircher, Athanasius 69
Knights Hospitallers of St. John 32
Knights of Christ 35, 40
Knights of St. John of Jerusalem 40
Koffler, Father 111, 112
Koresh, David 286

L

LaFalce, Rep. John 3
Lainez, Diego 56

Lambeth 148
LaValette, Father 106, 107, 108
laypersons 3, 10, 70
Leahy, Patrick 3
Ledochowski, Superior General Vladimir 71
LeFevre 46, 56
Leicester House 136, 137, 138
LeJay, Claude 56
Lexington Green 181, 185
Libera 10, 238
liberation theology 130, 132, 133, 150, 157, 197, 205, 251
line of demarcation 167
Liturgical Calendar xvi, 12, 196, 197
liturgical year 175
Livy 59
Llull, Raimon 33
Locke, John 131
London 37, 97, 100, 101, 103, 104, 121, 137, 142, 148, 152, 153, 162, 164, 167, 172, 175, 177, 182, 184, 185, 239
London Coffee House (Philadelphia) 142
Longfellow, H.W. 150
Lorenzo Ricci's War 97, 99, 100, 101, 103, 105, 107, 109, 111, 113, 115, 139
Louis-le-Grand (college) 104, 107, 177
Loyola St. de Ignatius 44, 46, 51, 69
Ludolph of Saxony 28
Luis Vives 44, 45
Luken, Rep. Charles 3
Lulworth Castle 151
Lynch, Thomas 189

M

mace 5
Madigan, Rep. Edward 3
magic lantern (laterna magia) 70
Magnificat 197
Main Street Journal xvi-xvii
Mainz (mentz) 20, 40, 156, 157, 160, 161
Majorca 33
Malone, Bishop James W. 10
Malta 32, 111
Manes, Grand Master Diego 32, 33
Manresa 31, 40
Maraniss, David 81
Marco Polo 168
Marduk 59
Maria-Theresa, Empress 111
Marie-Antoinette 112
Maritime War 100, 139
Mark of Cain 265, 267, 269, 271, 273, 275, 277, 285, 287

Markey, Rep. Edward 3
Mars 11, 161
Marshall, Justice John 239
Martin Luther 20, 21, 22, 23, 24, 29, 30, 65, 199
Martin, Malachi 87
Martinique 106, 108
Mary, Virgin 22, 28, 48, 175, 197, 198, 212, 235, 236, 237, 238, 257, 258
Maryland 4, 86, 104, 147, 151, 156, 170, 174, 175, 176, 177, 184, 185, 196, 197, 198, 230, 235, 242, 244
Masons 119, 121, 123
Massachusetts 1, 8, 10, 138, 142, 173, 178, 181, 182, 185, 189, 227
Mayhew, Rev. Jonathan 149, 150
Mazzini, Giuseppe 248
McDade, Rep. Joseph 3
Medici learning 33, 68, 124
Medici Library 23, 24, 73, 120, 216
d'Medici
    Catherine xii
    Cosimo 23
    Giulio (Clement VII) 18, 23
    Lorenzo "the Magnificent" 22, 46
Medulla theologiae moralis 79
megaphone 69
Meigs, Montgomery C. 249-250
Mein Kampf 71
Mendelssohn, Felix 290
mental reservation 50, 78, 79, 80, 82, 101, 120, 187
merchants 47, 51, 63, 82, 141, 142, 143, 144, 161, 164, 168, 169, 170, 171, 173
Mercury 5, 59, 60, 67, 240, 261
Merodach 59
Merrie Land 175
Messiah 38, 197
Michaelangelo 24, 247
Mifflin, Thomas 179
Mikulski, Sen. Barbara 3
milice du Christ 187, 199
militiamen 100, 181, 285
Miller, Rep. George 3
Miracle On Main Street xii, xvii-xviii
Miranda prorsus 71, 72
missionary adaptation 11, 13, 208, 211, 238, 256, 258
Mitchell, Rep. George 2
Molay, Jacques de 40
Moliere 67
Moneta 10
monetary system xii, xvii-xviii, 82

Montaigu 44
Montgomery C. Meigs 249
Montreal 194, 195
Morals and Dogma 118
Moses 203, 205
Mount Rothesay 137
Moynihan, Sen. Daniel P. 2
Mozart 67
Munich 40, 66, 67, 156, 238
Murtha, Rep John 3
Muslim 35, 36

N

Nabonidas 276, 277
Najera, Duke of 28, 30
Nantes, Edict of 64, 85
Naples 40, 111
Naram-Sin 266-267, 277
National Association of Evangelicals 9
National Association of Scholars 73
National Council of Churches 9
National Portrait Gallery (UK) 152
Navarette 30
Navarre 30, 110
Negrona 32
New Deal 107
New England 98, 104, 111, 122, 140, 164, 184, 195
New France 98
New Orleans xv, 139
New Testament 20, 22, 29, 31, 32, 39
New Wardour Castle 172
new world order 15, 220, 224, 265, 283
New York 142, 147, 148, 173, 178, 240, 243, 247, 248
Niccolo Machiavelli 23
Ninety-five Theses 22, 29
Noah Webster 78
nonjuring bishops 152
Norfolk, Eighth Duke of 123, 135
Norfolk, Ninth Duke of 135, 136
North Carolina 139
North, Lord 143, 174, 185
notariqon 51, 161
Nova Scotia 150
Novus ordo seclorum 15, 214, 220, 256
Number In Scripture 198
nuncios 97

O

O'Gorman, Thomas 152
Oakar, Rep. Mary Rose 3
oath xiv, 40, 48, 51, 52, 57, 95, 119, 121,

APPENDIX E   INDEX

152, 168, 187, 251, 274
oath of obedience 48, 51, 187
Obey, Rep. David 3
Odin 59
Ohio 99, 100, 108, 138
Oliva, Superior General John Paul 133
Olive Branch Petition 182, 185
On the State of the Church 113, 157, 159
opium 167
Osiris 11
Oswald, Lee Harvey 251
Othello 150
Otis, James 138
Our Flag 189, 192

Oxford 23, 102, 103, 112, 1 15, 177, 218

P

Paine, Tom 180, 185, 229
Pamplona 28, 32
Papal States 106, 111
paper currency 37, 100, 141
Paraguay 106
Paris 12, 19, 37, 40, 44, 67, 97, 104, 106, 139, 140, 157, 162, 164, 169, 170, 177, 184, 185, 208, 209
Paris, Treaty of 139, 141, 168
Parlement 106, 107, 108, 184
Parliament 68, 94, 106, 138, 141, 142, 143, 169, 171, 173, 175, 178, 181, 184, 185
Parma 111
Pascal, Blaise 79, 107, 232
Pastoral Letters 79, 106
Patriarcha (Robt. Filmer) 130, 131, 132, 133
Patuxents 176
Payen, Hugh de 35
Peculari quadam 70
Pell, Sen. Claiborne 3
penances 31, 43, 184
Penn, Admiral Sir William 101
Perm, William 100, 101, 102
Pennsylvania 85, 86, 100, 103, 121, 124, 139, 147, 152, 177, 178, 179, 181, 182, 184, 185, 211
pentagram 39, 210, 211, 213, 228, 257
Persephone 5, 234, 237, 238, 244, 258
personal liberty 85, 150
Petty, Robert (Lord Shelburne) 139, 168, 208
Pharaoh 203, 205, 206
Philadelphia 9, 102, 103, 141, 142, 162, 171, 177, 178, 179, 180, 181, 185, 194, 195, 197, 199, 211, 237, 244
Philadelphia, Charter for the City of 102

philosopher's death 190
philosophes 117, 118, 120, 129, 190
Pike, Albert Grand Commander 118
Piscataways 176
Poland 64, 103
Politics of Witchcraft, The xviii
Pombal, Sebastian the Marquis de 105
Pompadour, Madame de 108
Pontifex Maximus 6, 10, 13, 15, 16, 37, 82, 85, 86, 119, 120, 180, 182, 215, 216, 220, 221, 231, 256
Pontifical Institute 87
Popes
  Adrian I 21
  Adrian VI 22, 32
  Alessandro VI 167
  Alexander VI 46
  Boniface VIII 4, 37
  Clement V 38, 40
  Clement VII 18
  Clement VIII 1 30
  Clement XII 119
  Clement XIII 106, 110, 184, 185
  Clement XIV 179, 185
  Eugenius III 36
  Gelasius I 47
  Gregory IX 14, 16
  Gregory XIII 57
  Gregory XV 69
  Honorius II 36
  John Paul II 1,6
  John XXIII 71
  Leo I 11
  Leo III 21
  Leo X 21, 199
  Paul III 42, 46, 204
  Paul VI 72
  Pius IX 235, 252
  Pius V 113
  Pius VII 232
  Pius XII 80
  Sylvester 284
  Innocent VII 21
population, Roman Catholic 86
Portugal 36, 40, 64, 65, 105, 106, 112, 118, 119, 122, 168, 175, 184
powder plays 68
preachers 57, 148
Prefect of the Sodality 156, 161, 177, 195
Presbyterian 148
Primitive Christian Church 38
Princeton University 132
Proclus 237

Professor, the 189, 190, 191, 192, 193, 194, 195, 199, 200
Ptoprietors, the 100
Protagoras 23
Protestant xiii, xv, 5, 46, 49, 55, 56, 57, 58, 64, 65, 71, 77, 85, 94, 104, 113, 118, 124, 129, 130, 131, 133, 137, 144, 148, 149, 150, 151, 152, 153, 158, 159, 160, 162, 175, 176, 182, 188, 199, 200, 206, 210, 241, 242, 248, 253, 259, 284
Protestant Episcopal Church in the United States 153
Protestantism 18, 23, 29, 32, 44, 57, 66, 86, 87, 95, 111, 120, 157, 159, 254
Protestants xiii, xv, 5, 49, 50, 52, 55, 58, 67, 87, 102, 113, 121, 147, 152, 159, 176, 184, 233, 242, 254, 259
Psychopomp, the (Mercury) 54, 60, 261
purgatory 22, 57
pyramid 58, 118, 121, 136, 214, 222
Pyrenees 28

Q

Quaker(s) 100, 101, 102, 103, 181
Quebec 194
Quebec Act 173, 178
Queen
  Catherine of Aragon (England) 44
  Catherine of Braganza (England) 122
  Elizabeth I (England) 67, 130, 167
  Henriette-Marie (England) 174, 175
  Isabella 27, 28
  of Heaven 30, 212, 216, 256

R

radio 70, 72, 74
Rager, John Clement 132
Rangel, Charles 3
Raphael 249
ratio studiorum (method of study) 65, 66, 74, 120, 129, 159, 177, 180, 182
Ray, James Earl xviii
Reagan, Ronald 1, 9
Reconciliation 287, 288, 290, 291
Red Room 151
redcoats 143, 160, 181, 185, 194
Regimini militantis ecclesiae 51, 52, 82, 93, 95, 160, 201
Religious History *of the American People* 242
Remus 11
resurrection 23, 29, 39, 187, 189, 191, 193, 195, 197, 201, 213, 223, 224, 232
Rev. Samuel Seabury 152

Revere, Paul 177
Rhodes 32
Ricci, Superior General Lorenzo xix, 86, 87, 88, 94, 95, 97, 98, 100, 103, 104, 105, 106, 107, 108, 110, 112, 113, 114, 115, 122, 138, 140, 144, 148, 149, 150, 153, 156, 159, 161, 164, 170, 171, 179, 180, 181, 182, 183, 184, 185, 187, 188, 189, 190, 191, 193, 194, 195, 197, 198, 199, 200, 201
Ricci, Sebastiano 54, 59, 261
Rock Creek Farm 176
Rogers, Will 107
Roman College 80, 103, 190
Rome 1, 3, 4, 5, 6, 10
"Rome" (District of Columbia) 4
Romulus 11
Roosevelt, Franklin D. 107
Roothaan, Superior General John 247
Rosicrucian 68, 123, 160, 170
Rostenkowski, Rep. Dan 3
rosy cross *(rose croix)* 36
Rothesay, Isle of Bute 136
Rothschild 160
Rothschild, Meyer 161
Royal Proclamation of 1763 139
Roybal, Rep. Edward 3
rule of law 280, 281, 283

S

Sacraments, the seven Roman Catholic 21, 57
Sacred College 10
Sacred Heart 108, 109, 150, 184, 197, 213, 214, 223, 256
sacrifice 6, 15, 57, 69, 93, 216, 231, 232, 259, 265, 268, 269
Sacy, de 98
St. Alphonse Liguori 80
St. Apollinaris 11
St. Catherine 28, 30
St. Cecilia 197
St. Denis 12, 45
St. Francis Xavier 45, 48, 291
St. Isaac's Cathedral 242
St. John 39, 40, 173
St. John's Lodge 173
St. Martina 11
St. Omer's Jesuit College 4, 67, 101, 104, 170ff
St. Omer, Godfroi de 35
St. Paul 11, 48, 255
St. Peter 11, 22, 28, 38, 46, 114, 247

APPENDIX E   INDEX

St. Peter's Cathedral (Basilica) 22
Salmeron, Alfonso 56
Salzburg 67
Sarbanes, Sen. Paul 2
Sargon 271, 272, 273, 276, 277
Satan 16, 20, 236, 281-283, 289, 292
Satanael 39
Saturn 11, 67, 93, 220, 221, 224, 229, 234, 237, 238, 244, 256
Scottish Rite Freemasonry 40, 240
Scripture 13, 14, 15, 16, 21, 30, 39, 46, 59, 65, 66, 70, 73, 120, 150, 159, 204, 205, 206, 208, 209, 210, 212, 218, 223, 229, 260
Second Continental Congress 181, 194
Secret Teachings of All Ages (Hall) 123
Seventh Day Adventists 9
Sewanee, Tennessee xiii
Shakespeare 66, 67, 68
Sharpsburg 242
Shelburne, Lord (Robert Petty) 139, 168, 208
Sibylline 15, 59
Sidney, Algernon 130, 131
smuggling 141, 184
social communication 72, 73
Society of Dissenters 149
Society of Jesus xiv, xvi, 46, 47, 48, 50, 51, 60, 77, 78, 79, 81, 82, 86, 94, 97, 104, 106, 107, 110, 111, 112, 114, 115, 117, 121, 136, 137, 159, 167, 168, 169, 187, 188, 198, 199, 201, 204, 232
Solomon, King 30, 39
South Carolina 139, 240
Spain 18, 24, 27, 28, 30, 36, 40, 43, 44, 109, 110, 111, 112, 168, 175, 184
Spinelli, Cardinal 148
Spiritual Exercises 45, 66
Stamp Act 141, 142, 147, 148, 184
Stamp Act Congress 142, 184
Ste. Barbe, College of 44
Steinmayer, Father Ferdinand (alias Farmer) 147
Stevens, Rev. Thomas 168
Stourton, Charles Philippe 155, 157, 161, 164, 171, 177
Stuart monarchs 113
Sun-Tzu vii, 86-94, 98, 104, 105, 111, 113, 120-121, 130, 135, 149, 162, 185, 189, 286, 287, 289
Surratt, John H. 253
Surratt, Mary 253, 254
Swieten, Gerard von 118

Switzerland 30, 31, 49, 106

T

Tammuz 11
Taney, Justice Roger Brooke 239, 240
Tea Act 169, 172, 177, 185
television 71, 72, 74
Templarism 68
Tennessee Waltz: The Making of A Political Prisoner xviii
Terminator II 60
Test Act 148
Teutonic Knights 40, 58
Teutons 59
thirteen xix, 27, 38, 40, 85, 86, 87, 88, 89, 91, 93, 95, 122, 162, 172, 176, 177, 182, 189, 192, 193, 194, 195, 200, 210, 214, 233, 239, 257
Thirteen Articles Concerning Military Art 86, 87, 89, 91, 93, 95
Thirteenth Amendment 239
Thomson, Charles 123, 124, 125, 140, 142, 143, 177, 179, 181, 182, 183, 209, 211, 217
Thorpe, Francis xix, 172, 188
Thoth 59
"Tiber" 4
Tillot, Minister de 118
Tisbury 123, 172
Torgau 21
Townshend Acts 143, 168, 184, 185
Townshend, Charles 142
Trafalgar Square 152
Treasurer of the Apostolic Chamber 179, 184
Trent, Council of 54, 55, 56, 57, 60, 65, 160, 204
Trickster 60, 82, 261, 282, 286-287
Trier 154, 156, 157, 158, 160
Troyes 36, 37
Turks 20, 32
tyranny 115, 117, 123, 133, 141, 143, 148, 149, 150, 179, 185, 198, 203, 251, 257

U

U.S. Catholic Conference 10
United States foreign policy 1
United States Supreme Court 239
United States, Great Seal of the 16
University of Paris 44
University of Saumer 102
University of the South xiii
University of Trier 157

327

Unknown Superior 59, 98, 120, 137, 138, 191, 200, 223, 252
Unuk 271, 272, 277
usury 81, 107

V

Valladolid 28
Vatican 2, 3, 4, 5, 9, 32, 38, 46, 70, 104, 114, 120, 159, 160, 171, 180, 185, 194, 237, 241, 247, 248, 249, 255
Vatican II (1964) 3, 4
Venice xix, 32, 169
Vernon Howell 286
Vicar of Christ 21, 47, 125, 195, 200
Vienna 40, 66, 104
Virgil 5, 15, 183, 216, 217, 219, 256
Virginia 99, 140, 175, 177, 178, 184, 244
Virginia Declaration of Rights 132
Visitandines 197
Visitation 197
Voltaire 102, 107, 117, 177, 184
Voragine 28
Vox clamantis 40
Vulcan 5, 257

W

Waco 224, 285, 286
Waite, Arthur Edward 173
Walsh, Dr. James 227
Walter, Thomas U. 239, 242, 244, 250
Walters, Vernon 2
Wardour Castle 123, 174, 185
Wartburg Castle 22, 29
Washington and His Compeers (Hayden) 122
Washington, D.C. 8, 9, 248
Washington, George 153, 181, 182, 189, 193, 230, 245
Webster's Dictionary 78, 79, 82, 250
Weishaupt, Adam 170
Welds 151
West Indies 67, 141
West Point 240
White House 176, 226, 227, 228, 230, 241, 245, 254
White, Andrew 175, 176, 197, 235
Wiget, Father B.F. 253
Wills, Garry 68
Wilson, William 2
Wiltshire 123, 172, 185
Wittenburg castle 22
Woody Allen 279
World War II 71
Worms, Edict of 55
Wotan 59
writers 12, 72, 100, 117, 212, 222, 232
WWWebster 79, 81, 138, 139, 140, 184

Y

Yahweh 59, 205, 206, 212, 217, 260
Yom Kippur 39
Young, Notley 4, 232

Z

Zohar ("Book of Splendor,") 39
Zoroaster 118
Zwingli 56

www.ingramcontent.com/pod-product-compliance
Lightning Source LLC
Chambersburg PA
CBHW071229230426
43668CB00011B/1358